The Math of Life

a financial Life of

Living Life Debt Free

Trusting God for His Supply,
and Living On It

B. Lee McDowell

The Math of Life
Copyright @ 2023 by B. Lee McDowell
Published by Dowadad Press
    A division of Lee McDowell Christian Ministries, Inc.
    Nacogdoches, TX
    www.blmcm.net

ISBN # 978-0-9980359-7-0

All rights reserved. No part of this publication may be reproduced, stored in a retrieval system, or transmitted in any form or by any means – electronic, mechanical, photocopy, recording, or any other – without the prior written permission of the publisher. The only exception is brief quotations in printed reviews.

All Scripture quotations are taken from the King James Version of the Bible.

Printed in the United States of America.

Acknowledgements

In June, 1980, just after being Born Again in Pastor John Morgan's office at Sagemont Church, Houston, Texas, my wife, Barbara, attended a Church Training class taught by Pastor Morgan. He had compiled a Financial Freedom seminar and workshop while leading the church to get completely out of debt the previous year.

It was a game changer for our financial life and way of living. I have been fortunate to live these Truths, teach these Truths, and now share these Truths in book form.

I am grateful to God for His Truth and Life, and for Barbara and I getting to experience Him day-in and day-out, year-in and year-out. I am grateful to Pastor Morgan having been given Financial Life Truth from God, and sharing it with us.

Dedication

This book is dedicated to
those Saints desiring to Live Life financially free,
out of financial bondage…
and willing to make difficult choices & decisions,
along with taking difficult actions.

There is nothing like Financial Freedom.
Living Life Debt-Free.
Trusting God for His Supply,
and Living On It.

Contents

chapter	title	page
1	God Is Our Friend	11
2	Don't Buy The Lie	14
3	What Is The Real World?	18
4	This Is Not Rocket Science!	22
5	It's Our Choice: life or Life?	27
6	1 + 1 = 2, Usually	31
7	Financial Freedom	35
8	Life Is NOT *Fair*	41
9	God Is Owner, Man Is Steward	45
10	We Cannot Serve God & Mammon	49
11	Godliness With Contentment	53
12	The Love of Money	57
13	Desiring To Get Rich Quick	61
14	God Gives the Power to Get Wealth	64
15	Faithful vs Unjust	68
16	The Unprofitable Servant	69
17	If You Don't Work, You Don't Eat	72
18	You Are Worth More	77
19	Sell Yourself At All Times	82
20	Give Yourself Away	86
21	Poor vs Broke	89
22	Your Treasure Shows Which Heart	93
23	Your Spending Plan Portrays Your Priorities	96
24	A Monthly Spending Plan Is A Must	99
25	It's Reconcile, Not Balance	107
26	Keep Track of Every Penny	112
27	Know Your Personal Net Worth	115
28	The Bottom Line Each Month	119
29	Online Banking	124
30	Spend Every Penny You Make	125
31	God Supplies the Needs of His Saints	128
32	Pay All Your Bills On Time!	132
33	Making Future Purchases	135
34	Purchasing Autos	140

35	Purchasing a Home	142
36	Grace Giving	144
37	Give, Get, to Give More	148
38	Lay Up Treasures In Heaven	151
39	Honor the LORD With Your Giving	155
40	Proving God	160
41	Give From A Willing Heart	163
42	The Tithe Is Holy To God	169
43	Giving vs Loaning	172
44	Pay Yourself 2nd	176
45	A Channel For Another's Need	180
46	Start Saving By Age 12	184
47	A Living Savings Fund Is A Must	187
48	An Emergency Fund Is A Must	190
49	Typical Savings of Americans	194
50	Don't Incur ANY Debt	198
51	Getting Out of Debt	202
52	Never Co-Sign For Another	210
53	The Emotional Hooks of Money	213
54	The Devastation of Depreciation	217
55	Bondage – The Result of Greed	221
56	Investing For the Long Term	224
57	The Importance and Need For Insurance	228
58	Is A Will Worth Anything?	232
59	Funny & Fake Money	236
60	Pay CASH for EVERYTHING	239
61	Prepare For the Expected	242
62	Prepare For the Unexpected	246
63	Wise Counsel Provides Protection	250
64	I Can't Afford Not To…	253
65	Superlative Quotes that Give Guidance	255
	Sinner diagram	260
	Saint diagram	261
	On Being Born Again	262
	On Being Spirit-filled	265
	Scripture References	267
	Books by BLM	272

Foreword

Lee McDowell is a man saved and called of God to be "living proof of a loving God to a watching world." From the day Lee and his wife, Barbara, invited Jesus Christ into their lives, they have committed everything back to God that He has given them. Every page of this book will bless you and help you to be more like Jesus.

Today is the first day of the rest of your life, and the best is still yet to be. Thank God for leading you to read these words of wisdom sent to you by God through His faithful messengers, Lee and Barbara McDowell.

John D. Morgan
Pastor, Sagemont Church
Houston, TX
1966-2019, 53 years

About the Author

Since September of 2015, the author has been living in solitude with God in a relatively secluded country setting, removed from the daily hysteria of ordinary life. During this time, what God had poured into the past 43 years is now in writing. By reading B. Lee McDowell's works, you can experience the most uncomplicated, completely enunciated, and direly needed Truths that all Saints should know.

Born into a family of educators, B. Lee McDowell instead set his sights on other fields and first became a professional golfer before settling into a lucrative sales career. But God had different plans.

With a father who was a college tennis player and later a multi-sport coach, Lee was involved in athletics from an early age. An injury at age 12 re-directed his athletic plans, and he turned to golf, playing on the Texas A&M University Golf Team, ultimately winning the Texas State Amateur Golf Championship, and playing on the PGA Tour for a couple of years.

In his late twenties, he became a salesman, where he worked his way up to become a manager/vice-president of the world's largest small boat dealership, Louis DelHomme Marine in Houston, Texas.

But in 1981, God called Lee to a life of ministry. He studied at Southwestern Baptist Theological Seminary, and began his life's calling. Having been a minister in various forms in various towns for 40 years, his extensive experiences and acquaintances have given him a broad perspective of *Life as a Christian* showing in his writings.

Life changed in 2003 when Lee suffered a major heart attack. God then had him serving in part-time pastoral roles until his 70th birthday. At that point, God moved Lee into writing books and blogs, and doing discipleship training and counseling. From an encounter at a men's retreat with Greg Wray, a Saint from California, he got the idea of doing ministry at a local park on Sunday mornings. Lee led the ministry, *Christ in the Park*, at Festival Park in Nacogdoches for 5 years. Then he had *Christ at the Market,* on Saturday mornings at the Nacogdoches Farmer's Market with David & Diane Ruby (Ruby Farm). Today, he is writing, teaching, and speaking as God leads.

B. Lee McDowell is the president of Lee McDowell Christian Ministries, a preaching, teaching, discipleship-making ministry. Lee and his wife of 56 years, Barbara, have 2 children and four grandchildren.

Preface

I love math. Ever since I was a young boy, I enjoyed learning all I could about the *workings* of math. My father taught me all sorts of math that was *above my age grade*. Example: when I was in the 2nd grade, my school let out about an hour before my father's school did (he was a junior high math teacher and coach). Our schools were next to each other, so I went over and sat in on his 8th grade math class when my school day was over. Well, I started learning 8th grade math in the 2nd grade. As I moved a grade higher, it seems Dad's last class was a 9th grade class…therefore, I learned 9th grade math when in the 3rd grade. Math always has held my highest interest and esteem.

Life also has held a special place in my heart. When I was 3 years old, living in Commerce, Texas, my appendix ruptured. My parents rushed me to Doc Allen who had a hospital attached to his office, which was in the front of his house! He pronounced me dead at one point, but his wife, Coy Allen, also his nurse, *kept working with me* as the story goes. And she *got me back to life*. After that, she always called me one of *her boys*. Life took on a new meaning as I grew older and knew of the story of Coy Allen and my ruptured appendix.

Life took on another new meaning for Barbara and me on May 20, 1980, in Pastor John Morgan's office at Sagemont Church in Houston, TX (called Sagemont Baptist back then). After visiting on Sunday, May 18, and hearing Pastor Morgan's message, *Ye Must Be Born Again,* we were moved to call and make an appointment to see him to discuss the matter further. That led to our trusting the Lord Jesus Christ to be our personal Savior in his office that Tuesday morning. Christ's Life became our Life. His Supernatural Spiritual Life is greater than any physical life I may have.

Then, when I was age 57, I had a heart attack late one night, sitting in my recliner watching TV with my wife nearby. Long story short…a deputy sheriff heard the call for an ambulance, he was one block from our house, came immediately and got a pulse back in me with his cardiac training. His name? Brian Cross. I would have never made it out of the house alive that night without his being there. The ambulance couldn't have made it soon enough. I was without a pulse for 7-8-or 9 minutes. My cardiologist, Dr. Antoine Younis, gave my wife and daughters and my parents three options around noon the next day after he had put a stint in: *He will die later today, he will die within 2 or 3 days, or he will be a vegetable the rest of his life here on earth…based on all the tests and readings of his heart, brain, and otherwise.* But, by the Mercy and Grace of God, here I am 20 years later.

So, you can see where MATH and LIFE mean a lot to me. And, in wanting to share the many great TRUTHS God has given me over the past years, I honor Him, His Truth, His Math, and His Life in me with these pages that follow.

Everyone either follows God's Way of handling finances (walking in the Spirit) OR follows the devil's way (walking in the flesh). Truth or lies.

Unknowingly to most Saints, borrowing and debt is a spiritual statement of unbelief. Unbelief of God and His Word. When God has spoken, distrust involves the potential for disobedience. Distrust stems from unbelief (the withholding of belief, doubt). Mark 9:24. In Saints, this always comes from the residue, spiritual, carnal mind.

Credit takes away a dependence on God, the thoughts of God, communing (prayer) with God about financial issues. Credit is telling God, "I know You, but I don't believe You or trust You."

Chapter 1
God Is Our Friend

Henceforth I call you not servants;
for the servant knoweth not what his lord doeth:
but I have called you friends; for all things that I have heard
of my Father I have made known to you.
John 15:15

What a powerful and meaningful declaration by God. The Creator of the universe and all things, all people, has told us He Is Our Friend. And gives one awesome promise. *I will make known what I am doing.*

But God has also made other promises. One of which is: He will make sure to supply all you have need of (Philippians 4:19).

These are just two of the magnificent promises of our Friend and Great Shepherd for His Saints, His sheep.

When it comes to doing finances God's Way, we simply ask God and He tells us. He will give us His financial wisdom. He will show us all He is doing to ensure our needs are met, and we shall have no need to want. In addition, God will lead us every step of the way. Do you not remember the 23rd Psalm?

> The LORD is my shepherd; I shall not want. He maketh
> me to lie down in green pastures: he leadeth me beside the
> still waters. He restoreth my soul: he leadeth me in the
> paths of righteousness for his name's sake. Psalm 23:1-3

What beautiful, comforting, and encouraging words from God. Our Friend. Those first five words give us great insight into God's fellowship with His Saints. My Shepherd. My guide and leader. Anyone knowing the life of a shepherd and his sheep knows that sheep cannot be driven like cattle. Sheep must be led. God knows that better than anyone. He leads His sheep.

Do not confuse the word *maketh* as something God forces upon us. The Hebrew *shavah* means to avail, bring forth, bring to pass, cause, place, procure. Our Friend and Shepherd has green pastures picked out for us to enjoy plenty of food, shelter, rest, tranquility, safety, and peace. These include the work God wants us to have to be provided food and shelter. God's sovereign care gives us the bounty that His green pastures provide.

Twice more in these first three verses of the 23rd Psalm we see God speaking of leading us. *Beside still waters.* Sheep will not drink from running water. Sheep need calm, clear, peaceful, still waters. That is what the shepherd has scouted for and takes his sheep to. The Shepherd meets the need of His sheep. *In the paths of righteousness.* That which is just, that which is prosperity, certainly enough, needs met. No wonder God tells us we should have no *want.*

Let us think of more words describing our fellowship with our Friend.

If God be for us, who can be against us? Romans 8:31

Stop and think about all the battles everyone faces in realm of economic matters. Education, jobs, money, bills. It is wonderful to have a Friend who *owns the cattle on 1,000 hills* (Psalm 5:10) to be walking with us daily in our financial endeavors. Listen to this promise:

But my God shall supply all your need according to his riches in glory by Christ Jesus. Philippians 4:19

Let us wrap ourselves in this promise with no end in sight to God's supply. All needs met. According to God's riches in glory. By Christ Jesus. Is there any lack, any limit to God's supply for His sheep? And we can rest knowing the same God the Apostle Paul speaks of, is our God, our Friend. All our needs met. According to God's riches in glory. By Christ Jesus.

And never forget another of our Friend's declarations, *I will never leave thee, nor forsake thee* (Hebrews 13:5). So what have we to worry about, be anxious about, afraid of, stress out about? Let us remember the powerful premise from Philippians 4:13:

I can do all things through Christ which strengtheneth me.

When we know the parabolism of this statement, it ensures that God Himself will Live His Life through us, using His strength to follow through on all that He presents in this book.

Therefore, can we give any reason that we are unable to experience and enjoy God's leading, provision, and protection in our financial matters? Can we give any reason God, our Friend, is unable to provide for us in every way we have need? Can we give any reason that we are unable to see God take us through our days on earth without knowledge, wisdom, direction, and contentment with what He provides for us? I don't think so. I think you will agree.

In the pages of this book you will find a multitude of Scripture verses giving God's Word on finances. You will find many forms and charts giving practical information on handling financial issues. You will find abundant clear, concise, and complete ideas of how you can find the *Life of Christ* in your finances…You will perhaps find great encouragement from the multiple testimonies of God working in the lives of those knowing, believing, trusting, resting, and receiving Truth from God.

So let us begin a journey of discovering God's Financial Way. Living Debt Free, Trusting God for His Supply and Living On It. *The Math of Life. Christ's Life.*

Chapter 2
Don't Buy The Lie
…he was a murderer from the beginning,
and abode not in the truth,
because there is no truth in him.
When he speaketh a lie, he speaketh of his own:
for he is a liar, and the father of it.
John 8:44

Ever since the Garden of Eden, the devil has been the enemy of mankind. Always questioning God's Word. Distortions, diversions, detours, disguises, and disagreements. Just a few of his tactics. And giving his lies to further confuse any issue. Listen to those words in Genesis chapter 3:

> Now the serpent was more subtle than any beast of the field which the LORD God had made. And he said unto the woman, Yea, hath God said, ye shall not eat of every tree of the garden? And the woman said unto the serpent, We may eat of the fruit of the trees of the garden: but of the fruit of the tree which is in the midst of the garden, God hath said, Ye shall not eat of it, neither shall ye touch it, lest ye die. And the serpent said unto the woman, Ye shall not surely die: For God doth know that in the day ye eat thereof, then your eyes shall be opened, and ye shall be as gods, knowing good and evil. And when the woman saw that the tree was good for food, and that it was pleasant to the eyes, and a tree to be desired to make one wise, she took of the fruit thereof, and did eat, and gave also unto her husband with her; and he did eat. And the eyes of them both were opened… Genesis 3:1-7a

Adam & Eve both bought the lie.

The first words from the devil were a lie and deceitful. Eve spoke when she should have kept quiet. It is never a righteous moment to get into a discussion with the devil. Even though Eve spoke Truth when she said they could eat of any tree in the garden, she added the thought of not touching the fruit. Scripture never tells us God told her this. This conversation should have never taken place.

Temptation is not a sin. But James tells us:

> Blessed is the man that endureth temptation: for when he is tried, he shall receive the crown of life, which the Lord hath promised to them that love him. Let no man say when he is tempted, I am tempted of God: for God cannot be tempted with evil, neither tempteth he any man: But every man is tempted, when he is drawn away of his own lust, and enticed. Then when lust hath conceived, it bringeth forth sin: and sin, when it is finished, bringeth forth death. James 1:12-15

Detour, distort, deceive…tools of the devil. Very effective in those who are innocent, or not-so-innocent. Ask a question, add a lie, distort God's Word, insert a detour, and the deception can lead to destruction.

The same tool used by our spiritual enemy today. The devil will use these same tactics in so many different ways. And God's people have bought into his lies leading to financial destruction in many ways.

Perhaps you didn't make the connection of the temptation and deceit leading to Adam & Eve's sin being exactly the same as the Apostle John speaks of in 1 John 2:15-16,

> Love not the world, neither the things that are in the world. If any man love the world, the love of the Father is not in him. For all that is in the world, the lust of the flesh, the lust of the eyes, and the pride of life, is not of the Father, but is of the world.

The same three tactics in the very same order as Adam & Eve faced in the Garden. Amazing, isn't it. And you and I face these same tactics every day in our own financial world.

Deception can take the most ridiculous positions. There are highway billboards in our area that say, "Advertising doesn't work? Just did!" It did? No product is listed (advertising is insinuated), and how many buy something where we have no product mentioned or shown? Of course the billboard owners are trying to convince folks who do advertising that just seeing their billboard works and multitudes will buy whatever product they advertise on that billboard. I suppose if someone buys that idea and puts an add there, the advertising of the billboard to them has worked.

But I have seen these billboards numerous times. I have seen the billboards advertising products, places, and promise. Never bought anything shown on the multitudes of billboards. Why? I will not buy the lie. Advertising has one goal. Get us to do something that will destroy our contentment with God's supply for our need. It is intended to create a want, when God has told us He is our Shepherd, our more than adequate Provider, and with all needs met we shall not want.

Listen to this tactic of our enemy: "If your God will not give you this right now, just sign right here and I will." (John Morgan, Pastor, Sagemont Church, Houston, Texas, 1979.) See the tactics?

"Credit is your friend. You can have a greater lifestyle right now." See the tactics?

"You deserve a break today." See the tactic?

"Because you're worth it." See the tactic?

"Bet you can't eat just one." See the tactic?

"Have it your way." See the tactic?

All dispelling God's Way. All trying to get us thinking the world's way.

Another real consideration is the *emotional cost* of money *leaving you*, or of you *doing without* something. This can be a part of the *emotional hooks of money* or *emotional stress* surrounding financial items. *This factor* is very rarely ever considered even though we *all know* it is real. We can all agree that life on earth was never *intended* to be one of *fun and games, vacations, get-a-ways*, and *buying, buying, buying, spending, spending, spending*. But many have bought the lies of the devil, and *these are the realities of too many people*.

WHEN is the last time you took into consideration the idea of *real money leaving you* when you purchased a large ticket item brand new, then walked out of the store and thought, "I just paid $1,000 for _____, and now that I have it home it is worth maybe one-half (1/2) that much." Oh, it is nice to have that new item at home, but is it worth ½ of your money *leaving you* the same day? What if you paid $25,000 or $50,000 for a new vehicle (let's pretend…IN CASH), and you drive it home and think, "This is a great vehicle I paid $_____ for, and it is worth 3/4th that much now that I have gotten it home." How does that make you *feel?* Does the *feeling* of having that new vehicle justify (satisfy) the *feeling* of it being worth ¾ what you paid for it the day you handed over YOUR CASH and drove it home? What if you thought of it this way: *someone just STOLE $6,250 from me*. How would that make you *feel?* Or, *someone just stole $12,500 from me?* How about that?!? THAT IS THE DEVASTATION OF DEPRECIATION.

This book will give much Truth from God. This book will share how to endure and resist temptation from our enemy to turn from believing God will provide all our need, where we shall have no want.

It is high time the people of God know God's Truth, believe God's Truth, trust God's Truth, receive God's Truth, and rest in God's Truth. For Jesus said,
> And ye shall know the truth, and the truth shall make you free…If the Son therefore shall make you free, ye shall be free indeed. John 8:32, 36

This is *The Math of Life. Christ's Life.*

Chapter 3
What Is The Real World?
These things have I spoken unto you,
that in me ye might have peace.
In the world ye shall have tribulation:
but be of good cheer; I have overcome the world.
John 16:33

John 16 is the close of that beautiful gathering of Jesus with His closest disciples for the *last* supper and His intimate conversations with them of chapters 14, 15, and 16. In 16:33 God gives us Jesus' last words before offering His famous prayer to the Father (ch.17) prior to heading to the Garden of Gethsemane and the moment of being taken captive. He tells them He has spoken words to give them peace, but He also tells them things will be difficult in the *real world*.

Too many preachers and teachers make out Christianity to be some sort of inoculation against problems or enemies. Some even say Christianity is a hindrance against prosperity and health. And then, some go to the other extreme and say that being a child of God is a guarantee for wealth and health. We know all this is false teaching and does not give us the Truth. Jesus did.

However, notice two important points Jesus gave relative to facing this *tribulation* that all will face: *be of good cheer…*for *I have overcome the world*. No matter what we may face, we can do so with *good cheer* and *in Christ* who has overcome all tribulation the world has to offer. That is, to be confident and not discouraged, to be positive and not in despair but in God's peace, to be dependent in the One Who Lives in us.

But now listen, one does not have to be a child of God to practice the Truths found here. Believing, understanding, desiring to practice, and doing so will be much more prevalent in Saints. But Truth works always.

So, let me add the *piece de resistance* (a play on an old saying) that brings God's *peace* every day in the *Life of a Saint*. Our world is comprised of only two kinds of people…*sinners* and *Saints*. Sinners have only the *natural spiritual mind* that cannot grasp the Truths of God (God tells us this in 1st Corinthians 2:14). But God also tells His Saints we HAVE His Mind, THE *Mind of God*…1st Corinthians 2:16. Wow! God's Saints are equipped to read God's Truths in the Holy Scriptures and in a book like this sharing

Truth from Holy Scripture, and then take God's Truths and apply them to our physical life. *Living Life Debt Free - Trusting God for His Supply, and Living On It.* AND, enjoying the *Peace of God.* Well, amen!

The *real world* is that time in life when the *kid* enters the *adult* world. *Real life* happens when we come out of the child-youth-college life PREPARED or UNPREPARED for the *real world.* This book will help anyone at any age face the stress and strain the *real world* can throw at us with that *peace* and *good cheer* Jesus spoke of.

Leaving college can be stressful for any new college graduate. I can remember the years leading up to my graduating from college. I was ready to get out into the *real world.* After all, there were *dreams* I wanted to see experienced. I had never held a job that provided funds for me, or Barbara and me in our early marriage days, to purchase many things. There was *life* after college…or, so I thought. It was *life* all right, but not the care-free time I was thinking of.

I married my sweetheart, Barbara, about 9 months before graduation. We left our wedding the evening of June 3rd in Highlands, Texas, and went straight to San Antonio for the 1967 Texas State Amateur Golf Championship. And I won! That's what I am talking about! What's next!

Well, a summer with some golf, then back to College Station, the last semester before graduating with that Business Management degree from Texas A&M University. And in February, 1968, we headed to Ft. Worth, Texas, to a job for me at Ridglea Golf Club under Head Pro Raymond Gafford. I was one of four assistants, two of us at the new *men's only* course about 3 miles south of the main club's facilities. I was paid $400 a month. It was a great year or so, before several men at the club gave me support to give the PGA Tour a try. Long story short…4 years later, having not beat Arnie or Jack or Gary or Lee (another Lee who had won some tournaments), or very many others to be exact…we wound up back in Baytown, Texas, our hometown. At that point, our two daughters, Kelly & Jennifer, had been born.

I started working in sales at two different car dealerships. From there, a man my father had coached way back in the early 50's in junior high (Louis DelHomme, Louis DelHomme Marine, Houston, Texas) came and got me to go to work for him. Around 8 years later, I felt the desire to do something on my own, and tried to do a couple of business ventures. And then, God intervened and our life took a dramatic change of direction…the ministry. Now, here I am, *retired*, supposedly. But God never intends for one of His ministers to retire. Ministry can go on until our last breath.

Now…how does all this play into this book, this chapter, the whole scheme of things we call the *real world*? Let me share some basics:

- working for a living is daily…monthly…yearly. It never goes away. That is the *real world*.
- expenses, the cost of living, are daily…monthly…yearly. They never go away. That is the *real world*.
- savings, that pot of gold to buy what you want with. Is not an easy accumulation. That is the *real world*.
- retirement comfort, that life on a silver platter. Not many ever reach that place. That is the *real world*.
- DECISIONS…those day-in and day-out choices, then actions, affect every aspect I just mentioned. WHO we get our information from, WHO we really listen to before making those decisions and taking those actions which can affect us so dramatically. WHO is really the most important decision we make in this life. That is the *real world*.

WHY? Because the *real world* is a formidable foe. THAT is the *real world*, at least for 95%+ of Americans. Just hearing that *69% of all Americans have less than $1,000 in savings, and that the overall 'savings rate' of Americans is less than 2.3%* today. In 1966 that rate was 12%. (the personal savings rate measures how much of Americans' after tax, or disposable, income is left over after spending on bills, food, debt, and everything else). Just hearing that *most Americans are living from paycheck to paycheck, and could not pay their due bills if they missed one paycheck*. This confirms what I am getting at. I used to say in the early 90's in the pulpit in West Houston about ½ way be-tween I-10 and Hwy 290: *Probably 90% of the people in either direction are living paycheck to paycheck*. Who knows how many today.

Decisions made each and every day, sometimes each and every moment of each and every day, go a long way in determining just how close one person/one couple can have anywhere near that *retirement comfort* in their later years that most dream of in their early years. I have had some of the greatest *mentors* who have shared many great truths for Barbara and me. I have been given the privilege to pass forward (via being someone's pastor) what God has brought our way. *This book* is about 60+ ideas that have been accumulated along the past 60+ years to give you something to think about, or go one step further and make some decisions by. After all, someone has said, *Knowledge is power.* However, Albert Einstein said, *Any fool can know. The point is to understand.* I am no Einstein, but I must add: *To know is one thing, to understand is another, but to apply what you know and understand is most critical.* I have tried to know, to understand, and then to apply what I think I understand. Maybe you will do the same.

Let me encourage you, if you haven't already done so, to glance through the Table of Contents intently. Each chapter can stand on its own. Even though most interact in some way with others, each has its own truth to be examined and then exercised as you see fit. I imagine there is probably ONE chapter that YOU will go to first, and God will show you something you haven't known or used. Well, amen.

But, I promise you that once you have read the first two chapters, *practicality* is now about to enter your thinking processes, and decision-time is about to face you. When you have read the book, you will be prepared with God's Truth to embrace the Real World with Heavenly Truth from a Heavenly perspective and a Heavenly power. God's Truth does have Real Power. THAT is what I call *The Math of Life. Christ's Life.*

Chapter 4
This Is Not Rocket-Science!
Train up a child in the way he should go:
and when he is old, he will not depart from it.
Proverbs 22:6

It has been my observation for many, many years that too few people have ever had instruction in the basic, and uncomplicated Truths of:
- life
- financial stability
- God's economy
- God's Life in the finances of Saints.

This book will look at 60+ illustrations of various Truths that revolve around those 4 basic principles. Each will be defined and/or described over and over. Anyone with half the desire to live an uncomplicated and comfortable life will be given all that is needed to enjoy such pleasures as that lifestyle affords.

Basic math is not rocket-science. Basic economic principles and practices are based upon basic math. Even a child can learn and start to utilize what this book gives. However, God's involvement in one of His children's financial world can do things nobody in the physical world can understand or do. *God's financial Way* opens *His Spiritual World* to any of His children who are interested and will receive Him and His teaching.

For reference in this book,
God calls His children by the name of *Saint*.
I will use the term *Saint* when referring to God's children.

The scriptural text for this chapter is one that is often quoted, vaguely understood, eagerly avoided, and therefore very seldom followed. People like to laugh and say that *there is no instruction manual for raising kids, training them to be responsible adults*. Not so. God's Word is chock full of tremendous insights and instructions for doing so. You will see that by the time you are half-way through this book!

King Solomon spoke these words to give us one of the most profound expressions of parenting. Trouble is, many Hebrew educators are not quite certain whether *train up* means *dedicate* or *prepare*. I find no difficulty either way…a parent who *dedicates* a child to be trained is one who is at least interested in *preparing* a child.

Educators and unbelievers (not to indicate they are *equal*) may argue and debate over exact *interpretations*, but suffice it to say, every person (a Saint or not) needs some *training* or *preparing* to face life and deal with all the financial issues encountered each and every day. *But this book is different, in that we will do this from the perspective of just how God is involved in all the financial issues each Saint has to deal with.*

I think this training provides the fertile ground (re: parable of the Sower, Matthew ch.13) that gives God the opportunity to show one of His children *His Way* to handle the 4 principles this book builds upon. As a footnote: of the 38 recorded *parables of Jesus* in the New Testament, 16 deal with money or possessions. These do not include His many *parabolic* statements on finances in His other teachings.

It is important to know that a parable or parabolic teaching in Scripture is *a Heavenly Truth with a Heavenly meaning. Sometimes earthly illustrations are included.*

Three things must be addressed and acknowledged up front:
1. The **amount** and **quality** of training are important. There cannot be too much training in the early years of childhood about these 4 principles. The quality of training is just as critical. God has told us there is The Way, and all other ways are NOT The Way. And that His Truth shall MAKE us *free*. Financial Freedom is important for an uncomplicated and comfortable life. (Of course, defining and understanding Financial Freedom will be important – see ch.5).
2. Every Saint has **two spiritual souls.** Each soul has a mind, a set of emotions, a will (decider), and the sum total of these three acting together comprise a heart. Sinners have one spiritual soul, the *natural soul*. Saints have two spiritual souls…
    - the *Supernatural Spiritual Soul of God* given at the New Birth/New Creation (at being Born Again) which has the Mind of God, God's set of Emotions, God's Will (Decider), and God's Heart (which is the sum total of the Mind, Emotions, and Will acting together)

- the *natural spiritual soul* which is enmity with God, given at the first birth into this world. It is still in a Saint as a *residue* of the *old man*. It consists of the natural mind, natural emotions, natural will (decider), and natural heart. The *natural soul* cannot receive and understand the Truth of God (1 Corinthians 2:14).

For more detailed information on the makeup of *sinners* and *Saints,* see my book:
The Images of God & Man.

3. **I take God at His Word.** When functioning in the *Supernatural Spiritual Soul of God,* I can See, Receive, Understand, Believe, and Trust the Truth God is giving me. He says that with training in The Way, the child WILL NOT depart from it when he/she is old. What is *old*? Well, the Hebrew word for *old* refers to 50-60-70 years of age. The Psalmist tells us a *typical* life span was 70 years, or maybe 80 (Psalm 90:10). But, whatever the age you think is *old,* God says: *Train up a child in the way he should go: and when he is old, he will not depart from it.* Proverbs 22:6

As Pastor John Morgan says: "God said it, THAT settles it…we need to believe it!" But first, we need to be functioning in His Soul. Make sure you are doing that.

So, let us begin to find out just what God has to say about these 4 principles. When the Word of God says something, we will take it at *face value*, and not question it.

In this book, the **Spiritual** will always take precedence over the so-called **practical or physical**.

To end this chapter, let me give you a few of my most favorite quotes from some mentors from the past 35+ years…

John Morgan, "Man chooses the supplier of his need. God or Satan. Truth or Deception. Obedience or Disobedience. Freedom or Bondage. Deception & Disobedience always lead to Bondage."

John Morgan, "When God is able to supply any need, any time, any place, in any amount TO us or THROUGH us according to His will, we become free. Financial bondage is you having more trust in your material goods than you do in your eternal God."

John Morgan, "When your outgo exceeds your income, your upkeep becomes your downfall."

Dave Ramsey, "Live like no one else…so that later, you can live like no one else!"

Dave Ramsey, "Every dollar should have a name on it at the start of every month."

Spiros Zodhiates, "Money can't answer to your call and say, 'I love you': money can't respond and say, 'I love you, too.' Don't make money (that which is not responsive to your heart and to life) your primary concern in life. It can meet your need, but it cannot comfort you."

Spiros Zodhiates, "You cannot serve two masters, for while your attachment to one increases, your attachment to the other decreases. Choose God, or the things of this world will become a consuming fire within you."

Ron Blue, "The one ingredient that makes true freedom possible is generosity. Generosity and financial freedom are inextricably linked."

Ron Blue, "A family conference is a meeting where you review and discuss your estate plan with your heirs. Every family has a conference at some point. Usually this meeting takes place in the emotion-charged days following a funeral…by scheduling a family conference early on, you can discuss your estate plans with your heirs and avoid future problems and misunderstandings."

These are just starters to whet your appetite. By the way, God's Word tells us we should use all the Scriptural and experiential advice and instruction from those whom God is using to aid the children of God.

> Folly is joy to him that is destitute of wisdom: but a man of understanding walketh uprightly. Without counsel purposes are disappointed: but in the multitude of counselors they are established. Proverbs 15:21-22
>
> The way of a fool is right in his own eyes: but he that hearkeneth unto counsel is wise. Proverbs 12:15

How would you like to have a Father who owns the cattle on 1,000 hills? Or, a Father who has promised to supply your every need? The Holy Scriptures tell us our Heavenly Father is both of these to every child of God.

So, keep in mind, basic math is not rocket-science. Basic financial principles and practices are based upon basic math, God's Truth, and God's promises to His children. Every Saint can learn and utilize what this book gives.

Truth makes us Free. Truth is Life. Truth is the Way.

Are you experiencing financial freedom? Whose way are you travelling?

You will find PLENTY of God's counsel in these pages! It is *The Math of Life. Christ's Life.*

Chapter 5
It's Our Choice: life or Life ?
(the world's way or God's Way?)
It is the Spirit that quickeneth; the flesh profiteth nothing:
the words that I speak unto you, they are Spirit, and they are Life.
John 6:63

Every Saint has a choice: live life the world's way, or Live Life God's Way. And this is never more relevant than in the financial realm. (In case you didn't see it, the sub-title for this book is Living Life Debt Free - *Trusting God for His Supply, and Living On It.*)

So, these pages will focus primarily on *God's financial Way*. However, we will look at some ways the world tries to counterfeit God's ways. Just keep in mind, YOU will make choices based on WHICH way you wish to follow.

First, let's look at this word, *economy*, to start with. Listen, there is no such thing as *the economy* (don't believe me, just look at the various *definitions* available and see what I mean). That is like saying, "The *weather* in America today will be ..." There are at least 100 different *weather situations* every moment of every day in America. Guess what...there are over 1,000,000 different *economic situations* just for the population of America. *Economics* has been called *the science of managing money so it can be productive for its owner.* Therefore, for the sake of this book, let us talk about *economics* and not *the economy* and simply lump all the factors and situations into two definitions:

- **world's** financial way – the methods and practices the world suggests, or sometimes commands (someone has decided for us), that we engage in for the management of our financial resources. Figuring things out can get very complicated.
- **God's** financial Way – the Truths, methods, and practices that God gives for *Trusting Him for His supply, and living on it*. It really is that uncomplicated.

Second, you have noticed (I'm sure!) that I mention *life* two different ways in our title to this chapter. The *life* (with a small *l*) is indicative of managing our finances using the *world's way*. The *Life* (with a capital *L*) is indicative of managing our finances *God's Way*. Jesus is the Way. Jesus is Truth. Jesus is Life. Jesus makes us Free. Each individual, or couple, makes a decision of which *way* to proceed in all aspects of the financial realm.

That includes income, outgo, savings, retirement, insurance, wills...every which way. Sadly, some choose to do things *God's Way* for one aspect, then choose to do things the *world's way* for others. *Co-mingling ways* does not work well, even though the enemy may try to persuade some to do so. As my pastor, John Morgan (Sagemont Church, Houston, Texas) said back in 1984, "It is never right to do wrong."

Living Life Debt Free - Trusting God for His Supply, and Living On It is not a pick-n-choose method. It is a One-Way method where one totally abandons themselves to God and walks with Him day-by-day in handling and managing His resources. Notice I said *His resources*. We will see more on that in detail later. Suffice it to say right now: God owns it all. We are to Live in God's Truths, methods, and practices. This is *learning to listen to God's wisdom instead of man's logic*, and *doing what is right, no matter what it costs*. (John Morgan, 1984).

Third, Truth is Living God's Way, bringing the Life of Christ to be our Life, even in the matter of finances. As my friend, Michael Wells always said, "Jesus is The Way, and all other ways are not The Way." Well, amen.

Let me give you a couple of illustrations that show the power of the Life of Christ in our finances. R. G. LeTourneau is a man who as a young boy began to love the idea and wherewithal of moving dirt. It was about the time (1920) machinery was *invented* to move large amounts of dirt for all kinds of construction. He became a prolific inventor of earthmoving machinery. History reports his factories supplied LeTourneau machines which represented nearly 70 percent of the earthmoving equipment and engineering vehicles used by the Allied forces during World War II. His story is written in a fabulous little book called *Mover of Men and Mountains*. The whole essence of his story is that when he began his business as a young man he made a *deal* with God: he and God were to be *partners*. 50% - 50%. After a short time LeTourneau wondered why business wasn't too good. And then he thought, "I haven't been giving God His 50% of any profits." He started doing so, and business skyrocketed. Check out the testimony of all God did through R. G. Letourneau. It is incredible. LeTourneau University in Longview, Texas. Mission endeavors all over the world. He speaks of his later years where he was giving God 90% of his income! And it all began when LeTourneau lived up to his commitment to God by the Grace of God. And God poured His Life into everything LeTourneau did.

Sagemont Church (formerly Sagemont Baptist) in Southeast Houston, Texas, is another testimony to the Life of Christ in finances. Pastor John Morgan was convicted that God's people needed to do finances *God's Way*. In 1979, he wrote his Financial Freedom material. And then led 300 families to get out of debt, and to begin to trust God in their financial life. A short time later in a *40 Day* venture, the 300 families contributed over $1,000,000 to get the church out of debt, and to this day Sagemont Church still operates *debt free*. Thousands of people have joined the throng of people living *debt-free*. Many churches have followed suit.

While at a pastor's conference in Jacksonville, Florida, in January, 1988, I heard given the testimony of Pastor Homer Lindsay and the First Baptist Church of Jacksonville doing a similar thing: "Debt Free in '43." That's correct: 1943! Wow!

All this proves out in this Life the great Truth in Scripture:
> But Jesus beheld them, and said unto them, With men this is impossible: but with God all things are possible. Matthew 19:26 (In Mark 10:27 these same words are repeated).

> If thou canst believe, all things are possible to him that believeth. Mark 9:23. (Jesus telling a father who is desiring Jesus' help with his son).

Therefore, You and I must choose either to live a life of *worldly financial methods and practices,* OR choose to Live a Life of *God's financial Truths, methods, and practices.* (let me insert this bit of wisdom before going on…a *therefore* is always referring to what has just been said, written, given…it is good to go back and review what or why the *therefore* is there for)

My hope is that you will take the time to read all that is written to give God an opportunity to speak to your Heart about what He can do, and where He can take you, in your stewardship of His resources. Do you have another Father who owns the cattle on 1,000 hills?!? Will you commit to Live the Life of *God's financial Truths, methods, and practices?* It will add up to *The Math of Life.*

This book is written with expectations of you finding out the Truth of Ephesians 3:20,

> Now unto Him that is able to do exceeding abundantly above all that we ask or think, according to the power that worketh in us.

Be a steward of God's resources. It is *The Math of Life. Christ's Life.*

p.s. I will give you throughout this book, and in a list at the end of the book, over 100 Scripture verses speaking to God's Way of finances and His plan for Heavenly economics.

Chapter 6
1 + 1 = 2, Usually
Verily, verily, I say unto you, Except a corn of wheat
fall into the ground and die, it abideth alone:
but if it die, it bringeth forth much fruit.
John 12:24

Much fruit. One seed planted can yield *multiple* fruit. Exciting words! Anyone who has ever planted seeds knows the potential of a multiple yield. And that is a word from God as to what He can do with the seeds He provides us for daily living and what sort of yield He can give at harvest time.

It is so amazing as to how many of God's people never give one moment's thought as to God's potential with His resources He sends our way for us to be *faithful stewards* over…not owners.

In fact, Luke 16:10 gives a very important principle of God's financial Way: Faithful vs unjust.

> He that is faithful in that which is least is faithful also in much: and he that is unjust in the least is unjust also in much. Luke 16:10

Prepared people are multiple times more likely to be *faithful* in God's eyes than any unprepared person could be. So, this book is about helping some child of God, in particular, to have a great start at being *prepared* and found *faithful*. However, one does not have to be a child of God to practice the Truths found here. Believing, understanding, desiring to practice, and doing so might be much more prevalent in Saints.

Just a quick point (much more in chapter 15, page 68), God's use of *unjust* instead of *unfaithful* is a strong, parabolic statement from Him. There is a big difference between those two words, and the Truth of Matthew 16:1-13 becomes known when we understand the parabolic words spoken by Jesus. And the next 4 verses are independent of these, but…whoa!

Things add up. That IS a given in life. Life adds up. And it starts with the *little things*. And God says that those people who are faithful (the Greek word, *pistos,* means *dependable/trustworthy*) with the *least* ARE faithful IN *much*. Now here is an incredible Truth in 2 letters: **IS**.

IS means equals. 1 + 1 = 2. And 1 + 1 **is** 2. *Is* and = are the *same as*. So, why is that important? Because we must know and recognize that things that are happening all around us day after day are *adding up to (equaling)* something. We cannot ignore that.

This Truth can work for us in a mighty way when it comes to the *Math of Life*. For instance, if we will just ADD any amount to our savings on a regular basis...daily, weekly, monthly...we will end up with more than we have at the beginning. However, entering into this process in *God's Way* adds and multiplies amounts differently than the *world's way*. This is how Christ's Life is breathed into an individual's (couple's) financial status. It takes starting, then continuing, and more continuing with God to end up where you want to be.

IF we are spending instead of saving, that ADDS UP to having *little* in the bank later on. So, I am amazed at the staggering numbers given by those who research the spending and saving habits of Americans. Listen to these typical figures:

- "69% of all Americans have less than $1,000 in savings today." (Stuart Varney on the Stuart Varney Show, FOX Business Network, 10/10/16)
- "44% of all Americans making $100,000 to 150,000/year have less than, or easily available, $1,000 in savings." (Stuart Varney, 10/10/16)
- "Half of U.S. families have zero retirement savings accounts." (2016 GOBankingRates survey)
- "Over ½ of U.S. families have no savings at all." (2016 GOBankingRates survey)
- "And, 34% report having ZERO in savings at age 65." (2016 GOBankingRates survey)
- A note deep in my notes folder says "in 2010, 72% of Americans are living *paycheck to paycheck*...up 1% from 2009." (I didn't make note of who said that on what program)
- Paul Ryan said "78% of Americans are living paycheck to paycheck." (U. S. Congressional House Speaker Paul Ryan on FNC, Tuesday evening, 11-14-17). He went on to say that "57% don't have $500 cash in savings."

Are those last numbers incredible, or what?

Three notes before we move on:

1. A banker friend from back in 1975 gave me this advice: *Pay yourself first*. He explained: "When you go out to eat because you deserve to get something for all the hard work you have done...who ends up with the money the next morning? The food place. You have nothing, except a hungry stomach that needs to be fed again." Someone might say, "Are you saying I can never go out to eat?!?" No. My banker was saying, "Before you give someone else some of your money, make sure you have put some amount into your savings account." (I recommend a predetermined amount for a specific period of time...see Chapter 22)
2. Too many Americans have bought into (no pun intended) the advertising that tells us *we deserve a break today* (or, the many variables that have come and gone over the years) and goes on to tell us how we should spend our hard-earned money with their company to give us that *break*. Well, we DO deserve a break...put something into *our* account before we put something into *their* account.
3. Think of the unimaginable, unaccounted for, amount of dollars the typical American spends in a lifetime on things like drinks, chips, candy, entertainment, etc., etc., etc. (You and I could make a list of 500 things!). Not to mention cigarettes or booze or drugs. Now listen! **They rarely ever, if never, give one thought** about what they will have in the bank at age 65. I am saying we should never spend any amount on any of these *things* until we have put our pre-determined amount into OUR savings account for the time frame we set. I hear some saying, "But you don't expect me to go without, or to not have any fun, do you?!?" Is ending up at age 65 with no money in the bank your description of **F-U-N** ?

Things add up. Life adds up. Spending adds up. Saving can add up. We need to make sure we are in charge of the process of *adding up* into *our account!* It's what we do with the *little amounts* that determine whether we will be faithful with the *big amounts*. Remember? God says so.

Never forget, being *unjust* is the opposite
in God's eyes of being *faithful*.

Faithful – Grace Life – God living through our earthsuit.
Unjust – enmity with God's teachings - living in carnal mind.

Now listen...there is basically no excuse for anyone to end up at age 65 and not have a very tidy sum in savings. It really is difficult to have any empathy for those who have squandered a lifetime of possible savings. However, if you and I just take the majestic statements in Chapter 2 made by folks who have studied, practiced, learned, taught, & have seen results for themselves and others...take these and apply them to our life...we would have no problem facing life at age 65. Guaranteed.

How is that? In God's financial Way, reckoning with the Life of Christ, 1 + 1 = more than 2! It's there. We know it. We have the 3 pieces (1 + 1 + Christ). Listen, have we not heard, *give and it shall be given unto you*...to such an extent we cannot out give God...He gives back MORE than we give? *A seed must die before it can grow?* One seed planted can yield MULTIPLE fruit. $1 given to missions can yield numerous souls!

Yes! Figure on **God's formula** and ADD to your substance, not waste. And reckon with God to do the unimaginable and unfigurable with what you do not waste!

Be faithful with the *little things*. It is *The Math of Life*. *Christ's Life*.

Chapter 7
Financial Freedom
*And ye shall know the truth,
and the truth shall make you free.*
John 8:32

Soon after my wife, Barbara, and I became Saints in 1980 at Sagemont Church, Houston, Texas, she attended Pastor John Morgan's *Financial Freedom Seminar* during a 13-week Church Training course on Sunday evenings prior to the evening service. I can remember her coming home very excited to hear of the great Scriptural teachings on finances. They were contrary to all we had learned in the worldly environment we had always been in.

Actually, this was the first time I think I had ever heard of the phrase, *financial freedom*. Heretofore it had always been, *financial independence* or *financial security*. There is a HUGE difference between *God's thinking* and the *world's thinking*. What a difference *God's Way* is from the *world's way*.

Financial independence or *financial security* are about a person gaining some sort of level of supposed *independence/security* in a worldly, dollar way. With all the relative thoughts and decisions, it always centers on the individual gaining this *independence/security* by his/her own efforts. And, of course, many have that *so-called security* vanish in the blink-of-an-eye due to some force beyond their control.

In contrast, *financial freedom* is about God's capabilities and doing. It is a status and provision the individual is given through the promises, provisions, and protections of God.

There is NOTHING in the financial realm that compares to the *financial freedom* a Saint can enjoy who is completely dependent upon God for all aspects of the Life of provision, protection, and projection. And so many times, it is hilarious how God confounds the *wisdom* of the world (and worldly!) with His financial Way.

Let me share a remarkable testimony by the great pastor of the First Baptist Church of Dallas, Dr. W. A. Criswell, back in the early 1980's. In those days, many companies, institutions, churches, and individuals had *2% over prime* loan rates. That wasn't too difficult to swallow if they were of the mind to *borrow* UNTIL the prime rate started to rise to a very high number…18%! One Sunday morning, Dr. Criswell got up in the pulpit of

FBCD and said, "We no longer answer to God. We now answer to the bank." The people were aghast. Dr. Criswell said the church needed to get out of debt.

Let me share the marvelous story of how the First Baptist Church got out of debt back in 1982.

> In a recent conversation with Pastor John Morgan, 53 years the Pastor of Sagemont Church in Houston, Texas, he graciously gave the following story...

A group of pastors and their wives were invited to go to Hawaii with Dr. Criswell. Dr. Criswell had gotten word that Sagemont Church had gotten out of debt and was not going to borrow. He asked Pastor John Morgan to visit him in the hotel there to talk about handling finances in the church.

As the two men sat on the porch of the Criswell's room one night, Dr. Criswell said, "I want to tell you an idea I have about getting our church out of debt. I want to know if I have a good idea and if this came from the Lord." Dr. Criswell had given some of his staff the task of finding out the average income for the families of FBC Dallas and their average net worth. He knew the amount FBCD needed to get out of debt. His idea was to divide the need by the number of families who were faithful in their giving, and to ask them to bring a gift related to their financial status on a certain day. He was going to ask them to go to their bank and borrow whatever amount was relative to them. And then on a certain Sunday they would bring their gift to retire the debt of FBCD.

Dr. Criswell then said to Pastor Morgan, "What do you think about that, lad?" Pastor Morgan said, "Dr. Criswell, you've certainly done some research and thinking, but let me just run something by you with all due respect. I've learned that if the bank has money, we have money, because that is where they get their money...from us, including the children of God. So, if the members of FBCD have money in the bank, God has provided it. And if your people borrow from the bank, then they are going into debt."

When this rang a bell with Dr. Criswell, he looked over at Pastor Morgan with tears in his eyes. And Pastor Morgan said, "Dr. Criswell, if the people go down and borrow money, that puts them in bondage." Dr. Criswell got out his handkerchief, wiped his eyes, and said, "Lad, I never thought of that, but you're right." Pastor Morgan said, "Well, I am not right, but what God says is right." Dr. Criswell responded, "Well that's reason I want you to come and talk to my people. Our people are the best and finest people in the whole world, and they will bless you." And what the people of FBCD did thereafter was right.

Dr. Criswell then said, "You know, I believe you're right. Well, lad, would you come preach for me soon on a Sunday morning?" Of course, Pastor Morgan told Dr. Criswell he would be glad to. Pastor Morgan says he was so nervous about preaching at the great First Baptist Church of Dallas, he forgot his Bible and left it in Houston. He literally prayed for God to give him a room that had a Bible in it. This was at the hotel in downtown Dallas next to the church. He spoke to God, "Oh, dear God, I am preaching tomorrow and I have forgotten my Bible." And God spoke to him to look for the Bible the Gideons typically put in hotel rooms. Sure enough, there was one there. And Pastor Morgan got up in the famous pulpit of FBCD the next morning and preached using that Gideon-provided Bible.

Pastor Morgan thought, "My Bible is in Houston, but the same God Who wrote my Bible wrote this one here. I am on the right track." So he preached that morning with the red Bible and told the Sagemont story. Pastor Morgan emphasized two points: 1) as long as the people are in debt, the church is in debt. 2) Nowhere in the Bible did God use borrowed money. "He owns the cattle on 1,000 hills and the hills they graze on. My God will supply all my needs according to His riches in glory by Christ Jesus. If we don't have the money that we need to do God's work we're fixing to do what God doesn't want us to do, like going into debt for 20 years."

God worked in many amazing ways. FBCD owned a building next door to the church. A close friend of Dr. Criswell's came and told him, "Why don't we sell the air space above our Education Building. They sold the air space above that building to an insurance company. One member gave a large amount on the basis that for every dollar the members gave, the church could use a dollar from the member's money. Like a matching gift.

From that the church became debt free.

In a relatively short time the church had enough money to pay off the bank COMPLETELY! And Dr. Criswell got up in the pulpit once more and proclaimed, "We are FREE!"

Pastor Morgan concluded our conversation with, "The main thing is…when you get to the point in your life that God, our Heavenly Father, owns it all, and come to understand that it belongs to His children to be used…that's the story. It's not by your gambling in Las Vegas, or being made the President of the biggest company in the world. But when you let go, and let God, He will start you and He will stop you. The way He will stop you is Philippians 4:19. He has said He will supply all we ever have need of. Be sure of how you are fixing to use what God has supplied. There are many things we don't need."

Pastor Morgan has always taught, James 1:17, "Every good gift and every perfect gift is from above, and cometh down from the Father of lights, with whom there is no variableness, neither shadow of turning."

Numerous folks have told Barbara and I that they want to know what God has to say about how to do finances His Way.

The basic knowledge of the *Ways of God* that Pastor Morgan gave us through his seminar took us on a journey that has now spanned over 40 years. We pay CASH, or we don't buy it. It has been one of continuous learning, experiencing, and joyfully trusting in God.

Let me give you the beginning statements from Pastor Morgan, as he opens his conference…

John Morgan, from his Financial Freedom Seminar, 1980…
"When God is able to supply any need, any time, any place, in any amount to us or through us according to His will, we become free. Financial bondage is you having more faith in your material goods than you do in your eternal God."

John Morgan, from his Financial Freedom Seminar, 1980…
"Financial freedom is:
- Freedom from financial debt
- Freedom from financial worry

- Freedom from financial selfishness
- Freedom to obey God financially"

Soak on those two statements for a while. They will give you a grand idea of just how peaceful, calm, and comfortable your financial Life can be under the direction of God, with His Hand on all you do.

God is able to supply any need, any time, any place, in any amount to us or through us according to His Heart.

We are to have more trust in our eternal God than we do in our material goods.
We are to be free from ANY financial debt.
We are to be free from ANY financial worry.
We are to be free from ANY financial selfishness.
We are to obey God in ALL financial matters.

Since Pastor John Morgan's seminar involves so many ideas and scriptures, it would be impossible to cover hardly more than a handful in this short chapter. I may have whet your appetite for what Pastor Morgan has to say with the above quotes. I hope so. His teachings from the Word of God and the applications of God's Truths literally changed the course of our finances for the rest of our lives. Let me encourage you to be sure and contact Pastor Morgan and obtain his workbook:

John Morgan
PO Box 8894
Bacliff, TX 77518

Barbara and I have been LIVING *God's financial freedom* since those days of 1980! Yes, there have been a time or two of *waiting* instead of instant gratification. But, oh, what a glorious testimony to our great God when we see His answer to prayer and supply come onto the scene!

No financial debt.
No financial worries.
No financial pressures.
All from obeying God and trusting Him for His supply, in His time, in His will…and Living on it.

And a wait in time that really is more expectation (to see *what* and *when* God will provide) WITHOUT any exasperation, exigency, or exhaustion during the wait.

Be encouraged to trust God. It is *The Math of Life. Christ's Life.* Living Life debt free. Trusting God for His supply, and Living on it.

Chapter 8
Life is NOT *Fair*
...the just shall live by His faith.
Habakkuk 2:4

Many people always go around saying, "That's not fair!" "You're not fair!" "Life is not fair!"

They have it right...they're just missing the point.
LIFE is NOT *fair*...
 Being born blind, or deaf, or deformed is NOT *fair*.
 Being born with any handicap is NOT *fair*.
 Being born into different cultures or families (some say) is NOT *fair*.

But, the point is: GOD is **JUST**, NOT *fair*.
God picked out the perfect parents for YOU and ME!
God picked out our family heritage.
God decided our sex.
God chose our socio-economic situation for us to grow up in.
God even picked out our location to live while young.
God...
God...
God has even numbered the days we will have in this life.

The list can go on and on.

Therefore, are we going to *give up* in living out the days He has numbered for us? Are we going to be *defeated* before we ever get into the game? Are we going to be *mad, angry, bitter, hold grudges,* etc.

Or, will we make the most of what God has given us and led us through? Will we make the most of how we have benefited:
- through education, including many Truths of God
- through learning from others, gaining the financial wisdom of God
- through experiences, experiencing God's Life in our finances

Will we be the *just*, Living the Life of God and His faith?

Proverbs 3:33 tells us *He blesseth the habitation of the just.* As God is *just*, so should we be. It brings His blessings.

Proverbs 9:9, *Give instruction to a wise man, and he will be yet wiser: teach a just man, and he will increase in learning.* Notice that education is a good thing for a *just* man.

Proverbs 10:6. *Blessings are upon the head of the just...* Wow!

Proverbs 11:1, *A false balance is abomination to the LORD: but a just weight is His delight.* There are so many aspects of life that are relative to our deciding to walk as a *just* person!

Proverbs 11:9, *...through knowledge shall the just be delivered.*

Proverbs 16:11, *A just weight and balance are the LORD's: all the weights of the bag are His work* (concern).

Proverbs 20:7, *The just man walketh in his integrity: his children are blessed after him.* Aha! God even tells us that OUR CHILDREN are blessed by OUR walking in His *justness*.

What does it mean to be *just*? Basically, it speaks of one who is lawful, honest, righteous, right. Truth is, God's Nature is His being all these. He is the standard of ethics. 2 Chronicles 12:6, "...The LORD is righteous." *Is* means *equals*. One who is living out a *just* life is experiencing all the Nature of God through his earthsuit. That one believes God. That one trusts God. THAT is being JUST. I want to be *that one*, don't you?

Let us look from the perspective of a *just* Life at some steps that follow God's instructions:

Get an education...keep learning until you die! Study the Holy Scriptures. Learn from those who have gleaned God's financial Truths. And every one that has gone to school through high school has learned a lot. But, I am not talking about going to another school and taking expensive classes. I am talking about getting books or asking family and friends to find out the best ways to buy a car, shop for higher-dollar appliances, save on vacations, make wise investments, etc.

Grow by learning from others who have learned the financial wisdom of God. One of the greatest opportunities in living is to be around older folks who have gone through some of the financial issues and decisions we are dealing with. Their knowledge is valuable. God has given me so many *older* folks who have taught me numerous truths that have yielded great results and increases in our financial realm. *Am I crazy or what...how few people ever ask ANYONE ANY question about insurance, certain products, particular companies to do business with, some individual to buy/sell a home with, or numerous other financial matters???* Isn't that insane, really! There is so much to gain, so much to avoid, so much to enjoy by *rubbing elbows* with folks who have *learned the hard way*, as our parents used to say. It is a great tragedy to miss out on *growing* by learning from others God has graciously brought across our life's path.

Gain from our experiences...keep some sort of record of all the experiences God has taken us through. Make notes on what yielded good or the best returns. And make note on what subtracted from our storehouse! Invaluable lessons (an *education* in themselves!) can be gained through our experiences. It is a great loss to miss out on gaining from our experiences of God's Life in our finances.

Taking the risk of possibly sounding a little negative, let me mention two things that we should always avoid:
- Making excuses. NEVER do this.
- Blaming someone or some thing. NEVER do this.

The *excuse* and *blame* games never yield any positive gains in any aspect of life. To move forward, we need to steer clear of such distractive and destructive efforts.

It is exciting to really see what a *just* Life can do for us. Let me recommend that you take the time to read and meditate on Daniel 1:1 through 6:28...see if you can list several principles of the *just* Life (God's Life) that stand out in the actions of Daniel, Shadrach, Meshach, and Abednego exemplifying being *just*, and how God protected them every step of the way.

It would be a good challenge for you to find several instances where God honored those who practiced His *just* Life in handling His resources. He will do the same for us IF we are *just* in our financial endeavors.

Dare to be a *just* Saint. It is *The Math of Life. Christ's Life.*

Chapter 9
God Is Owner, Man Is Steward

*And the Lord said, Who then is that faithful and wise
steward, whom his lord shall make ruler over his
household, to give them their portion of meat
in due season? Blessed is that servant, whom his
lord when he cometh shall find so doing.
Of a truth I say unto you, that he
will make him ruler over all he hath.
Luke 12:42-44*

It is very interesting Jesus gives a couple of parables about covetousness, greediness, trust, watchfulness, and readiness. Then Peter asks, *speakest thou this parable unto us, or even to all?* And the Lord tells us clearly there is a difference between being *owner* and being *steward/ruler* over what is the owner's.

Let me introduce the manner in which a Saint decides *who* is *what* regarding possessions and finances…

Since the old slang excuse of Saints for all our troubles *(the devil made me do it)* is from the pits of hell, it is high time Saints take responsibility to start making Scripturally wise choices originating from the Truth of Scripture. Nobody…certainly not the devil…makes a Saint DO anything. It is always our CHOICE! God's Word is chock full of directives for God's children to CHOOSE…

> And if it seem evil unto you to serve the LORD, **choose** you this day whom ye will serve; whether the gods which your fathers served that were on the other side of the flood, or the gods of the Amorites, in whose land ye dwell: **but as for me and my house, we will serve the LORD**. Joshua 24:15
>
> **I have chosen the way of truth**: Thy judgments have I laid before me. Psalm 119:130
>
> For God so loved the world, that He gave His only begotten Son, that **whosoever believeth in Him** should not perish, but have everlasting life. John 3:16
>
> *(my boldness in all verses is for emphasis)*

It is interesting that God introduces a new word for *choosing* in the New Testament…*to believe*. And the Greek word behind *to believe* is *pisteuo*, which carries with it more than a mental idea, but a mental persuasion, really a moral action, a choosing. This persuasion always leads to *action* based on the *belief*. Truth is: what we perceive, we *believe*; and what we truly *believe*, we act upon.

I will never forget some of Pastor John Morgan's first words to Barbara and I right after we were Born Again in his office: "Here's some good news, you have a NEW CHOOSER. Much of what you used to choose will no longer be what you choose. It is because the New Man in you is your NEW CHOOSER, and He (Christ) chooses the things of God." WOW! How beautiful it has been these 40+ years to Live with our NEW CHOOSER, Holy Spirit's Mind. This New Man *Believes* and acts upon His Beliefs. That is how the Life of Christ is carried out in Saints.

Guess what…one of our first NEW beliefs led us to our decision to acknowledge that God is OWNER and we are just His *stewards (economists/business managers)* of everything. Pastor John was well-known for his Scriptural financial teaching. It was in this area of life that we began to make drastic changes in our financial realm.

First, let us know for sure what a *steward* is: *oikonomos*, one who is a manager of the household or domestic affairs of a person, their *business manager*. It can be a physical (coins and other possessions) or Spiritual (Truths) management. God says He has given to Saints this management of all that He has given us, both physical and Spiritual. In the realm of financial management, handling the money/resources God gives us is a Spiritual matter. We either believe and trust as He directs, or we go against God and believe our own way (a matter of serving other gods). Listen to God's Word in 1 Peter 4:10…

> As every man hath received the gift, even so minister the same one to another, as good stewards of the manifold grace of God.

Saints have the responsibility of management in the *manifold grace of God*. This is an exciting testimony of God working through His Saints to be His stewards. Him carrying out the responsibility, when He is allowed to rule and reign in our life. (Do yourself a favor, and look up the Greek and meanings behind *manifold grace of God*.)

So, let's narrow down this stewardship life to three things:
1. a **decision**. It is a **confirmation**. We believe and trust God's Way, or another way (which is never The Way!). It is incumbent upon Saints to find out WHAT IS *God's Way* in the matter of financial stewardship, if we are going to believe and trust *His Way*.
2. a **direction**. It is a **conviction**. Once we know *God's Way,* and have believed and trusted to act upon *God's Way,* we must be convicted we are doing His Will. Only through convictions do we continue in a direction when pressures come against us. Time and time again, people find out they have preferences, and not convictions. They just will not stick with what they have said they *believe and trust* in God's Word.
3. a **determination**. It is a **compelling**. Convictions lead to this compelling desire and determination to continue on and carry out *God's Way.* One of the most difficult challenges facing Saints is to stand firm and continue on in The Way when the world, the devil, and the pride of life come against everything God says to do. Standing firm and continuing on to the finish is accomplished ONLY when we believe God to the extent that He has sealed *our belief* with *His Faith.* His Faith will carry every Saint to the finish line who possesses such. His Faith only comes when we believe with our Heart of God, and Holy Spirit seals our believing with His gift of His Faith.

So, where do we stand: as a STEWARD, or as an OWNER?

Do we own our car, or does God? Do we own our golf clubs, or does God? Do we own our sewing machine, or does God? Or, worse still, does the bank or finance company *own* these? No one *owns* a home, car, etc., IF they *owe* money on any of these. The financial institution *owns* them until the debt is completely paid off. Do we own our check book, or does God? Do we own our savings accounts, or does God? Do we own the hours of each day, or does God? It can be a startling thing to think of being on God's clock and figuring how we are spending the hours each day He gives us. See? Everything comes into play in the realm of ownership vs stewardship.

But, there is still the issue of faithfulness. Are we being a good steward (business manager) of all that God owns? OR, will He find that being a slacker, or sluggard, or simpleton has been the rule in stewardship for us?

Try taking the time to make a list. On the left side, write down an item, or issue. In the next column list *who* is the owner. In the next column show on a scale of 1 to 10 just how well you are at being a steward of God with each item/issue. Last column, make note of any beliefs/actions you should take to correct any *wrong* entries! Then ask the Lord to come and BE in and through you the things you noted in the last column. THAT is what abiding in Christ and seeing His Grace Life Lived out in you is all about!

A confirmation, a conviction, a compelling…these are the pillars of *financial stewardship God's Way.*

Be a good, faithful steward of God's resources. It is *The Math of Life. Christ's Life.*

Chapter 10
We Cannot Serve God & Mammon
No man can serve two masters:
for either he will hate the one, and love the other;
or else he will hold to the one, and despise the other.
Ye cannot serve God and mammon.
Matthew 6:24

Mammon is a word that speaks of the *god of riches or wealth*. It refers to all sorts of various material things…earnings, possessions, something of material value.

Everybody knows that *mammon* is a key player in the life of so many on this earth. It has always been. The Scriptures speak clearly about trade, coins, crops, flocks, houses, and work…all so often connected to that *god* of so many people's lives. And Almighty God steps in and says, "Ye cannot serve God and mammon."

Mammon (Greek: *mammonas*) appears only 4 times in the NT. Here in our text, and again in Luke chapter 16 (in the closing verses of the parable of the Unjust Employer, vs 1-13).

> He that is faithful in that which is least is faithful also in much: and he that is unjust in the least is unjust also in much. If therefore ye have not been faithful in the unrighteous mammon, who will commit to your trust the true riches? And if ye have not been faithful in that which is another man's, who shall give you that which is your own? No servant can serve two masters: for either he will hate the one, and love the other; or else he will hold to the one, and despise the other. Ye cannot serve God and mammon. Luke 16:10-13

The context of Luke's passage indicates a connection to the *god of materialism*, as does Matthew's verse. Almighty God is declaring that everyone has to decide, then direct their life toward HIM or the *god of riches or wealth*.

So, this is one of those battle grounds where actually the *natural spiritual mind* of a Saint (the one from our first birth that is left still inside the Born Again Saint) is at war with the *Supernatural Spiritual Mind of Christ* that the Saint was given as a part of the New Birth. *This* is a *real* battle that can continue to be waged for virtually as long as Saints remain on this physical earth. (The reality that a Saint can be so abandoned and controlled on a constant basis by Holy Spirit, and therefore *Live* out of the *Mind of Christ* is another discussion for another place and time. Look up my writings in other books.)

Therefore (I like that word, don't you?!?) appears hundreds of times in the Holy Scriptures, meaning check your premises as mentioned beforehand. Two of the greatest teachings Saints can be given are:
- the importance to our God of *what* is said in our text
- the *how* that Christ's Life in Saints can avoid the false god, and serve God

Actually, our God makes Himself very clear and very profound on this matter. He unequivocally states that:
- no man can serve two masters
- either he will hate the one, and love the other
- or, he will hold to the one, and despise the other
- no one cannot serve God and mammon (the *god of materialism, riches, or wealth*)

Each individual must decide to whom his affections and decisions and activities will be centered upon and submissive to. Who will guide the Saint's life? Will it be *The Life* or *a life*? But, God makes it perfectly clear that *very strong emotional ties* will dictate a profound clarity of decision-making and action-taking activity in each person's life. Emotional bondage can derail a Saint's Spiritual desire to serve God financially.

How does this practically work out in our day to day financial experiences? It is one thing to know we must serve God, and to decide to do that, but what are the steps we take to put that into practice? Let us look at a couple of examples:
- One thing is this, be good and just stewards. Jesus is finishing His parable of the Unjust Employer. We must remember a *Scriptural parable* is *a Heavenly Truth with a Heavenly meaning,* sometimes using an earthly illustration. Many have faltered at this parable for its seemingly confusing statements. One thing causing this *seeming* confusion is that the Greek word, *dieblethe,* translated *accused (v.1),* should actually be translated *falsely accused.* Therefore, we see Jesus

is simply commending the wise steward for his practical wisdom of using whatever personal means he had in ways to secure his future on earth. In doing so, Jesus drew the ire of the Pharisees, who were covetous, which gave Him opportunity to get right in their faces with a few challenges in verses 25-34. Actually, a just steward today would be more concerned about helping unbelievers to know The Way of salvation and eternal Life than his own earthly future.

- Another thing, as a good and just steward we honor God with our substance and our first fruits. God is the greatest *giver* of all. And we cannot out-give Him.

King Solomon told us this in Proverbs 3:9-10...

Honor the LORD with thy substance, and with the firstfruits of all thine increase: so shall thy barns be filled with plenty, and thy presses shall burst out with new wine.

Malachi has told us this in Malachi 3:8-12...

Will a man rob God? Yet ye have robbed me. But ye say, Wherein have we robbed thee? In tithes and offerings. Ye are cursed with a curse: for ye have robbed me, even this whole nation. Bring ye all the tithes into the storehouse, that there may be meat in mine house, and prove me now herewith, saith the LORD of hosts, if I will not open you the windows of heaven, and pour out a blessing, that there shall not be room enough to receive it. And I will rebuke the devourer for your sakes, and he shall not destroy the fruits of your ground; neither shall your vine cast her fruit before the time in the field, saith the LORD of hosts. And all nations shall call you blessed: for ye shall be a delightsome land, saith the LORD of hosts.

Luke has told us this in Luke 6:38.

Give, and it shall be given unto you, good measure, pressed down, and shaken together and running over, shall men give into your bosom. For with the same measure that ye mete withal it shall be measure to you again.

So, let us show our love and service by giving cheerfully and bountifully as He directs His Heart in us. Our giving can include the financial resources God has trusted us with, the talents He has equipped us with, and the time He has allowed us to have, but always our giving begins with our substance and our first fruits financially. Serving God is being a *ready and cheerful giver* as God is.

- Another is that we be found faithful in doing so. Faithfulness is such a huge issue. In all walks of life, especially in the work arena, employers are looking for the faithful workers/employees. There are so many ways to apply v.10, but always keep in mind God has declared that the faithful in the LITTLE things IS faithful in the BIG things. The faithful in those things with less value WILL BE faithful with those things having larger value. Wow! A great Life Truth! And, the faithful in *the little* can be trusted with *the big*. And the next verse tells us our degree of faithfulness will determine whether He will commit to our trust the *true riches*, Spiritual wealth. Woe to those who are unjust…

- And another is the acknowledgement and putting into practice of the use of God's Heart in financial matters, and not the heart of the world. That war previously mentioned must be decided for God's side. God requires such. Practically speaking, it is imperative that Saints LEARN God's Ways in the financial world, and then USE His Ways in every encounter. As one will quickly learn, God's Way is often, if not almost always, an opposite Way from the world's way. The end result is either we are enjoying *righteousness* or *unrighteousness*.

Therefore, our decision as to whether we will serve God or mammon is a definitive one. It will take us down a path of God being #1 in our life, or mammon. The latter is getting dangerously close to exposing the heart that *loves money/things/wealth*. Remember, Saints have two hearts from which to choose. And God has more to say about that…see chapters 12 and 41.

Choose to serve God, and not mammon. It is *The Math of Life. Christ's Life.*

Chapter 11
Godliness With Contentment
But godliness with contentment is great gain.
1 Timothy 6:6

Wow! Who among us reading these words does not want contentment? Peace? Joy? How can we not appreciate and get excited when OUR LORD tells us *godliness with contentment* brings GREAT GAIN? *Peace* and *Joy* are among the GAIN that contentment brings. But, contentment can work financially as well.

I remember the first time I went to church as an adult really looking for something that the world could not offer. Barbara and I were not *rich*, but we sure had things pretty good for a young couple at that time. But there was something missing. It was like we just didn't have *enough*. And there was no real *peace*. What we didn't realize was that this *enough* was not money or things or riches...but that which only the LORD can bring and give.

Isn't that hilarious?!? *bring and give*. Hasn't that been missed by almost every living being in this world, including so many Saints? Listen to the next few words God spoke to young Timothy concerning this *godliness with contentment*, OR about those without it!

> For we brought nothing into this world, and it is certain we can carry nothing out. And having food and raiment, let us be therewith content. But they that will be rich fall into temptation and a snare, and into many foolish and hurtful lusts, which drown men in destruction and perdition. For the love of money is the root of all evil: which while some coveted after, they have erred from the faith, and pierced themselves with many sorrows.
> 1 Timothy 6:7-10

Those who don't possess and LIVE by *godliness with contentment* are those who will fall into temptation and a snare (entrapment, bondage, debt), and into many foolish and hurtful lusts, drowning in destruction and perdition, because of their LOVE of money, coveting after such, and ultimately err from the faith, piercing themselves with many sorrows. WHAT A LIST OF SAD NEWS!

What will it take for Saints to listen and heed the Words of God, and let His Life be Lived through us with *godliness and contentment*?

Do you know someone who is Living a Life of *godliness and contentment*? What does their Life look like? Do they look like they are missing anything? Do we really think that if someone doesn't have all the world's *things* that they cannot be satisfied, have any joy, live not in peace, and certainly not be content? Oh, what a sad day it is in Christianity in so many ways.

What is it about *godliness and contentment* besides just being a gift from our Lord when we let His Life be our Life in our finances in particular? God gives us a direct word in His letter to the church at Philippi. Look for the 5 things emphasized below:

- peace of God
- our hearts and minds
- Christ Jesus
- a list of virtues
- God of peace

> Rejoice in the Lord always, and again I say, Rejoice. Let your moderation be known unto all men. The Lord is at hand. Be careful for nothing; but in everything by prayer and supplication with thanksgiving let your requests be made known unto God. And the peace of God, which passeth all understanding, shall keep your hearts and minds through Christ Jesus. Finally, brethren, whatsoever things are true, whatsoever things are honest, whatsoever things are pure, whatsoever things are lovely, whatsoever things are of good report; if there be any virtue, and if there be any praise think on these things. Those things, which ye have both learned, and received, and heard, and seen in me, do: and the God of peace shall be with you. Philippians 4:4-9

Is it any wonder that the Apostle Paul (actually Holy Spirit speaking through Paul) gave us 4 of the most pertinent, meaningful, and powerful verses regarding this idea of *godliness with contentment* relevant to finances before he ended this chapter and this letter to the church at Philippi? Read them closely...

>Not that I speak in respect of want: for I have learned, in whatsoever state I am therewith to be content. 4:11

Holy Spirit used the Greek *husteresis* for *want*. It is not what we commonly think of as *something I really want or think I can't live without*. It is a *falling short*. Paul was telling the Philippians he was not doing without (falling short), but was satisfied, or content, with what he had, especially how God was providing for him through them.

>I can do all things through Christ which strengtheneth me. 4:13
>
>But I have all, and abound: I am full... 4:18
>
>But my God shall supply all your need according to His riches in glory by Christ Jesus. 4:19

Now before we close this chapter, let me expound just a bit on the difference (definitions) and discernment of what we typically *want* and *need*. These two have everything to do with contentment...

want – *I think I can't live without it.* Isn't that the sad state (no pun intended) we find too many folks living in today? It didn't just start yesterday either. I can think back to my teen years and hearing my parents speaking of a common phrase in that day, *keeping up with the Joneses*. How did that enter life in our day? CREDIT. It really hit our generation in the early 1950's when credit cards came into being. Fake money (see Chapter 59). And almost everybody began to *want* what they truthfully could not buy with CASH, but with CREDIT they could have it NOW. And contentment *went out the window* (a phrase I used to hear my grandparents speak of when talking about something that had gone away...that gave way to *Elvis has left the building*...lol!). Gone.

Think about this. Our enemy has taken the word *want (husteresis)* and distorted it into a "me" discontentment. With God supplying every need, Saints can never *fall short*. Just as Paul stated. Scriptural contentment is nowhere to be seen or found in the lives of way too many today.

We may *want* something, but God has told us He will supply *our need* WHEN we NEED it (or, sometimes He provides in advance expecting us to save for a future need) and *we shall not want* (Psalm 23:1). And when we can't live without a *want*, waiting on God to supply our *need*, trouble is just around the corner.

need – *everything we must have to live according to God's financial Way*. Ever since Barbara and I heard the teachings of Pastor John Morgan in his *Financial Freedom Seminar*, and we decided to *Live Life Debt Free - Trusting God for His Supply and Living On It*, we have had the peace, joy, and contentment that God gives to those who trust Him and honor Him in their financial lives. We have been fortunate to experience the testimony of the Apostle Paul. God has provided at times, and protected at times, in the most unbelievable way. God has always made sure we had plenty. Well, amen.

What does God tell us is *contentment?* Having food, raiment (clothing), and housing in whatever is God's supply.

Let me encourage you to try *Living Life Debt Free - Trusting God for His Supply, and Living On It? Peace* and *contentment*. It is *The Math of Life. Christ's Life.*

Chapter 12
The Love of Money
*For the love of money is the root of all evil:
which while some coveted after,
they have erred from the faith,
and pierced themselves through with many sorrows.*
1 Timothy 6:10

This is a verse that rarely do many Saints take seriously, much less really *know*, comprehend, and understand the tremendous impact it should have in every life.

Holy Spirit penned through the Apostle Paul one of the most quoted verses from the end of this first letter to Timothy, Paul's beloved companion. Paul sent Timothy to Ephesus to deal with false teachers evident in the church there. Timothy, who was apparently of a timid nature, was encouraged to boldly stand against these evil men by upholding Truth God had given.

And one of God's most profound Truths is v.10 in which God tells us it is the *love of money*, not just money itself, that *is the root of all evil*. Wow! Double Wow! Think of all that is expressed in these 29 words:

- love of money
- root of all evil
- while some coveted after
- they have erred from the faith
- they have pierced themselves through with many sorrows

Incredible! What a monumental picture, declaration, description, and warning of perhaps our enemy's greatest foothold in the lives of people on this earth. Let us take a look at each of these positions Holy Spirit so eloquently puts forth.

Love of money. What exactly is this? The word **love** comes from the Greek *philarguria*. THIS is not the ordinary Greek word for LOVE! This is a major instance where the Greek word behind our English translation carries a dramatic meaning different from that which many Saints interpret and understand in any casual reading. LISTEN TO THIS: this is the ONLY place in the New Testament this Greek word is translated *love*, out of the 179 times *love* appears! All 178 other times it is either *agape* or *phileo*, or a derivative of each. WOW!

So, what is so critical about this Greek word at this exact moment in Scripture? Remember, a reading of 1 Timothy must take into context that Paul was emboldening young Timothy to stand for Truth. Some don't. These folks, God tells us, are

> proud, knowing nothing, but doting about questions and strifes of words, whereof cometh envy, strife, railings, evil surmisings, perverse disputings of men of corrupt minds, and destitute of the truth, supposing that gain is godliness: from such withdraw thyself (6:4-5).

Don't miss these 5 key words: *supposing that gain is godliness. Supposing?* Yes, more. *I don't have enough. I want more. God is really blessing, I want more resulting in godliness.* Never *content*. Remember from our previous chapter? Verse 6: *godliness with contentment is great gain.*

In v.9, Paul goes on to say,

> But they that will be rich fall into temptation and a snare, and into many foolish and hurtful lusts, which drown men in destruction and perdition.

Now listen, we get to the text of our chapter here. This Greek word, *philarguria*, specifically relates to money, or silver. It carries with it the meaning of accumulating these, retaining what is gathered, to multiply it. It can go so far as to indicate covetousness. Don't miss this…to be *covetous* or live in *covetousness* is to be greedy, one who will defraud for gain/engage in plans for fraud or extortion. God is telling of the *root* of what drives any person to do evil things: *having a lack of contentment with God's provision.*

That is why Paul had written in the midst of this discourse, *But godliness with contentment is great gain* (v.6). The whole warning here is for Timothy to preach and teach against the accumulating and multiplying of riches just for the sake of the *love* of such. THAT is a bad kind of *love*. And then, Paul goes on to tell us what *that love* leads to…

Root of all evil. Root…*rhiza*. That which springs from. The cause or the manufacturer of. It speaks of the primary perpetrator, that which commits, of evil. The *philarguria* of money springs forth evil. But note *what evil* is perpetrated. Evil…*kakos*. This is a word specifically meaning *content to perish in one's own corruption*. How interesting is this! When one has the *philarguria* of money, they are perpetrating upon themselves corruption. Knowingly or, most likely, unknowingly. Wow! Let's go further…

While some coveted after. The word *coveted* is interesting. Coveted…*oregomai*. It means *desiring*, but in an extended way. It is where someone will go to extremes, or a stretching out/longing for, to get something. This longing will cause the person to do strange and odd, and oftentimes evil things to obtain what they long for. Now listen to the horrific and sad end result of this *philarguria*-ing for money or silver or riches…

They have erred from the faith. Erred…*apoplanao*. The meaning here is that these have gone away from the faith, strayed, because of their *philarguria* of money. It is interesting that God uses another word for *erred* in v.21, *astocheo,* deviate

Which some professing have *erred* concerning the faith.

Here the erring is about what is spoken of in v.20, *profane and vain babblings, and oppositions of science falsely so called.* Nothing to do with money. And, in 2nd Timothy 2:18, the erring is about *profane and vain babblings* again (v.16). Same Greek word for *erred, astocheo.* Again, nothing to do with money…

Who concerning the truth have *erred*, saying that the resurrection is past already; and overthrow the faith of some.

What is important is that God is telling Timothy, and us, to beware of these dangers that are giving a wrong goal, or wrong track, for people to follow. And, in doing so, are taking others away from the faith. *The faith* is Fruit of Holy Spirit. Related to God's Life and Truth. *And we today,* are to avoid at all costs *the philarguiria of money.* Now listen to the last item God mentions…

They have pierced themselves through with many sorrows. This means just what it says. The ones erring from the faith have caused their own trouble. Wow! This is a sad testimony, especially when it comes to money. But life proves Truth. And, as a pastor I have seen over and over where individuals who come for *financial advice* are really their own answer to *their problem.* As I heard not long ago, *Quit shooting yourself in your foot when* *you have no toes left!* Sounds ridiculous. Sounds impossible. But it happens more than most want to admit.

So, how can we conclude this study of a verse that doesn't sound much like a track for a Saint to run on to get to a God-honoring end with His finances? Well, this is like something we need to know, and be warned of, as we are getting into the *starting blocks of our life's financial run*. Don't shoot ourself in the foot by ever having a *philarguria of money*! Don't let money, or silver, or gold, or riches, or *things* (anything) get us so consumed with the accumulation of those that they take us away from the awesome Spiritual Truths of God in the realm of being a steward of what God entrusts us with. Let me assure you, the lure of *getting rich quick* or *making more than you can imagine* or *an easy way to make a bunch* will look you square in the face at many points in your life. And, in a blink of an eye, a Saint can be snared by a false idea contrary to God's methodical, practical, God-initiated practice of stewardship.

Do not let the *love of* money (covetous of, greediness for) become a part of your life. Be content with God's provision. It is *The Math of Life*. *Christ's Life.*

Chapter 13
Desiring To Get Rich Quick
He that hasteth to be rich hath an evil eye,
and considereth not that poverty shall come upon him.
Proverbs 28:22

Before we look at the real issue of this chapter, having *a desire to get rich* QUICK, let me mention something this discussion is NOT about…
- *being rich*. Does God have a problem with someone, particularly His kids, being rich? No. However, a lack of contentment(ch.9), having an evil *love of money* (ch.10), can enter into a sinful desire to get rich quickly.

Solomon shares great wisdom in verse 22: *"he that hasteth to be rich hath an evil eye."* Ophthalmos poneros, an evil eye, or unsound eye. Anyone who is a studier of people knows from the wisdom of God that much is to be found out about someone by looking into their eyes.

The light of the body is the eye: if therefore thine eye be
single, thy whole body shall be full of light. Matthew 6:22
Ophthalmos haplous, a sound, righteous eye as opposed to *ophthalmos poneros* (an evil eye). The *eye of the Soul* is a phrase that speaks of the *Light* (or *darkness,* small *s* soul) that is transferred to the earthsuit that yields a performance of *righteousness* or *good/evil.*

There is so much to be known about the *two spiritual souls* that yield *two spiritual hearts* when it comes to talking about *Life as a Saint*, particularly in regard to financial activities. Turn to page 261 and see the Spiritual diagram of a Saint. When we know the 2 souls in a Saint, we can see where one minute we can be thinking in the *Mind of God,* and the next minute we can be thinking in the *natural mind.* What Solomon is speaking of is someone thinking in the *natural mind.*

All of the discussion in Scripture needs to be looked at from a pre-Pentecost and post-Pentecost perspective. That moment differentiates a *child of* God prior to Pentecost without Holy Spirit/Holy Soul OR a *child of* God post-Pentecost with Holy Spirit and Holy Soul within. Therefore, we can determine *today* (with *Holy Soul* along with the *natural soul* within a Saint), which *heart* and which *eye* we are using!

We must know and remember that Saints have *two spiritual eyes*. The *eye of the natural soul* and the *eye of Holy Soul*. Now, did you know there are people who do incredible studies of eyes and eye movement (involving the direction our eyes move) who can tell *what* someone is thinking or feeling? Well, God got ahead of these modern day *eye-watchers*.

Think also about the reason of wanting money quickly to do something, whether it be honest or crooked. There is still a price to pay by those who hasten to be rich for this realm of reasoning.

> A faithful man shall abound with blessings: but he that maketh haste to be rich shall not be innocent. Proverbs 28:20

The Hebrew word translated *innocent* here is *naqah*: pure, without guilt, free from punishment. In the context of Proverbs 28:20, Solomon says the man who makes haste to become rich WILL NOT be pure, without guilt, or free from punishment. No case could be made that God *winks* at this type of person, and perhaps because of the way in which they have pursued a *get rich quick* action.

Something else that is interesting is the number of Saints who desire to *get rich quick* because they are not walking with God, listening to *His Mind,* are susceptible to the devil's direction, and in many cases these Saints fall prey to vanity in their *natural mind,* an emptiness of the Grace of God to work as God leads to add to their pocketbook.

> Wealth gotten by vanity shall be diminished: but he that gathereth by labor shall increase. Proverbs 13:11
>
> The getting of treasures by a lying tongue is a vanity tossed to and fro of them that seek death. Proverbs 21:6

God makes it perfectly clear that any effort to gain riches by vain, deceitful, or any form of wickedness is something He is not pleased with. And the end result is not good for our bottom line! Take a moment to meditate on *shall be diminished, shall not be innocent, poverty shall come upon him,* and *seek death*. None of those sound like something we would want, AND we should take heed to avoid the *desiring or hasting to get rich in a quick way.* Gathering by labor and being found faithful is God's way to prosper and gain.

Whatever the reason for desiring to *get rich quick,* God tells us this is not one of His mindsets, ideas, attitudes or methods. And He does not look upon our walking this route in life with grace or grant.

I think it wise to conclude with a mention of something God has told us that IF we ever enter into a life of wealth, richness, or *plenty*:

> Charge them that are rich in this world, that they be not high-minded; nor trust in uncertain riches, but in the living God, Who giveth us richly all things to enjoy; That they do good, that they be rich in good works, ready to distribute, willing to communicate; Laying up in store for themselves a good foundation against the time to come, that they may lay hold on eternal life. 1 Timothy 6:17-19

As is a well-known fact: no matter how *fast* we get rich, we can't take it with us into the next life. We are to be willing, be ready to distribute (share) and be rich in ministry…but most of all keep hold of our Spiritual foundation…while being a prudent and careful financial planner. It is *The Math of Life. Christ's Life.*

Chapter 14
God Gives the Power to Get Wealth
*But thou shalt remember the LORD thy God: for it
is He that giveth thee power to get wealth...*
Deuteronomy 8:18

This is just one of the verses in the Scriptures that is clearly explicit in stating something God has done, is going to do, or only He can do, FOR US. "...**it is He** that giveth thee power to get wealth." Man thinks it is himself that has the power to get wealth.

Think not? Look back to verses 11 thru 17 (especially v.17):
    And thou say in thine heart, My power and the might of
    mine hand hath gotten me this wealth.

Well, Truth makes us free. We know that. So, what are we going to do with this verse 18 in *The Math of (our) Life*? First, let me suggest we take a look at that word translated *power* in the English Scriptures. The Hebrew *koach* speaks of someone having strength or force. It describes a capacity to produce. Incredibly, *power* appears 120 times in the Old Testament, with **26 different** Hebrew words translated into *power*. Amazing! The exact Hebrew (or, Greek in the NT) word in their language spoke to them the *specific meaning* the speaker or writer was trying to state. Holy Spirit, through Moses, gave us THE word to show *God's power, God's capability*, to produce wealth as no human can. In fact, I would say it is a MUST that you, reader, go to your Scriptures and read ALL of Deuteronomy chapter 8 (as I have done several times) to fully get what God has for us, and to completely grasp just what God can do for us. Many teachings throughout the Scriptures are for a specific time in history, and others are timeless. The principles in this chapter are timeless. How they were carried out in OT days can be different from how they are carried out today in NT days. Know that difference also.

Second, look at what God tells us in the rest of v.18...
    ...that He may establish His covenant which He sware
    unto thy fathers, as it is this day.

A covenant. *berith*. A contract of one party to another. God promising His people a certain stipulation. Deuteronomy chapter 8 was given by God to His people as they entered into the land He promised to give them. Each of us today, as Saints, are entered into a land with God indwelling us; a land with His presence that is a *promised land*. God has promised to be ALL to His children, today of which are His Saints.

Here is my summary of God's promise to His children, if we allow His Life to Live through us:
- we will possess the land He gives us
- we will remember ALL that God has done for us
- we will be humble
- we will be tested, to know which heart we are functioning in, to know if His Word is kept
- we will be led to depend on His supply, especially His Word
- we will have things that don't deteriorate
- we will think on these things again and again
- we will walk in His ways and trust Him
- we will constantly bless the LORD for the good land He has given us
- we are to beware to not forget our God, and to beware of not allowing His Life to Live in us
- we are to beware to not let our hearts (wrong heart) be lifted up in pride
- we are to beware letting pride steal us away from His Heart and forget God's provision
- we are to beware of reaching the point of saying in our heart (wrong heart!), "My power and the might of mine hand hath gotten me this wealth"
- we are to remember the LORD our God and His power to have given whatever is our gain, and to have whatever we have
- we will have PLENTY.

HOW are *we* going to do all these? *We* are not. God will do them through our earthsuits. When we are abandoned to Him.

So, how does this *work out* for us in *The Math of (our) Life*? Are we all going to be rich? Are we all going to have all our needs provided for? Are we owners or stewards? Which of these premises depicts a position God has taken regarding our financial matters? The answers being, according to Holy Scripture, the first is not Truth...the second is Truth...the third is *we are stewards, God's financial managers*.

God never promises His Saints will be rich, either by doing certain things, or just by being a child of God. However, some of His children will be. That is an issue between God and them. But, for ALL Saints the Truth is God promises to provide all our need, and that He is owner and we are stewards of what He sends our way.

Before we get into the practice of what we do with any *wealth* God sends our way, let me once again mention that it is imperative for each of us to KNOW and put to PRACTICE the Truths in Deuteronomy ch. 8, for they bring Life, *Christ's Life,* to our stewardship of God's resources.

Here are some practical steps to know:
- whatever wealth we might have is a gift from God to be used in His service (2 Corinthians 9).
- we are to provide for brethren that are in need (1 John 3:16-17 give us thoughts to meditate on).
- we are to *be not high-minded* (arrogant in our wealth), nor *trust in uncertain riches, but in the living God, Who giveth us richly all things to enjoy* (1 Timothy 6:17).
- we are to guard against greed in all instances (see story in Luke 12:13-20, and God's stern assessment in v.21).
- as we are doing all the above, do so *ready to distribute, willing to communicate* (liberally giving); *laying up in store for themselves a good foundation against the time to come…*
(1 Timothy 6:18-19).

Well, amen. Sounds like a promising future for all of God's children, correct? Not so fast. *Forgetting God and His provision* yields a different practical experience. Did not God say so???

> And it shall be, if thou do at all forget the LORD thy God, and walk after other gods, and serve them, and worship them, I testify against you this day that ye shall surely perish. As the nations which the LORD destroyeth before your face, so shall ye perish; because ye would not be obedient unto the voice of the LORD your God.
> Deuteronomy 8:19-20

Wow. Sad ending for some. What is most sad is that it doesn't have to be that way. To reject God's promise by turning from Him to other *gods* is a terrible decision.

So, let me close by saying this: I know that everything written in this book may not be absolute truth. But a whole lot is. And as my pastor, John Morgan, told me as I went off to seminary, "A lot of what you hear will be good, green grass, but some will be sticks. Eat the grass, and leave the sticks." Dear Saints, anything God hath said, pick it up and eat it. Perhaps some of the rest may be sticks.

Be certain to *remember the LORD thy God*...it is *The Math of Life. Christ's Life.*

Chapter 15
Faithful vs Unjust
He that is faithful in that which is least is faithful also in much: and he that is unjust in the least is unjust also in much.
Luke 16:10

At first glance this may seem like a simple verse that couldn't make that much difference. I mean, who doesn't know that *faithfulness* is important, and anything different is bad. Well, true. But God's Truth is more than that here. And can be applied many ways in our financial dealings.

So, let us begin by looking at the two key words: *faithful* and *unjust*. Notice carefully that the second word is not unfaithful. Aha...big difference.

Faithful in the Greek is *pistos*. Trustworthy, observant of and steadfast to one's trust. Not too much difficulty here, except we must make note that God tells us He is watching for our being *faithful in that which is least* because He knows that is a pre-requisite for our being *faithful also in much*. The context of this verse is God dealing with how we handle *mammon* as well as how we will handle the *true riches* (Truths of God). Wow.

So being *faithful in that which is least* takes on a much higher priority when we know this.

Now we need to look at the opposite statement God makes. *Unjust in the least. Unjust* in the Greek is *adikos*. Can include wicked, treacherous, unrighteous. Wow. Falling short of the righteousness standard of Divine laws. Listen to this...being fraudulent, false, or deceitful is included in its revelation, particularly in its context in Luke 16:10. What a difference than just thinking the opposite would be *unfaithful*, without justice or not trustworthy, etc.

We must pay great heed to how God Sees those who handle the *mammon* AND the *true riches!* It is *The Math of Life. Christ's Life.*

Chapter 16
The Unprofitable Servant
So, likewise ye, when ye shall have done all those things
which are commanded you, say, **We are unprofitable servants**:
we have done that which was our duty to do.
(bold, my emphasis)
Luke 17:10

Since there is a *so* at the beginning of verse 10, let us back up a couple of verses and see why Holy Spirit said that…
> But which of you having a servant plowing or feeding cattle, will say to him by and by, when he is come in from the field, Go and sit down to meat? And will not rather say unto him, Make ready wherewith I may sup, and gird thyself, and serve me, till I have eaten and drunken; and afterward thou shalt eat and drink? Doth he thank that servant because he did the things that were commanded him? I think not. vs.7-9

Whoa, Nelly! At first glance our text is a staggering statement from Jesus. We read where someone who is a servant does ALL they are commanded to do, and then they are said to be an *unprofitable servant*. How is that? How would you feel if your boss told you that each day at work?

Well, what is underneath the surface of these words from our Lord and Savior (the parabolic *Heavenly Truth with the Heavenly meaning*)? First, let's take a look at the word, *commanded*. In the Greek, it is, *diatasso*, with a reference to an *order* or *appointment* by the master to his servants of things they were supposed to do. We would call it a *job description* in today's world. It is that which we are hired and paid to do.

The word *duty* is the Greek *opheilo*, which basically means *to owe, to be indebted*. Wow! That puts this into a whole new perspective for us also, doesn't it? If we don't believe in indebtedness, then we definitely would not want to be caught working less time or to an undesirable level for what we are paid for. But, then to realize that if we do JUST what we are paid for, we *owed* that to our master/employer and are not getting paid anything extra, nor making him/her anything extra.

The key word in Jesus' illustration is *unprofitable*, *achreios* in the Greek. It speaks to one who has actually fulfilled their usefulness. It can designate someone who is set aside because they are no more useful. But, there can be no mistake that Jesus was talking about the former...one who has actually fulfilled their usefulness. This is a servant (employee) who has done all that they are paid to do, no more...no less. We would at first thought say this is a *good* employee.

However, what Jesus is saying here, in light of His other teachings about *going the 2nd mile*, and others, when we have JUST done what we are paid to do, THAT constitutes an *unprofitableness* for our master/employer.

Now, listen, and think this through. Yes, the employer has *made a profit*, supposedly, when we do what we are paid to do (assuming we did a *good work*), BUT in the overall economics of things WE just produced what we were paid to do...and gave nothing more to our employer. To Jesus, He is saying WE did nothing to be *profitable* (do more and make more) for our master/employer looking at what WE have done and been paid for.

So, how do we respond to Jesus' illustration and declaration? Let me show you...

I am hired and told what my responsibilities are, what time I am to be at work, perhaps what time I have to take a break in a couple of hours, what time I have to take for eating (lunch, supper, etc. depending on my *work hours*), and maybe another break in the 2nd half of my *work day*. I follow all the rules, do a reputable *good work* for my employer, am always on time, etc. I have done ALL I was paid to do, and did it well. I am an *unprofitable servant/employee* according to Jesus.

HOW THEN, can I BECOME a *profitable* servant/employee?

First, I can get to work several minutes before *start time*. In this time, I say hello to my fellow workers, drink some coffee or another drink, take care of any personal business that arises, AND I am at my work station a couple of minutes (or, more!) before the appointed start time to work.

Second, I do very little, if any, *personal business* on company time. That includes any type of electronic activity (phone, texts, emails, Facebook, Twitter, etc.) or conversation with anyone.

Third, I take my breaks, but do not infringe upon the appointed amount of time.

Fourth, I take my meal break, but do not infringe upon the appointed amount of time.

Fifth, I take any other permitted breaks, but do not infringe upon the appointed amount of time.

Sixth, I DO NOT quit working on my appointed jobs/work activities UNTIL *quitting time*. I even GIVE some additional minutes *off the clock* to my employer before shutting down my work station or desk.

Seventh, I DO EXTRA WORK without compensation.

NOW, then, I have become *profitable*. My employer is making *extra profit* on what they are paying me to do.

WHY would I do ALL this??? There are numerous reasons. The one that comes to my mind right off the bat is this: *God has been gracious enough to provide me with a good employment.* My employer has been gracious enough to have a business and provide for me a job. If they had not given me the job, I would be out of work with NO PAY, until I could get another place to serve/work. That alone is enough to warrant my doing more than what I am paid to do.

But, stop and think of all the benefits of having THIS job. Make a list of all the reasons that quickly come to mind as to why it *pays* to do more than what we are *paid* to do.

And stop to think of this: any employer that treats his/her employees *justly* is worthy of working for. Think of what they think of you for being that kind of employee. How *profitable* do you think it might become for you IF you turn into one of the most *profitable* employees your employer has? Soak on that for a while...

As we close this chapter, why not take a look one more time at the *Parable of The Talents* in Matthew chapter 25. Notice an *unprofitable servant* is mentioned at the end, and what Jesus said should be done to that one. Ah, be a *profitable servant*...profitableness is *The Math of Life. Christ's Life.*

Chapter 17
If You Don't Work, You Don't Eat
*For even when we were with you, this we commanded you,
that if any would not work, neither should he eat.*
2 Thessalonians 3:10

These are the words of a faithful servant after saying (2 Thessalonians 3:6-9) he didn't eat anyone's bread for free. He worked for what he ate, laboring and travailing night and day, so that he would not be burdensome to any of the folks at Thessalonica. What a great testimony! God goes on further to tell us:

> For we hear that there are some which walk among you disorderly, working not at all, but are busybodies. Now them that are such we command and exhort by our Lord Jesus Christ, that with quietness they work, and eat their own bread. 3:11-12

What could be any more plain and uncomplicated: *we don't work...we don't eat*. The Greek *ergazomai*, to acquire by labor (work). That is pretty clear, isn't it? Long before our complex and complicated society got here (something the devil has been working on for a long time), folks just worked to provide for themselves and their family. A global *economy* was the farthest thing from their mind. In fact, it never had entered their mind! And the idea of *welfare*, or *social services* was not a factor either.

So, we have gotten ourselves into a dilemma that is compounded by the *help me* (I am a victim) mentality that has ensued. Things are so out of kilter now that the typical hard-working, self-providing, *if I don't work, I don't eat* person is surrounded by many family members and friends, not to mention perhaps some neighbors, that are not like-minded. And certainly many of these others are not God-minded. Of course, take God out of society (schools, government, and most businesses) and *God-mindedness* is not present in most lives. Another of our enemy's ploys.

All of this has gotten us to a point that *life* is not anywhere near what God designed and ordained it to be. In Genesis 2:15, following the days of Creation, God tells us:

> And the LORD took the man, and put him in the garden
> of Eden to dress it and to keep it.

The Hebrew for *dress* is *avad*, meaning primarily to serve, work, toil, to till, plow, to become fatigued. Context would determine its exact usage. Well, here God was using a combination of thoughts, but the idea was for man to work for food for themselves. Actually, this work was to be *fun* in the Garden of Eden. But, along came sin, and work ceased to be *fun*. The simple point is that all humanity was designed to work to provide the necessary food for existence. And that existence could include enjoyment. Eating for many is an *enjoyment*.

Now listen, there can be no reason for any capable Saint once grown into adulthood to not do their own *providing*. To be reliant upon, or even expect, someone else to provide food, or raiment, or any other necessity while not working ourselves is inexcusable, or even heretical. However, many *bleeding heart Saints* (as I call them) allow some to make excuses, have all kinds of reasons, and even allow blatant lies about how or why they can't work or can't *make it* (provide) in today's world. All the while both sides are ignoring God's specific instructions and promises concerning needs, work, and provision.

There is another perspective that we Saints must consider. My good friend, Michael Wells, in his book *My Weakness for His Strength* (vol. 1), Day 330, p.561, says this:

> It is clear in the Scriptures what is man's responsibility and what is God's. Often the two meet. "If a man does not work, let him not eat," yet, "Why do you worry about what you will eat? Look at the sparrow!" Man is to work, but not for the reason that he thinks. Work is not to secure food but is in obedience to the commandment of God. Work makes us healthy, happy, and content, as well as less anxious and depressed. If a man is fed when he does not work, he will be discontented. Man works for different reasons, all good, but it is still God that provides the food.

Michael draws attention to the core issue: obedience to God. However, what most do not know or consider is that the two primary Greek words in the New Testament for *obey* and *obedience* are *hupakouo* and *hupakoe*, respectively. They primarily carry with them the thought of *abandonment*. Abandoning, or yielding (as most recognize), to an authority is the thought. As in abandoning to the Heart of God and His desires. Our obedience (abandoning) is the result of that positive issue: Holy reverence in union with an awareness of possible chastening for disobedience (not abandoning to His Heart) results in our being obedient/abandoning. But (and this is a Holy *but*), our obedience/abandoning always makes us *healthy, happy, and content, as well as less anxious and depressed*. Well, amen! Hallelujah!

Listen to some more of God's Word regarding this premise:
> Go to the ant, thou sluggard; consider her ways, and be wise: Which having no guide, overseer, or ruler, Providing her meat in the summer, and gathereth her food in the harvest. How long wilt thou sleep, O sluggard? when wilt thou arise out of thy sleep? Yet a little sleep, a little slumber, a little folding of the hands to sleep: so shall thy poverty come as one that traveleth, and thy want as an armed man. Proverbs 6:6-11

> The sluggard will not plow by reason of the cold; therefore shall he beg in harvest, and have nothing. Proverbs 20:4

> Love not sleep, lest thou come to poverty; open thine eyes, and thou shalt be satisfied with bread. Proverbs 20:13

And listen to this:
> Even a child is known by his doings, whether his work be pure, and whether it be right. Proverbs 20:11

And lastly,
> Also unto Thee, O Lord, belongeth mercy: for Thou renderest to every man according to his work. Psalm 62:12

What all has God spoken to us concerning work and provision? Let us take a glance back and summarize some of the things God has told us…
- God designed, created, and commanded people to work to bring in a harvest of food for survival and sustenance.
- God expects people to work.
- God will *work* alongside people to see that provision is a given.
- When people decide (and it is a *decision!*) to *sleep, slumber*, close his eyes to the situation and/or work, poverty and *having nothing* will

come about. Even an ant knows that one! Even a child knows that...
- And, God renders to every person according to his work.

It has been my privilege to follow the leading of the Lord these past 6 years in being in ministry to some homeless and jobless people. My wife, Barbara, and I, and another couple, Rick & Abby West, take something to drink, a little food, an offer of friendship, and a Scripture study (of an uncomplicated combination of a verse or two of Scripture and an application or two) to a local park on Sunday mornings. Every Sunday morning, no matter the weather. Let me give you a few observations:
- most of those I have met are living the result of their family environment and upbringing. They are living with very little of God's Truth to guide them.
- many have become full of anger, unforgiveness, bitterness, and a closed mind.
- most have no idea how to take the *Next Step*.
- most have an uncanny awareness of a lot of Scripture, albeit that most of what they know is what we would call the *angry side of God*, the *judgmental* verses, the most difficult *to do* verses, and nothing to do with love, mercy, and provision...except a few verses they *know* but don't *believe* due to their experiences. They even *know* 2 Thessalonians 3:10, and the *ant story*, but they can't wrap their minds around getting a job.
- most are getting financial assistance from some government agency and/or religious organization.
- most are receiving more in some sort of financial assistance than my wife and I receive from our Social Security checks (we have no income from any church retirement program).
- most do not actively seek work. More than one local merchant has confirmed this in their experiences with them.
- many ignore even the slightest ideas I give them as to how they could make a few dollars *today*...they come around with blank stares, empty hearts, looking for any kind of handout they can get (I give no money, just drink and small amounts of food, and the Scripture study on one page), and a mind to continue as they have been doing.

- many have no idea what the future holds, or where they are headed.
- some have walked away from any hope of a life like God intended.
- they really need more of an *organized life* than the varied helps of the many *ministries* that try to aid them. (But I have talked to business, government, and religious leaders about a place and a plan…none have been attracted to organizing and sustaining such)
- thank the Lord, a few at the park have grabbed hold of Truth and seem to be moving forward. God's Word does make an impact with some.

You may be asking, "Why have you included this chapter in your book?" Well, we must never forget that from the beginning of time, God ordained that man should work for his food.

> And the LORD God took the man, and put him into the Garden of Eden to dress it and to keep it. And the LORD God commanded the man, saying, Of every tree of the garden thou mayest freely eat: But of the tree of the knowledge of good and evil, thou shalt not eat of it: for in the day that thou eatest thereof thou shalt surely die.
> Genesis 2:15-17

Did Adam & Eve physically die that day they ate of the forbidden tree? No. They *died* spiritually. The greatest need they immediately had was to be restored to a Spiritual fellowship with Almighty God. But, they then had to go to work to get physical food to eat.

It really is inexcusable for Saints, as adults, to even think, much less expect, others should provide their need while they stand lazily by and idle. There is no excuse for not working to provide for self and family. Truth makes us free. The Truth of this chapter can keep us from living a lie. Well, amen.

It is very freeing to acquire by labor that which we have. Be a laborer. It is *The Math of Life. Christ's Life.*

Chapter 18
You Are Worth More
Than You Are Making Right Now

Are not two sparrows sold for a farthing?
and one of them shall not fall on the ground without your Father.
But the very hairs of your head are all numbered.
Fear ye not therefore, ye are of more value than many sparrows.
Matthew 10:29-31

Don't you just love the pictures God gives us in Scripture of how He sees and values us in every comparison with creatures like the sparrows of this parable? Sparrows. Tiny little birds. Plain colors. Simple life. In Jesus' day, two sparrows were worth *one farthing*. A *farthing* is estimated at a value of ½ of 1 penny in today's coin. Suffice it to say, it was the *least of value* of coins back then. Of little value. And Jesus tells us, no sparrow falls on the ground without our Father knowing it. And Jesus tells us, we are of more value than *many sparrows*. Even the very hairs of our head are numbered, if you want more evidence. You and I matter to God.

So, how does this parable relate to *The Math of Life*, particularly our *work*, and *being worth more*?

Your work (acquiring by labor) matters to God. When you begin to value yourself as God values you, you will begin to value the Life of Christ in your work. And with *Christ's Life* in your work, you can *Make More, Save More, and Live Free*.

Valuing the *Life of Christ* in your work will give you a desire to be aware of all that you have accumulated that prepares you to step up to new heights in your career. I am amazed at the number of folks I have met the past 50 years that have **no clue** what their education, experience, and talents are **worth** in the work world. Some of it is simply having not been taught or shown what is available. Some of it is simply having not been led to see what they are capable of. Some of it is simply accepting life just as it is and not looking for anything more.

Listen, if you are not earning what you **need,** or what you really are **capable** of earning, **LEARN** HOW to be *worth more*:
- Survey your capabilities and potential
- Undergird your education

- **C**ultivate enhanced abilities
- **C**reate a specialization
- **E**xpand your horizon
- **S**earch out new possibilities
- **S**ell yourself

Survey Your Capabilities and Potential

We need to be honest with ourselves and know what we are capable of, which leads to also knowing and evaluating our potential. So, it is good to take the time to write out and examine all of our capabilities. That involves education, training, history, experience, and accomplishments. (note: history involves listing our past jobs and positions, while experience involves listing our assignments, activities, and actions).

Put these five categories with appropriate detailed actions IN WRITING. In order to BUILD for the future, we have to know our past and who we are in the present. This is not looking backwards, but acknowledging and evaluating the past with an aggressiveness toward moving to the future. Too many folks have an *idea* of these things, but no definite *picture* of them.

Remember, a picture is worth 1,000 words (ideas). There is nothing like knowing WHO you are. Confidence and self-control come from knowing your *capabilitie*s and *potential*.

Undergird Your Education

Everybody knows something. You know something. But what is it that YOU know that no one else knows? That can be a vital link to your making more money. However, you can always enhance what you know. So, begin looking for, tweaking, and adding to what your *education* has you already equipped to do.

Education is only as good as it can take us to the next level. Every one of us has used what we have been taught to get us to where we are (with the exception of those who are going nowhere; they are not ever going to use what they know to get ahead of where they are!). So you and I have to have more in our *working knowledge*. Listen…we can increase our *book* knowledge. Book knowledge is good. However, increasing our *working knowledge* elevates our future! We can really never get enough from *books* that will enhance our *capabilities* and *potential*.

But there is another knowledge that can greatly advance our worth: *the experience of others*. Jack Welch, Chairman and CEO of General Electric between 1981 and 2001 gave us an *electric* thought: "To be the best you must learn from the best." Wow! How insightful and inspiring. So, I must find out who is the *best* in what I right now am doing, and desire to do, then undergird my education from what they know and have put into practice (their *working knowledge*)…and have gotten results that everyone would desire.

Cultivate Enhanced Abilities

We are now ready to move forward to the next level. I use the word *enhanced* because we have taken the abilities we started with and have added to them more *book* knowledge and more *experience* knowledge. Now it is time to *make better* our abilities.

Listen to this remark from a movie on TV…art teacher to art student:
> I don't see you in your work. Your feeling, your perspective. Without that, it's just putting paint on canvass. If it doesn't *move* you, it's not going to *move* the viewer. Every artist you admire *felt* it was worth the risk.

Do you grasp what that art teacher was saying to his student? Put yourself INTO your work. *Feel* what you are doing. *Like* what you are capable of doing. Yes, you are able to do certain things, but with practice, with fervor, and with commitment, you can develop your abilities to a level of expertise that the marketplace will take notice.

Create a Specialization

Everybody can do an ordinary job. Everybody can do what others can do. But you need to be able to do something out of the ordinary…something no one else can do, or do as well as you. And it pays well to be able to do what someone needs done that only you can do!

Mike Rowe on the Tucker Carlson program (Fox News), 5/26/17:
> "Learn a skill that is actually in demand. That negates any conversation about pay. You can work where you want, and you can write your own ticket. SKILL goes where you

go...it is inherently mobile. Keep one thing in mind: automation is coming."

People with a specialized skill that is wanted and needed will always be in demand, and be able to demand more pay. I knew a fellow once that was so skilled he was able to put whatever amount he wanted in his paycheck each month. The owner signed a blank check and handed it to him...every month!

Expand Your Horizon
When is the last time you took some time to just dream of what you might become? What have you always wanted to do? What would be your *dream job*? How much money do you want to be paid? It would be wise every FEW years to evaluate where you are, what you are being paid, what you have done since the last evaluation to enlarge and enhance your resume, and then to spend time asking God what He thinks of your potential. Make sure you are SEEING what God thinks of you and what you could become!

Search Out New Possibilities
It takes effort and initiative to get off your duff and get out to look for those opportunities for increased pay. Just remember: they are out there! Why settle for what you are making now? Armed with all of the benefits you offer some employer, keep a constant search for new possibilities ongoing.

Ask around to find out what others are doing to find job openings. Read materials that show positions available. Network with friends, church acquaintances, neighbors, and just about anyone to find out what they know about possible work opportunities. And use your technology resources to search for the personnel needs matching your resume that are unfulfilled.

The secret of many who are making more money than they were 6 months or 1 year ago is simple: they were seeking spots they could move to that paid more.

SELL YOURSELF

This is one of the most critical aspects of becoming a *success*. If no one knows you. If no one knows your abilities. If no one knows your capabilities. If no one knows your education, training, history, experience, and accomplishments, HOW DO YOU THINK YOU ARE GOING TO GET AHEAD OF WHERE YOU ARE RIGHT NOW?

First of all, your **name**. Your name needs to be invaluable. People need to recognize your name when mentioned, or at least have some sort of prick in their mind that your name means something to them.

And then your **record**. Have an available, convenient, uncomplicated, and attractive preparation of your record ready to be seen or shared with everyone. In this day of electronics, media, and social networking you should constantly be in front of as many people as possible. Do not use these resources for worthless, timewasting jabber, but for positive promising presentations of yourself.

However possible, and whenever practical, PUT YOURSELF IN FRONT OF OTHERS. Be diligent to PROMOTE YOURSELF at all times. One *bad* incident can undo a lot of positive other events. Someone has said, "How you spend your days matters more than how much it pays." I would add: "Well spent days increase income."

This subject of *You Are Worth More* always reminds me of a fellow I once told that he was worth twice what he was making. He started looking for another job, and within a couple of weeks he was making twice what he had been making! He just needed someone to bring his attention to how much he was worth. He just needed to SEE what His potential was. Is that YOU?!?

What you are worth in the marketplace is a matter of *The Math of Life. Christ's Life.*

Chapter 19
Sell Yourself At All Times
*A good name is rather to be chosen than great riches,
and loving favor rather than silver and gold.*
Proverbs 22:1

Isn't Proverbs 22:1 a great verse! It really puts God's Mind into perspective in connection with finances, resources, thoughts, plans, abilities, etc. when comparing *a good name* with *riches*, or striving to have riches. A GOOD NAME.

I mentioned this idea at the close of the previous chapter, but let's expand on this. Because I think *a good name* and *selling ourselves at all* times is so important. And so does God!

How many people think of *a good name* like folks used to years ago??? Let me begin this chapter with a wonderful story told by one of my family's greatest friends: Mr. W. D. Hinson.

I remember sitting in the Hinson's living room back around 1992 or 93. We were talking about the *old days* and that brought up deep Northeast Texas, Commerce, Winnsboro, Quitman, and Lake Lydia. Those places held many memories of events of days gone by. Mr. Hinson had graduated from high school in Winnsboro and gone to Commerce to attend East Texas State Teacher's College in 1925, a forerunner to his being in Texas' education field for almost 50 years. God has an incredible way of weaving and orchestrating the lives of many folks into one gathering!

Mr. Hinson's first residence at college was the rental of a garage apartment at my mother's home (she was a baby crawling on the floor!) and her parents (my grandparents), O. B. and Mildred Bradford. Brad, as my grandfather was called, was a professor at the college, and built the 2-story house the family lived in, plus the garage and apartment above. This began a life-long fellowship (it still exists between kids, grandkids, great-grandkids, and great-great-grandkids).

Laughing and carrying-on for who knows how long in the Hinson's living room, Mr. Hinson began to tell of a time when he and Mrs. Hinson had graduated, taken their first jobs in Weinert, Tx, and at the first opportunity made their way back home to Northeast Texas to visit family. Mr. Hinson and his father went to town, as people would call the small community in those days. The local gas station was also a small grocery and the local car dealership. Of course, the Hinsons knew the owner very well, and he knew them likewise.

While Mr. Hinson's father was getting some groceries and gas, Mr. Hinson and the owner got to talking about a NEW car beside the station. Mr. Hinson always said, "New always smells much better than what you currently have." One thing led to another, and eventually Mr. Hinson *made a deal* with the man. Keep in mind, he hadn't said a word to his wife, Lillian. He just thought that with their jobs and income *stable*, they could afford to trade, and he would surprise Mrs. Hinson when he got back to his parent's home.

WELL…as Mr. Hinson and his father headed back home, his father asked him if he had discussed a car deal with the man who owned the businesses. Mr. Hinson said he had. BUT…Mr. Hinson then said, "Father, I agreed to make a trade, but I think I had better discuss this with Lillian first. And I am not sure we need to do this at this time. I am not sure we should go through with that trade." A GOOD NAME. Mr. Hinson's father uttered 6 words in 1 short sentence: "Son, you have bought that car." After a moment, Mr. Hinson's father said, "You gave the man YOUR WORD that you agreed with the price and agreed to get the new car. Son, you HAVE bought it." Well, Mr. Hinson said, "No father, I just talked to the man about it." His father said once more, "Son, you've bought that car." Then added: "You told that man you would buy it. You gave him your word. That's a done deal."

Yes, Mr. Hinson HAD bought the new car, because in those days a *man's word* was as good as *his name*.

And, yes, things were a little difficult when Mr. Hinson had to explain to Mrs. Hinson just what had taken place…

Do you see the wisdom and Truth of God's Word that was lived out in Mr. Hinson's father's words and life? Do you see the wisdom and Truth of God's Word that was lived out in Mr. and Mrs. Hinson's life? Do you see how the wisdom and Truth of God's Word is so seldom played out in most folks' lives today, including *devout* Saints?

It is easy to see how this plays right into this chapter's title: *Sell Yourself At All Times*. But, the story has another moment that needs mentioning, one that took place in my life about 20 years prior to Mr. Hinson telling me all about the *car deal*, and also involved the Hinsons. For sake of space, I have to leave out years and years of that family fellowship I mentioned, plus other pertinent info, but in 1974, the man who had married the Hinson's only daughter, and played ball in Baytown at Horace Mann Jr. High for my father who was a coach, called me about going to work for him. We met at a restaurant on the east side of Baytown. As we walked in, many folks recognized the man and waved or spoke to him. After we had finished eating and discussing my leaving my present work and going to work for him, the man made his way to several tables and spoke to all who had greeted him earlier. I noticed how he was very friendly, cordial, and making the folks feel special. We made our way to his car upon leaving the restaurant, and the man told me something I have never forgotten (and still share today, especially to family members including my grandkids). *Always sell yourself. Sell yourself at all times.*

Mr. Hinson had *sold himself* for many years growing up in that small Northeast Texas town. So had his parents. And so did Mr. Hinson when he ultimately made the trade for that new car and drove it back to Weinert. The man knew WHO Mr. Hinson was, and his parents. The man knew Mr. Hinson's word was as good as he was.

One other tidbit that connects to this idea…
NAME IDENTICATION. Another important aspect of *The Math of Life*, is the idea of always *promoting* YOUR NAME…not your nickname, or some *catchy name*.

I did go to work for the man who bought me lunch that day. His name was Louis DelHomme, of Louis DelHomme Marine in Houston. And, I remember eating at restaurants many times in the years to follow, where Louis handed a credit card to the waiter/waitress and they said, "Are you the guy with the boats?" Most of the other boat dealerships in the Houston area had *catchy names*…Marine Products, Mount Houston Marine, etc. Not one time would the owner go anywhere and introduce themselves (personal name), or give someone a credit card to pay for something, and the other person know they were the owner of one of those boat places. Think about that.

One last reminder, from the book of Ecclesiastes: A good name is better than precious ointment… Ecclesiastes 7:1

Lord, help us to desire greatly and trust You to Live through us to maintain Your Great Name You have bestowed upon us.

Make sure your name is a *good name*, and *sell yourself at all times*. It is the *Math of Life. Christ's Life.*

Chapter 20
Give Yourself Away
For God so loved the world,
that he gave his only begotten Son,
that whosoever believeth in him should not perish,
but have everlasting life.
John 3:16

How many read this text verse and think of God giving Himself away? That is what He did. Jesus is God. The Greatest Giver and the Greatest Gift of all time. All out of His Heart of Love. The Heart of God filled with the Love of God. This same Heart filled with His Love is IN every Saint…wanting to be given away.

There are many ways a Saint can give this Heart away. In this chapter I want to draw attention to one practical way we Saints need to be thinking of.

It has been many years since I heard a phenomenal story from one of my church members about his father NEVER going WITHOUT a JOB during the Great Depression. That's correct. His father never went without a job during perhaps the most *jobless* time in the history of America.

Data from several historical accounts show that the Great Depression lasted from 1929 to 1939, and was the worst economic downturn in our history. It began after the stock market crash of October 1929, which sent Wall Street into a panic and wiped out millions of investors. Over the next several years, consumer spending and investment dropped, causing steep declines in industrial output and employment as failing companies laid off workers. Look at these figures:

1929 – Population, 88 million. Labor force, 49.5 million. Unemployed, 1.5 million. 3% of labor force.

1933 – Population, 92.5 million. Labor force, 51.8 million. Unemployed, **15 million. 29%** of labor force.

Think about this! One-third of all banks closed/vanished. By 1933, when the Great Depression reached its lowest point, some 15 million Americans were unemployed and unemployment had risen to 29%.

In spite of such disastrous events, and the even more disastrous results, the story of this one man's father's remarkable job history during these years bears listening to. HOW did the father always have a job? Well, the story goes like this:

> My father said he was laid off from work one day as things got bad for the person he was working for. Instead of worrying about unemployment pay, or soup kitchen lines for family members, he immediately set out to go and knock on some business doors. When told they weren't hiring, he asked if he could work for the company *without pay* (He would work without getting paid for working 8 hours each day). The owner or manager thought he was crazy. Well, it didn't take long before one business said, "OK, here's what you can do (job assignment)." After he had been at the company 3 or 4 days, the owner called him into the office. "Sir, you have been here 3 or 4 days, and have worked harder than any one of my employees I am paying to do what you are doing. I have decided to let go one of my paid people and put you on the company payroll." My father always had a job.

GIVING HIMSELF AWAY proved to show his heart and his abilities to the company that ended up with his being rewarded with pay commensurate with his work ethic. This same story was repeated a few times during this difficult economic period as a couple of the companies he got work from also went out of business, but the father never went without a job the entire time of the Depression era.

How many would do the same today if presented with the same scenario?

Well, I have a ministry with the homeless and jobless at a park on Sunday mornings in the town we live. One of the first things I tell someone who doesn't have a job: *I have a plan for you to get hired.* (To my knowledge, not many of the persons I have shared the above story with, and told them they could try the same plan, have gone and approached a business owner/manager with that idea).

But, let me give you another thought that could be just as productive and prosperous for you. In chapter 16 you read of the *Unprofitable Servant*. That story in the Book of Luke tells us that when we have gone to work, done the job assigned to us (and let's add that we have done a *good job),* we are an *Unprofitable Servant or Employee*. That is simply because we have been paid for what we were given to do, and not gaining our employer a *gain* above what he has paid us. Here is where *Give Yourself Away* can come into play every day at a job you are getting paid to do: DO MORE THAN WHAT YOU ARE PAID TO DO. GIVE your employer something of yourself that they are not paying for. Do not think that will go unnoticed!

How many people get raises and promotions for simply doing what they are paid to do, without ever GIVING THEMSELVES AWAY to their employer? Think about it. It is a fact that the ones who *go the 2nd mile*, come early and stay late, work on days no one else wants to work, etc., etc., etc., are the ones who most often get the raises and promotions.

Here's one more *giving yourself away* tip: employers take note of those who get to work EARLY (before the assigned *start* time). Nothing was a job-killer back in the days I was a manager at a company than an employee who wouldn't show up at least a few minutes before they were supposed to be at work. For most employees get some coffee, read the paper, or talk to another employee about yesterday's news/games/personal life. Do you do that on *personal time* BEFORE *clocking in*, or AFTER being *on the clock*? We always operated on a *get here 15-20-30 minutes before we start work, and don't shut down until closing time*. It didn't take long to know who was going to be a dependable, loyal, long-time employee who would be PROFITABLE for the company.

Besides, God has promised that those who are *faithful in the least WILL BE faithful in the much*. Those are the ones who GIVE themselves away, just like our Lord does to ones who are GIVERS like Him. Besides, perhaps the grandest and most well-known characteristic of God is that of generosity. It is His desire that His kids be the same way.

Be one who *gives yourself away*…it is *The Math of Life. Christ's Life.*

Chapter 21
Poor vs Broke
...a foolish man spendeth it up.
Proverbs 21:20b

In all my years of pastoring, there is one thing the majority of church members were positive about. That was helping other members financially who were *in need*. Very little was ever said or discussed about whether these folks were *poor* or *broke*. And not a word about whether the members were truthfully *in need*, or how they got into the situation they were in. In other words, not much was said about how the person's situation compared with Philippians 4:19,
> But my God shall supply all your need, according to His riches in glory by Christ Jesus.

Or, what God has said about His sheep and our always having a supply for every need, and no want...
> The LORD is my shepherd; I shall not want. Psalm 23:1

Wow! It is interesting how so many can evade, ignore, or deny the Word of God when addressing a situation. God has given so much wisdom for His people to use in handling financial issues.

Being *in need* is an interesting idea. Just exactly WHAT does that mean? It could be said of almost everyone that at some time or another each could be *in need*. Are all people who are *broke, in need*? Are all people who are *poor, in need*? Name any item you can think of, and someone could be *in need* of it. A house, a car, some clothes, food, medicine, school supplies, a haircut...see the unending possibilities??? And what sort of specifics are considered when determining that someone is *in need*?

Add to this discussion the words *poor* and *broke*, and we introduce a multi-faceted picture of someone's situation that most people cannot adequately describe. Now we add in a few *favorite* scriptures of some, and we begin to get into heated arguments about WHAT to do and HOW Saints are supposed to handle these financial dilemmas some folks have gotten themselves into. And my, oh my...just mentioning *these financial dilemmas* **some folks have gotten themselves into** can add fuel to the fires of what is right, and what is wrong...what is Godly and what is ungodly.

I always said during these times that we need to talk about whether the Scriptures tell us the Church is to help the *poor* and/or the *broke*. There is a VAST difference between the two! And it may seem incredulous to some, but the Scriptures NEVER mention someone being *broke*. That concept seems null and void with God, since He tells us over and over He will supply the *need* of His people! That's the verse above. Which might beg the question, how is a Saint ever *poor* or *broke*? OR, *in need*?

Aha! Perhaps we should first take a look at how some come to be *broke* or *poor* and *in need*:

1. *the result of bad choices.*
   The way of a fool is right in his own eyes: but he that hearkeneth unto counsel is wise. Proverbs 12:15
2. *the result of laziness.*
   Go to the ant, thou sluggard; consider her ways, and be wise: Which having no guide, overseer, or ruler, Provideth her meat in the summer, and gathereth her food in the harvest. How long wilt thou sleep, O sluggard? when wilt thou arise out of thy sleep? Yet a little sleep, a little slumber, a little folding of the hands to sleep: So shall thy poverty come as one that travelleth, and thy want as an armed man. Proverbs 6:6-11
   A slothful man hideth his hand in his bosom, and will not so much as bring it to his mouth again. Proverbs 19:24
3. *the result of following vain people & wild dreams.*
   He that tilleth his land shall have plenty of bread: but he that followeth after vain persons shall have poverty enough. Proverbs 28:19
4. *the result of ignoring good instruction.*
   Poverty and shame shall be to him that refuseth instruction: but he that regardeth reproof shall be honored. The desire accomplished is sweet to the soul: but it is abomination to fools to depart from evil. He that walketh with wise men shall be wise: but a companion of fools shall be destroyed. Proverbs 13:18-20
5. *the result of ...* (the reasons are numerous).

Do any of these reasons, or any not mentioned, call for a response to provide financial support or aid to those who are *in need*? Is there any instance where personal financial responsibility should trump help from others? At what point do well-meaning folks take care to help those *in need* to learn personal responsibility, learn financial discipline, learn how to handle the resources God has promised (and given) to meet all their *need*?

A real possible problem for the community is that of a lack of teaching as to just what the original writers God spoke through were telling us. A quick glance at any concordance shows us there are 12 Hebrew words translated *poor* in the Scriptures, 6 of which show up in Proverbs. What is critical is to know the meaning of the words of the original languages that can give specific instruction that is different from the use of one word to another word translated the same.

For instance, in Proverbs 27:7, we find the Hebrew word *ruwsh*, meaning *to be poor, have a lack, be needy, or to be destitute*, also carries the meaning *to make oneself poor*. Now, listen to the wisdom applied to this word:

> All the brethren of the poor do hate him: how much more
> do his friends go far from him? he pursueth them with
> words, yet they are wanting to him.

Wow! One who is **known** to *make himself poor* is treated with disdain by his own brethren and friends. But listen! Without us knowing the use of *ruwsh* in this sentence, meaning *make himself poor*, we could see this person as one who has had a rough time, a bad situation, mistreatment, etc. AND feel we need to help him. His REAL need is not financial aid, but financial counsel and whatever it takes for him to get his financial stewardship straightened out and use some personal discipline.

However, in Proverbs 29:14, the Hebrew word *dal* appears, meaning *weak, thin, lean, needy, or poor*. Listen to the wisdom God passes on to us here:

> The king that faithfully judgeth the poor, his throne shall
> be established forever.

Wow! Here God points out that a KING who *shaphat*, gathers evidence and determines a *truthful need* is rewarded by God for helping that person, giving them financial aid. Determining a *truthful need* should be done with the appropriate and adequate research of a person's financial life.

Now, listen. When God tells us He will supply *all our need*, and we find someone who is in a life situation that evidence deems they *truthfully need help*, God will supply their *need* through someone who has an *abundance*. (see chapter 45 for a detailed look at such situations)

So, let me summarize…

- God never intends for us to be *broke* (Philippians 4:19). Most need financial counsel and financial discipline, not financial aid.
- Determining a *truthful need* is a very Scriptural responsibility, and it should be carried out with great wisdom and prayerfully.
- Being a *wise steward* of God's resources is a huge responsibility.
- God wants us to understand that a person with a *supposed need* might just be *poor* or *broke* because of their *irresponsibility*.
- IF you or I are one who is *poor* or *broke*, we must do a *self-examination* before we go asking someone else to help us. WE might have a *spiritual*, as well as a *practical*, problem.

I believe two quotes I have gathered will give some great practical advice to close this chapter with:

"99% of the failures come from people
who have the habit of making excuses."
George Washington Carver

"Things had to happen the way they did.
I had to hit rock bottom before I could change.
Now…we are going to have a wonderful life together."
movie: *Smash Up: The Story of a Woman* (1947)

Be diligent to be a good steward. It is the *Math of Life*. *Christ's Life*.

Chapter 22
Your Treasure Shows Which Heart
For where your treasure is, there will be your heart also.
Matthew 6:21

I'm going to start this chapter with a discussion that might shock you, or at the least may be a little startling to you. It has nothing to do on the surface with *your treasure* or *your heart* except that it is the undergirding of both. It is the question of what *is* is.

What is *is?*

Most people never really give any thought to that question. Some think we cannot really know what *is* is. They just have something in their mind as to what the answer is (no pun intended), and go on about their business. Not me. Almost 70 years ago when I was in the 3rd grade, my father (who was a coach/math teacher) taught me what *is* is. It means *equals* or *same as*. Always does! That may not sound like a particularly astounding revelation, but it really *is*. Whenever we say something *is*, followed by another declaration, we are *equating* the two. God is the One who gave us this premise. Many times in Scripture God tells us *a* equals *b*. We sort of take it with *a grain of salt*, as folks used to say in days gone by (meaning, not a big thing, just ordinary). But when one thing equals another, and particularly when God has said so when speaking of our treasure and our heart, WE MUST TAKE NOTICE! And, remember that all that God says is done *parabolically*. Only with His Mind can we understand Truthfully.

Let us go deeper with this definition of *is*. The Greek word translated *is* is *esti*. For each Saint, what we think, believe, and act upon (even with feelings) should come from our Holy Soul (the residence of God's Mind, Emotions, and Will). When God says something *is*, He is saying something that comes from the Heart of our Holy Soul. Yet, as Saints, we have *two souls*. So, there can be a double-mindedness in each Saint. (No wonder so many have such battles at times going on INSIDE them that they realize little about!). Only when something gets settled inside us is the war over. The battle has been *won* only when we function in God's Soul.

(see the trichotomy diagram of a Saint on page #261)

Just as a coin has two sides making up the one coin, the *two sides* of this verse make up the one Truth.

So, let's discover the importance of taking a look at Matthew 6:21. God tells us something really important: the connection between our innermost thinking, believing, feelings, acting (the *heart* we are functioning in) and our treasure. This is not just a generic verse occupying space in the Holy Scriptures. It is a critical statement of what is going on INSIDE US, in a place not many know about. God is expecting all Saints to always be functioning in our Holy Heart.

First, let us look at the Greek word translated to *treasure* in our English versions. *Thesaurus*. It is our riches, our wealth, anything laid up in store. It can have multiple meanings of *treasures*, relating to physical treasures or Eternal Life/Spiritual wealth in our Holy Soul. However, here, God is definitely talking about our riches or wealth as in *financial treasures*, in context of vs. 19 and 20 just before.

> Lay not up for yourselves treasures upon the earth, where moth and rust doth corrupt, and where thieves break through and steal: But lay up for yourselves treasures in heaven, where neither moth nor rust doth corrupt, and where thieves do not break through nor steal. 6:19-20

Proverbs 3 says our *treasure* is what we have IN the bank, and what we have COMING to the bank (in store, and income). Look at Proverbs 3:9-10…

> Honor the LORD with thy substance, and with the firstfruits of all thine increase: So shall thy barns be filled with plenty, and thy presses shall burst out with new wine.

Second, let us look at the Greek word for *heart* in our English versions. *Kardia*. A whole host of scriptures correlate the *heart* to those parts of us such as our thinking/thoughts, understanding, all sorts of emotions like love & affection & joy & fear & anger & sorrow, plus our decisions/will. These comprise the *totality* of the soul. The *heart* is the summation of all in the soul working together. Now, for a Saint we have to choose whether we will live in the soul (lowercase *s*) we were originally born with, OR in the Soul (capital *S*) we were given at our New Birth. God's Soul is the latter. Can you see the difference between the two souls? Can you begin to see and determine WHICH soul is functioning within you from time to time?

The term, *the heart,* is a nebulous term. The parabolism of Matthew 6:21 tells us we should know which *heart/Heart* we are functioning in by the way our finances are managed and the story they tell, compared with the Word of God.

Now, listen to this: God tells us our *treasure* and our *heart* are *in the same place.* OK. But, He also tells us in many places that our *heart* is the controlling factor in dictating where our *treasure* is…even though they are BOTH *in the same place.* If I am honest with myself, I can know *which soul* is managing my finances. If we are honest with ourselves, we can know *which soul* is managing our finances. THIS IS WHAT GOD IS TRYING TO TELL EACH OF US IN MATTHEW 6:21.

So, now IF we want Life, Christ's Life, in the Math of our finances, we must CHOOSE to Live in *His Soul.* We must choose His Mind, His Thinking, His Knowledge, His Wisdom, His Understanding, His Ways, His Emotions…HIS HEART…instead of the enemy's. The Good News really IS that we GET to choose! And that *His Heart* IS a possible choice for us a child of God.

Bad choices are NOT forced upon us. Bad choices are made in the wrong soul! Circumstances can NEVER make us choose *death* to our finances. Evil forces are not in charge of our finances. WE ARE, and by the Grace (working) of God we can make wise choices. AND WE MUST ALWAYS KEEP THIS IN MIND: the results or figures that the world thinks is *success* in finances IS NEVER what matters. It is the PATH we have taken to get to the results or figures we have IS what matters. We have arrived either by GOD's WAY or the devil's way, GOD's HEART or the devil's heart…no matter the numbers.

We must let GOD determine the numbers. Our Life is to be one of *choosing Life* in all financial decisions. That is *The Math of Life. Christ's Life.*

Chapter 23
Your Spending Plan Portrays Your Priorities
But seek ye first the kingdom of God, and His righteousness,
and all these things shall be added unto you.
Matthew 6:33

It has been said that a portrait is a picture of the soul. It is a portrayal of the innermost thoughts one has of what is being portrayed. A person's Spending Plan is simply a portrait or picture using numbers to reveal their soul. However, Saints should never forget that each Saint possesses two souls. Each soul (*natural soul* or *Christ's Soul*) has vastly different thoughts and desires relative to Spiritual matters which will impact our financial matters. Our Spending Plan/Priorities give definition/reveal WHICH soul a Saint is acting out of. Knowing of and being able to identify and differentiate between the two souls is of great importance for a Saint to *prioritize spending appropriately and in a God-pleasing way.*

Any person who does any type of *financial coaching*, or some sort of more sophisticated counseling/advising (one with a degree to do so), knows that it only takes a quick look at someone's *spending plan* or spending record/habits to see just what that person's priorities are in life. Money talks. That includes how we spend our money. Let's face it…we spend the money in our control on what we deem to be important to us!

The portrayal/picture of one's spending is as picturesque as an exact replica portrait/picture of the person. The old saying, *put your money where your mouth is*, is spot on when *listening* to what is really important to someone. So, what does our Spending Plan portrayal reveal about our priorities? What does your Spending Plan speak of you?

Let me paint a picture for you. When I was at the seminary back in the early 1980's, our family rented a small house not far from the campus. It was an older neighborhood. And right across the street from us was an elderly couple that had lived in their home for many years. They had a 2nd lot adjacent to their home that was vacant, except the wife had a beautiful garden taking up quite a bit of the space. My wife talked with the lady several times about growing vegetables, which my wife did so in the small confines of the back yard of the house we lived in.

This elderly couple attended a small church nearby. One day the neighbor lady asked my wife about whether I would come talk to their church about being their pastor (we never knew why the church was without a pastor at that time). I asked my wife to ask the lady for a copy of the church's budget. Church budgets tell us a whole lot about the priorities of the church. Well, one quick glance at that church's budget told me they were not interested in really providing for a pastor or any staff. They made very little provisions for Spiritual education or evangelism. Their main interest was to send a large portion of their tithes and offerings to missions, both to the convention they belonged to and to entities around the world. Now it is important for a church to support missions. But not at the expense of the local mission of the church at its present location. They had very little money budgeted for any local ministry of the church. They had no money budgeted to plan for the procuring of any future needs. When the woman indicated that she didn't think the church would be interested in changing any *spending priorities*, I did not think further about talking with them.

Priorities speak of where the *heart* is. Just as in chapter 22 on *treasure and heart*, spending priorities are just as clearly portrayed. In fact, our spending priorities show our *heart* and the heart's determination where our *treasure* will be spent. That is the link between our *heart* and our spending *priorities* and our *treasure*. Get this picture solidly settled in your thinking so that you will be cognizant of the driving forces of the *where* and the *why* of all financial decisions you make.

Now listen, you or I could look at any church's budget and see the heart of the people as it pertains to their priorities of ministry. It is that simple. It is that clear. AND, the same can be said for ANY and EVERY individual's or couple's family financial priorities.

So, when is the last time you took a look at your Spending Plan, that is – if you have one? Or, when is the last time you sat down and evaluated your *stewardship priorities* in how you are spending the resources God is sending your way?

If you don't have a Spending Plan or similar record of how you have been spending money each month, why not take the *15-15-25-45 Plan* (chapter 24, A Monthly Spending Plan Is A Must) and log your expenditures for the past 3 months (each month separately) according to the ways in which I have listed for the various percentages? That is at least a start toward a visual picture of where your money is really going, and what your monthly financial priorities really are.

Some of the percentages are simple, so far as logging your expenditures. Where needed, or would best give you a clearer picture, add a few *line items* to show what you are putting your money in.

Once you have done the above exercise, you can readily see what your expenditures show you regarding your financial priorities! This can be quite a shock for a lot of folks. However, it is a starting point for really evaluating what you have been prioritizing, and where you might want to start RE-prioritizing your money.

The more detailed your recap, the more explicit your *prioritizing* can be!

What this really does is give you a more specific look at where your *heart* (which heart? diagram on p.261) has been when it comes to your financial stewardship. And any way you look at it, this is a good thing.

What should really matter are two things:
1. Do my priorities reveal that I am reckoning with God for His provision and then direct how I administer His resources He entrusts to me?
2. Am I willing to make some *heart* changes, leading to *priority* changes, where re-prioritizing should occur?

In order to experience the Life of Christ in our finances, we must be abandoning ourselves to Him for His leadership and trusting Him to work however, wherever, and whenever to meet all our needs with an abundance to also give to every good work (including missions He leads us to give to). To that we can say, "Well, amen!"

Make your Spending Plan reveal the priorities of God. It is *The Math of Life. Christ's Life.*

Chapter 24
A Monthly Spending Plan Is A Must
A Sit Down & Count the Cost Plan
The thoughts of the diligent tend only to plenteousness;
but of every one that is hasty only to want.
Proverbs 21:5

"When your outgo exceeds your income, your upkeep becomes your downfall."
Pastor John Morgan - Sagemont Church, Houston, Texas, 1979

Pastor John Morgan was years ahead of the day of so many people beginning to get a grip on the effects of credit and free spending, with what amounts to *fake money*. There is no honest way of calling it other than to say that *credit* is NOT REAL MONEY. It is a GAMBLE against the future, period. It is a LOAN as a 2nd best scenario. Both are real! Period. Both are not *God's Way*. Whoever is extending the *credit* is *loaning* an individual/couple *the so-called purchasing power to buy something they are not paying for with real money (cash) that God has provided at the present.*

What it amounts to for most folks using credit is this: their *outgo* IS EXCEEDING their *income* for a given period of time. What most never take into consideration is this: they are *spending* the entire amount of the purchase, even though they are *paying* a prescribed minimum amount each month once the credit is incurred, and maybe zero the first month. They *owe* the full amount, *pay* the minimum each month, and *incur* interest on the unpaid amount. Those are the characteristics of any loan. In the end, they PAY MUCH MORE for the originally incurred *expense* item than what it *cost* at the moment of the *obtainment by loan*. THIS IS NOT A GAME WITH PLAY MONEY! The game of Monopoly, and others like it, may have skewed the buyer's mind into thinking REAL MONEY is not real! Or, who knows what they are thinking. They are thinking with the *wrong mind*, at the least.

If anything, the parents of the buyer have not taught the buyer the reality of their having to pay the full purchase price PLUS the interest over some prescribed period of time in the future. Nowhere in the American financial world is this more obvious than in the purchase of a house (which we will look at in detail in chapter 35). For now, just know that the *total paid* for a house in most cases is almost twice as much over the long-term loan as what the house could have been bought for, *with cash*, at the original purchase date. THAT IS SHOCKING when we consider most houses have a sale price of more than $150,000, perhaps more than $200,000 in 2023! Think of how much of a dent that makes in someone's *retirement funds*. (Oh, perhaps you have never thought of that aspect.)

So, what does this look like in many American households and their checkbooks? We will see many statements made by those in financial circles before we get through this book!

Here's one for starters. The typical family in America in 2023 is living *paycheck to paycheck*. In fact, Paul Ryan said (in 2017), "78% of Americans are living paycheck to paycheck" (U. S. Congressional House Speaker Paul Ryan on FNC, Tuesday evening, 11-14-17). He went on to say that "57% don't have $500 cash in savings."

And Speaker Ryan's statement is just one of hundreds of similar statements that show the status of America's households in this day. (Throughout this book I quote many sources giving dated surveys, studies, etc. on *savings amounts* and *savings rates* of Americans. Keep that in mind when some figures and dates seem to conflict.)

How do we escape being one of those statistics?!? Easy. We MUST have a *Monthly Spending Plan* (some call this a *budget*, but that word has a bad reputation & it is not as specifically descriptive as my *Monthly Spending Plan*). I will give the plan that I have developed after years and years of attending conferences, reading books, and perhaps more importantly, working with folks trying to get a grip on their family's financial matters.

I have taken into consideration God's Word for being a steward of the resources He allows to pass through each person's/couple's hands. I have taken into consideration ideas, advice, and practical application offered by some in the world's financial domain. And, I have taken into consideration many years of personal financial matters, especially *spending*. Barbara and I operating as *Mr. & Mrs. Lee McDowell, Unincorporated* have gone to great lengths to keep track of **every penny** of money that passes *through* our hands each month! YES…EVERY PENNY. Barbara keeps all the financial records mentioned in this book for our personal finances. She does a wonderful job of keeping our financial picture up-to-date.

Does the corporation you work for keep track of every penny? Or, does the smaller, perhaps, unincorporated business you work for do likewise? Does your bank keep track of every penny? Give me one good reason that each family should operate any differently if they want to be good stewards? (being a good *steward* is discussed in many chapters)

After all these years of helping church members evaluate and get control of their personal/family financial spending and saving activities, I can tell you that there are four (4) basic categories of *spending* that really make a difference.

The numbers I use are all *guesstimates*, with individual spending plans varying depending on different incomes, varying tax brackets, varying saving needs, and spending preferences. But interestingly, the more gross income a household has, the more expensive items (or, more total items) the household purchases. Therefore, typically the %'s are virtually the same. My chart shows my idea of how you might divide your GROSS income (allotments for each category).

Now we will take a look at what I call the *15-15-25-45 Plan*. There are two perspectives we will consider…mentality and actuality. Mentally we plan putting God first. But we live actually with government controls. However, we can live with **actuality** when our **mentality** is in accordance with God's Ways and **dictating** what **actually** takes place, recognizing in most cases Uncle Sam TAKES his share first!

Planning the spending of your Gross Income

15 - 15 - 25 - 45 PLAN

Mentality
pay God first
pay yourself second
pay Uncle Sam third
live off the rest

Actuality
pay Uncle Sam first
pay God second
pay yourself third
live off the rest

Details of the 15-15-25-45 Plan

15% Uncle Sam	15% God	25% Savings*	45% Living**
income tax	tithes	living savings	monthly expenditures
SS & Medicare	offerings	future purchases	fixed expenses
		emergency fund	variable expenses
		retirement	

GOOD NEWS… In **reality, you are actually LIVING monthly on about **55-65%** of your gross income.

*Keep in mind that the **living savings fund** is to set aside funds for things you will need on a regular basis, but not every month.

*The **future purchases fund** is to set aside a large amount of funds for things you know you will have to replace or repair, but not on a monthly basis, perhaps even a yearly basis.

*The **emergency fund** is not touched except for that extreme event that may or may not happen in any year. The **emergency fund** is there in case of a disruption of income.

*The **retirement fund** is not touched until retirement. With the typical person/couple living 15-20 years+ past the age of ceasing work, we must plan for those years just like we are planning for the year at hand.

INCOME and OTHER PAYROLL TAXES (15%)

It is somewhat interesting to know that in America there are many citizens who pay income taxes to *Cousin Jimmy*. Who is he? The Governor of the state in which those citizens reside. Many other U.S. Citizens DO NOT have state income taxes; only federal income taxes payable to *Uncle Sam*. Therefore, the *percentage* of one's Spending Plan allotted for Income Taxes may vary. And, with different folks often having much different deductible amounts to consider, again the *percentage* may vary from family to family. As you will see in all my ideas, good records of past experiences gives great information, knowledge, and *expertise* in making wise decisions for figuring your own personal *Monthly Spending Plan*. Other payroll taxes include amounts for Social Security, Medicare, etc.

One thing to remember, we are operating from your Gross Income. This is the pre-tax, pre-deduction for anything amount. So, to begin with, we are using 15% as a starting point only. If you can go back and figure how much ACTUAL income and other payroll taxes you have paid in recent years, you will be able to figure an *exact* percentage to acknowledge in your personal *Monthly Spending Plan*. Whether the total amount is taken out of your check on a monthly basis, or you pay quarterly or a lump sum at the end of the year, you need to figure what the 1/12th amount would be to include in your Monthly Spending Plan.

TITHES & OFFERINGS (15%)

For all intents and purposes, the *tithe* is 10%...*one tenth* of our gross income. Offerings are the additional giving to missions, special love offerings, and any other opportunities God brings our way and leads us to participate in (maybe to support a youth going to camp or give to a designated fund to build a building or instrument/equipment for a ministry). Therefore the 15% is a guideline of the amounts to figure for tithing and offerings. Since some of the offerings may be different each month, some sort of savings device might be used to handle the total amounts given as needed.

The main thing is to PLAN for an estimated amount to give cheerfully and abounding in God's Grace bountifully to every good work causing thanksgiving to God. This involves purposing in the Heart of God to first giving ourselves to God, willing to be a vessel of His Power working through us.

SAVINGS (25%)

The Living Savings Fund is for accumulating the amount of money for things that will be needed in the near future. Instead of having to write a large check out of our Monthly Spending Plan, we plan to set aside these funds regularly to be able to make the periodic purchases without disrupting our typical monthly expenditures. Examples might a new coffee pot, medicines, clothing & shoes, etc.

The Future Purchases Fund would be for larger purchases that we might incur during any year (other than every year). Examples would be auto tires and maintenance, a television set, kitchen appliances, vacations, retreats, special fees, etc.

The Emergency Fund is to be used for emergencies only. Job loss, job change, unexpected catastrophic events, or some emergency need of this sort. This fund is not for ordinary expenses of any kind and/or retreats/vacations/etc. It is monies to live month to month during an emergency period.

The Retirement Fund is for accumulating funds to live on when we retire from regular jobs. The age we do so will vary from person to person, couple to couple. IF one retires with a comfortable fund from the company worked for (direct company fund or an IRA/401k fund), then these monies will provide additional comfort in living. The latter would mean there are less funds each month that need to be set aside. However...with the change in companies and careers that many make these days, it is wise to begin early for a personal fund to provide for comfort in the retirement years.

LIVING EXPENSES (45%)

Living expenses include all regular monthly expenditures, including fixed expenses and variable expenses. This section will require much thought, evaluation, emotional considerations, some difficult decisions, and an open-eyed recognition of the multitude of ways that income can be spent other than the three categories previously mentioned.

This category really shows us just how much it takes to exist in modern times, and how careful and consistent we have to be to watch our pennies, nickels, and dimes...not to mention our dollars!

Note that I speak of our actually living on more than the 45% share of our gross monthly income. This involves the use of the Living Savings

Fund and Future Purchases Fund that we have been putting some of our gross monthly income into. A small portion each month to be used when the larger ticket items come due.

It is definitely advisable and necessary to give a detailed look, listing, figuring, and evaluation into the so-many ways funds are needed for simply existing in life today. Without careful and complete research and planning, way too many people find themselves HAVING to go to a credit card to make an expense BECAUSE they didn't THINK AHEAD.

It really is an eye-opener to see all the ways our money can seemingly *disappear*. This is one of the primary reasons that this type of *planning for spending* can make a huge difference in *our being in control of our money* instead of *our money being in control of us*.

IF YOU HAVE ANY PAYMENTS that are made quarterly, bi-annually, or annually, you need to take the $1/12^{th}$ (of the annual amount) needed for EACH MONTH, put that amount into one of your savings accounts, and then be ready to disperse the total with the funds already figured, set aside, and readily available at the moment the total is due. Fantastic, isn't it!?!

Oftentimes the seemingly insignificant expenditures can add up to a large amount over a period of time. And, the small amounts of charges to a credit card (or, multiple cards) can definitely add up. Listen to the wisdom of one of America's founding fathers:

"Beware of little expenses.
A small leak will sink a great ship."
Benjamin Franklin

Let's get real serious for a moment. Most of us are aware of the big outlays each month. It IS the small cash disbursements that drain our pockets and checkbooks so quickly. Keeping records *to the penny* is challenging at first, but it becomes very apparent it is the only way to really get control of our cash flow. Barbara and I keep a certain amount in our billfolds. We get receipts for ALL expenditures. And go to our Petty Cash bag for reimbursements. If it is impossible to get a receipt (as it is sometimes…), we make out a *chit* to get paid back from Petty Cash. That Petty Cash fund is a life-saver for keeping record of the small cash disbursements.

There are many folks who have what we could consider an *unstable income*. They do not receive the *same* paycheck week after week, month after month, etc. You may be one of many with jobs where your income varies from one paycheck to another. Such as:
- salesmen who work on commissions
- construction workers where weather or other delays affect paychecks
- or, someone in a job that is *seasonal* with great variances of income in different periods of the year.

A Monthly Spending Plan is easy to maintain even with these factors. So, what do you do?

First, write down your income (however) from the last few years (month by month). Is your annual total pretty much the same from year to year? Find your *average income* for the number of years you are calculating. Divide by 12. Yes, this gives you your average monthly income for the last _____ years. From this figure you determine your Monthly Spending Plan.

I know what you are thinking. "What if…?" It doesn't matter. In months where your income is *more* than your *average,* you put the *extra* into a *savings account* and call it *variable income protection.* That month you *use only* what your *average* amount is. When a month's income is less than your average, you use the amount needed from your *v.i.p. savings* (isn't that a cool acronym!) to make up the difference between *actual* and *needed* income for one of those months (but using no more than the *average* spending amount).

All of this removes any worries, fears, hassles, and stress from causing trauma with your *Monthly Spending Plan* and financial management.

Be diligent with your Monthly Spending planning…it is *The Math of Life. Christ's Life.*

Chapter 25
It's Reconcile, Not Balance
And all things are of God,
who hath reconciled us to Himself by Jesus Christ,
and hath given to us the ministry of reconciliation.
2 Corinthians 5:18

How does this verse enter into this financial chapter on *reconciling, not balancing*? Well, the word *reconcile* is about *changing from one state to another* (to be as one to the other). This is what has taken place in sinners when God has reconciled them to Himself through their trusting in Jesus Christ (the whole salvation thing), and becoming New Creatures (Saints). When Barbara and I were Born Again, Pastor Morgan told us we were no longer the same persons who had walked into his office that morning! Christ's LIFE entering ours gave NEW LIFE to us. We had a new **status** with God! *Reconciling* is a whole different matter than *balancing*. God did not *balance* our sins with any good things we had ever done.

This chapter will be about our checkbook, our personal hands-on record of our current financial *status* at a given bank or other financial institution. It is how we accurately know our *status* between our checkbook and our FI (short for *financial institution*). Every Saint with a checkbook has a *ministry of reconciliation* between their checkbook and their financial institution! The Greek *katallasso* means to bring into agreement, or harmony. That is what the process of *reconciling* our check register to our bank statement is all about. It is VERY IMPORTANT!

How many of us RECONCILE our checkbook ONCE EACH MONTH??? It is a critical action to take that can go a long way in *preventing* overdrafts or overdrawn accounts!

I am sure most everyone reading this book *knows* what a checkbook is, but I am not sure most everyone *knows* the difference between *reconciling* their checkbook versus *balancing* their checkbook. And, they often use either word when they are entering checks (debits) and deposits (credits) into their checkbook and getting a figure they think they have in the bank. These two words DO NOT mean the same thing, they ARE NOT the same activity, and both definitely have VERY IMPORTANT functions for keeping track of our financial accounts at the given institution and what funds we think we have available for our use.

So, let's begin with defining and describing the two words, making clear the different action required by each, and the importance of each.

BALANCING our checkbook. When we write a check or some sort of debit is made to our account, we *must* enter the activity into the *minus* column. The amount is to be *subtracted* from the *running balance* (the existing balance we have figured). When we make a deposit, or it is made by an electronic method, we *must* enter the activity into the *plus* column. The amount is to be *added* to the *running balance.* The *running balance* figured after the entry is important. First, this gives us our new *running balance*, and it is what we call *balancing* our account as our checkbook shows. This should not be difficult, but for those who have not been taught the basic function of numerical columns it can be an effort of great angst later in the week, or month.

For instance, in financial numerical column-speak, the farthest column to the right is the singles column. The next column to the left is the tens column. The next column to the left is the hundreds column. The next column to the left is the single-thousands column. This is probably as far *left* as most of us ever go! Here is the KEY thing: (my father was a jr. high math teacher and coach, and taught me this when I was in the 3rd grade) IF we don't enter all figures in a proper columnar manner, it highly increases the possibility we will make a mistake in either adding or subtracting figures, thereby coming up with an erroneous *running balance*. Uggghhhh! This can lead to all kinds of financial problems!

Another huge truth to take into consideration: the *running balance* in our checkbook is *almost never* what the *balance* is in our account on the FI's records. HOW is that?!? Simple. We have activity in our checkbook that is a *day* or *days* ahead of that activity showing up at the FI. *It is NEVER advisable to simply go into our FI and ask them "How much money do I have in my account?"* I could give you numerous reasons for not doing this...trust me! You will not believe an illustration I give you at the end of this chapter!

For now, keep in mind, what we just discussed was the *running balance* in our checkbook. Not a *reconcile* or *reconciling* of our checkbook. Total different activity and result!

RECONCILING our checkbook. It is imperative that we take this next step with our *checkbook* and *account* at our FI. The process should be done

once/month, soon after receiving our *monthly bank statement*. On the backside of almost every monthly bank statement sheet is a process that walks anyone through writing down:
- starting balance
- deposits & credits, since starting balance date
- checks & debits, since starting balance date
- then calculating the adjusted balance, of our bank account.

This is activity for a given period of time in our account. It gives us an *adjusted FI account balance*. It is important to note that the *adjusted FI account balance* MUST MATCH the *current checkbook balance* when we are finished doing all this figuring. And now we know the difference and importance of *balancing & reconciling* our checkbook!

Do you believe in *financial miracles*? Well, here's one to ponder (and never repeat!). This is the illustration I told you earlier that I would give at the end of this chapter. I know a person who had *never reconciled* their checkbook, but *never* had an *overdraft balance* occur. That, in and of itself, is a miracle due to the numerous and probable possibilities of an over-drafted account happening. What is more incredulous is the activity that occurred without an overdraft!

> This person had a reasonably good amount of income each month. They used only one credit card to obtain the maximum number of airline miles they could get. They deducted each credit card purchase from their checkbook at the time the card was used. (This is a good practice for those using credit cards a lot and wanting to pay the credit card bill in its entirety each month. When the bill is received, a check can be made out and entered into the checkbook WITHOUT DEDUCTING the check amount because the individual amounts have been already entered. Make sure to *mark* those amounts that apply to the payment to the credit card company.)
>
> *However,* this person also deducted the check sent to the credit card company. Wow! This is double-entering of the credit card charges! You might quickly ask: HOW did they not show a *negative* amount very quickly in their checkbook??? Seems impossible, doesn't it? Well, with the

convenience and ease of living in the country a short distance from a small town with the bank located next to the post office (and getting all their mail at the post office), they went to their bank a few times a month and did what I earlier said, "Don't do!" They reported that the bank was so kind as to give them an update on their account each time they went into the bank and asked for it. *And they entered the balance the bank said they had in their account,* ignoring whether there were any checks outstanding, or any other activity for that matter (like deductions for credit card charges), no matter what their checkbook balance was at that time! SOMEHOW, over a number of years, this process had somehow *covered* the *double-deductions* I previously mentioned involving the credit card charges. WOW!

If this doesn't make sense to you, that's perfectly OK. It makes no sense to me, but it is a truthful report of what had occurred for years!

I couldn't believe it when I was working with the individual and discovered it! DO NOT try this procedure for yourself. It cannot work twice!

So, just be aware of, and remember: *always* enter a *new running balance* into your checkbook after every item of transaction made to your account, and *always reconcile* your *checkbook balance* with your *FI statement each month* And, *never* just walk into your FI and ask them what the *balance* of your account is. THEY DON'T KNOW! *Your checkbook only* should show you your *accurate balance!* The *reconciling* once a month is to make sure your *checkbook balance* reflects what the bank shows without all the *un-cleared* activity of your checkbook considered.

Actually, I like to think of *reconciling my checkbook* as a way to make sure my bank has not made any mistakes! And I have had more than one instance where my bank has made a mistake.

A *reconciliation* equals a *new life* for your checkbook. Christ's Life in our finances *always* leads to & leaves a *positive balance!*

Be one who *reconciles* your checkbook with your monthly bank statement at least once each month! It is *The Math of Life. Christ's Life.*

Account Reconciliation

OUTSTANDING WITHDRAWALS/DEBITS
NOT YET CHARGED TO ACCOUNT

date	$	
TOTAL	$	

HOW TO RECONCILE YOUR STATEMENT
1. Mark your account register of each deposit or withdrawal that are listed on your statement.
2. Subtract from your account register any service, miscellaneous or automatic charges posted on your statement…but not yet on your register
3. Complete the form to the left (withdrawals/debits that haven't cleared bank).
4. Complete calculations on bottom right.
5. The final "RECONCILED BALANCE" should agree with your account register, if it doesn't, see "Hints for Finding Differences".

HINTS FOR FINDING DIFFERENCES
- Recheck all additions, subtractions, and corrections.
- Verify the carryover balance from page to page in your account register.
- Make sure you have subtracted miscellaneous service charges.
- Make sure you have added interest earned.

_____ Ending balance shown on statement

+_____ ADD deposits not shown on statement

+_____

+_____

+_____

_____ Subtotal

_____ Less Outstanding withdrawal/debits

_____ ***RECONCILED BALANCE**

*this should agree with your account register balance

Chapter 26
Keep Track of Every Penny
Be thou diligent to know the state of thy flocks,
and look well to thy herds.
Proverbs 27:23

It is interesting to stop and think that virtually all Saints work at companies that keep specific and detailed financial records, to *the penny*. In fact, some are the keepers of those records in their companies.

It is also interesting to stop and think of how many Saints belong to churches that keep specific and detailed financial records, to *the penny*. In fact, a few are the keepers of those records in their churches or they are on a committee that *organizes* the handling of the monies or they are in positions of authority that *control* the use of those monies.

It is also interesting to stop and think of how many Saints go to church business meetings who aggressively argue or attack the arrangements and appropriations of funds to particular accounts in the church budget. All it takes is a couple of such meetings to see that these folks are incredibly interested in how *every penny* is spent/used in the different church ministries, especially the ones they are most involved with, or dislike.

AND YET, ALMOST NONE have any such record keeping at home. Very few have virtually any history of handling their personal financial things God's Way. And still less can show any type of *good business* decisions in the appropriation, use, and distribution of the resources God allows to pass into their hands in their personal financial world at home. *How is that?* What could these people be thinking? I don't have time or the need to go into that mindset. That is a horse of a different color!

In over 40 years of ministry, I have yet to find a handful…that's five, counting fingers and thumb…who had a budget/spending plan at home to use in the management of their personal finances and kept records each month to the nearest dollar…incredible! Forget the idea they would do so *to the nearest penny*.

God speaks directly to the *record-keeping* of those things dearest to our hearts. In this day and time, it is sad that so many Saints today have so little knowledge of sheep, shepherds, shepherding, etc. It was so much a part of the life of God's people in the days the Scriptures were written, and God speaks incredible Truth to His people through earthly

associations of the shepherds and their sheep. The beloved 23rd Psalm is a marvelous statement of the fellowship between God and His people.
    The LORD is my shepherd. I shall not want. Psalm 23:1

    John ch.10 is unbelievable in the precise statements Jesus Himself makes about His being the Good Shepherd and His fellowship with His sheep/Saints. Proverbs 27:23 specifically states that God's people *must know* (that's what *be thou diligent* means) anything and everything about their personal belongings. Now listen, WE are the *personal belongings* of Almighty God! And He keeps track of everything we are involved with *to the penny*! Just think about God having His *Book of Life*.

    Listen to King Solomon's words in the verses following v.23:
> For riches are not forever: and doth the crown endure to every generation? The hay appeareth, and the tender grass showeth itself, and herbs of the mountain are gathered. The lambs are for thy clothing, and the goats are the price of the field. And thou shalt have goats' milk enough for thy food, for the food of thy household, and for the maintenance for thy maidens. Proverbs 27:24-27

God makes it perfectly clear that His Saints are to *know* and *understand* the in's and out's of their personal belongings and finances. Notice the details God gives us relative to life. Riches, crown, hay, tender grass, herbs (what a tiny, seemingly insignificant thing compared to the others mentioned), lambs, goats, and goats' milk…these were the heart and soul, so to speak, of the everyday physical life of God's people in those Scriptural days. They are an example of the detailed thinking we today are to give to our livelihood/income, our day-to-day involvements, our accumulated assets, our giving, our very being when it comes to the issues of food, clothing, all kinds of provision and preservation.

    Now, this chapter is all about a position. A position we must take daily in regards to knowing and keeping track of ALL that God has given us to be stewards of. Look throughout this book for, and use, all the types and forms of record-keeping we can and should keep.

    My wife, Barbara, *does keep* these types of records of all our assets, income and outgo, etc. All of this for the McDowells goes back to our thinking in the first place that we see ourselves as *Mr. and Mrs. Lee*

McDowell, Unincorporated, when it comes to handling the resources God passes through our hands...a form of good stewardship.

We have found that by keeping track, *to the penny,* of all that God brings our way, we honor His Word, and His Life continues to show forth in the provision and protection of His belongings of which we are just His stewards. Let me encourage you to be diligent record-keepers, to *the penny.* It is *The Math of Life. Christ's Life.*

Chapter 27
Know Your Personal Net Worth
Be thou diligent to know the state of thy flocks,
and look well to thy herds. For riches are not forever...
Proverbs 27:23-24

It follows that as we *keep track of every penny* we should keep track of our *personal net worth*.

I would venture to say that perhaps 90% of the people I have had contact with in the past 40 years have NO IDEA as to what is their *Net Worth*. Many don't even know what we are talking about. Sadly, it is just something that isn't talked about, isn't defined or enumerated, and doesn't hold much interest for too many people. And yet, it is one of the most important financial teachings the Word of God gives. Our text verse shows that.

A constant update of one's *personal net worth* is a very important part of being the good financial steward of the resources and riches God sends each person's way. It is definitely a part of being a *faithful* financial steward.

Basically, every business does some sort of *net worth statement*, and often many other financial statements, to be able to evaluate whether their business is prosperous or not, succeeding or not, growing or not, and all sorts of other determining factors in making present and future decisions for the company. In fact, how *up-to-date* these statements are can often lead to success or failure.

Once a person/couple has the statement form in place, it is a matter of research and posting the appropriate figures to complete the statement. And, the form makes it easy to do another *current* statement at a future date. Personal computers and uncomplicated personal financial programs make it SO easy!

So, let us begin with a look at a typical *net worth statement*:

PERSONAL FINANCIAL STATEMENT

_____ Date

ASSETS: (What God has entrusted to you)

Cash on roll	$_____
Checking account(s) balance	
_____	_____
_____	_____
Savings account(s) balance	
_____	_____
_____	_____
_____	_____
Credit Union savings	_____
Bonds, stocks, securities	_____
Cash value, life insurance	_____
Cash value, retirement plans	_____
Real estate (market value)	
Home	_____
Other real estate	_____
Automobiles (market value)	_____
_____	_____
_____	_____
Equipment	_____
Jewelry	_____
Collections	_____
Heirlooms	_____
Recreation vehicles	_____
Money owed to us	_____
Other assets	_____
TOTAL ASSETS	$_____

LIABILITIES: (What you owe)

Home mortgage	$_____
Credit cards	
_____	_____
_____	_____
_____	_____
_____	_____
Installment contracts	
_____	_____
_____	_____
_____	_____
Family loans	
_____	_____
_____	_____
Bank loans	
_____	_____
_____	_____
Credit Union loans	
_____	_____
Finance Company loans	
_____	_____
Real Estate loans	
_____	_____
Doctors/medical bills	
_____	_____
_____	_____
Other debts	
_____	_____
TOTAL LIABILITIES	$_____

Q. How often should we do a "Personal Financial Statement"?

A. At least once every 6 months!

I would recommend that one of these statements be done AT LEAST once each year, if not bi-annually. If more people would operate their personal finances like good businesses do, things at home would be on much more solid and sound financial ground.

This is a *longer-term* picture, whereas our *Income/Outgo Statement* is *shorter-term*. In fact, because asset and liability figures can (and, will) change over a few months or years, this makes it that much more important that we do one of these statements on a regularly scheduled basis (once/twice each year) just as we do the *Income/Outgo Statement* typically once each month, right after the month ends.

Net Worth is determined very easily by subtracting our Liabilities from our Assets, with the balance being our *Net Worth*. It doesn't take a *rocket-science* degree to know that we want to have a positive balance from that equation! Yet, far too many people do not realize that they have a negative balance. If the value of your assets exceeds the value of your liabilities, you will have a positive net worth. However, if your liabilities exceed your assets, your net worth will be negative. Without knowing what liabilities are, and the effect they have on our financial life, it is easy for people to be in a situation with a negative balance. And that can be the situation without them knowing it.

ASSETs are our entire property valuation. It is a statement of items that have some sort of economic value. Notice the sample statement for some of the more common assets people possess. It is proper on a *Net Worth Statement* to list ONLY those items whose value could be easily (you determine that meaning for your statement) turned into CASH, if not already such. And these values need to be *market value*, that amount which can easily become CASH. It is not proper to list clothes or miscellaneous items just because you paid an amount for them. They cannot be turned into CASH quickly, easily, or for any amount close to what you paid for them. Some things have great sentimental value, or we paid a certain figure for, or we *think* they are worth a certain amount. But, it is the amount we can quickly get if we try to turn them into CASH.

A LIABILITY is a given amount of indebtedness for an asset when *funds were borrowed to obtain* the asset. If we borrowed money (signed a *note of indebtedness, charged to a credit card*) at the *purchase* time and still owe any amount...that is a liability. Our liabilities are another word for our DEBTS. The outstanding balance of our credit card charges are a liability.

The liability figure listed on the *Net Worth Statement* would be the amount owed (outstanding) on an item. Our liabilities could include amounts owed on a personal loan, owed to a credit card company, owed to any other financial institution, or perhaps taxes of any kind. *A debt is a liability.*

One of the reasons I like for folks to do a *Net Worth Statement*, and update once each year, is that this gives a listing of all outstanding debts. I have always been amazed at folks who have come for some simple, pastoral financial coaching who cannot give a complete listing of their outstanding debts at the first conference. I have had people call back 2-3 times, and more, after our first meeting to tell me they just got a bill from someone and realized they had not listed that debt on the form I gave them to show me their outstanding debts.

When anyone – a company or a family – does not keep adequate, accurate, up-to-date financial records, the end result is typically very disastrous!

This important statement is simple, practical, and critical to having a sound and solid financial structure. It also keeps the main principle in our minds on a constant basis: *Living Life Debt Free – Trusting God for His Supply, and Living On It*. Each time we see we still have debts outstanding, we can move to take steps to eradicate them and move to being out of *financial bondage*. That, my friend, is *Living Life Debt Free - Trusting God for His Supply, and Living On It. THE Math of LIFE! Christ's Life.*

Chapter 28
The Bottom Line Each Month
Outgo Never Exceeds Income
There is treasure to be desired
and oil in the dwelling of the wise;
but a foolish man spendeth it up.
Proverbs 21:20

For half my life I was taught, "Don't use your own money; use another person's money." That was the teaching of investing, progressive accumulation, and just about any mathematical aspect of financial life. That included the use of personal credit cards to buy, spend, blow, and go. *Live life like there is no tomorrow.* And, by the way, *You deserve a break today!*

Nothing was ever mentioned or taught me about *owe no man anything* or *paying CASH for everything.* Not until we became a part of Sagemont Church (Houston, TX) and Pastor John Morgan's Scriptural teaching on doing finances God's Way.

When we first became members at Sagemont, we heard of the church's story of it becoming Debt Free the year before. There were absolutely incredible testimonies of how God worked in people's lives to get them personally out of debt including paying off home loans, to getting the church completely out of debt for buildings built years before. And how the people and the church began to LIVE Debt Free!

Pastor Morgan's Scriptural financial teaching was based on God's Word speaking of how God wanted to, and would, supply His children's needs each day, each month, each year. And with that Truth, Pastor Morgan put together some very interesting points and quotes that began to energize the people to start living with Christ Living His Life through their financial life. And the end result is worth looking at and implementing in our lives!

Let me begin by giving one of my favorite quotes from Pastor Morgan:
> "When your outgo exceeds your income, your upkeep becomes your downfall."

Think about that for a moment. IF our monthly expenditures (outgo) exceed our monthly income, we are doing so by one of two ways:

- taking CASH out of savings to pay for some things (over and above our month's income).
- BORROWING money to pay for those things our income could not cover…especially including amounts charged to credit cards and not *totally paid off* in the time allotted on each monthly statement.

There is no way around those Truths.

And, it naturally follows then: *our upkeep* (keeping on doing things the same way) *becomes our downfall* (ultimately, our financial doom, or bondage). There is no way around that Truth.

So, beyond any shadow of a doubt, we MUST NOT *spend* more than our income in any month…unless we want to use some of our SAVINGS. Therefore, the *bottom line* must show either a positive balance (income > spending) or neutral balance (income = spending).

Now listen! When *total spending* for any given month is added up, *all charges to credit cards* must be included in the total amount *spent!* A *charge* is an *outgo*, even if it is not physically expended at that time. **THIS** is where most folks LOSE SIGHT of their *total spending* for a given period of time. And really, they do not want to keep track of charges *as expenditures* at that moment!

So, let's look at a *typical* monthly income/outgo statement for someone. And particularly notice the variables shown, and know that each person/couple MUST fill in the variables and/or blanks as appropriate. The main issue is for each person/couple to keep track of their own income/outgo figures, and be honest with themselves as to accurate numbers.

DISCOVERING MONTHLY INCOME VS OUTGO

INCOME

SALARY A	
SALARY B	
OTHER	
TOTAL	$

OUTGO

CHURCH	
Tithes & Missions	
HOME	
Mortgage or Rent	
Insurance	
Maintenance	
AUTOS	
Loan payments	
Insurance	
Maintenance	
Fuel	
HEALTH	
Insurance	
Other medical expenses	
FAMILY	
Food - groceries	
Eating Out	
Clothing	
Mobile Phones	
Entertainment	
Vacations	
PETS	
Food	
Vet costs	
CHILDCARE	
CREDIT CARDS	
SAVINGS	
TOTAL	$

"When your outgo exceeds your income, your upkeep becomes your downfall."

Financial Freedom Seminar 1979

John Morgan
Former Pastor
(1966-2019)
Sagemont Church
Houston, TX

These are general areas of income and outgo. Personalize this to fit **your** monthly activity. Detailed amounts may need to be calculated on a separate page for any area itself (putting the typical monthly sum figure on this sheet).

Now, a proper *bottom line* is important to leading us to *increasing our net worth*. And, remember, there is a statement in Chapter 27 that gives us an accurate picture of the amount of our *net worth*.

It is wise to sit down and decide upon how to obtain and maintain a *progressive increase* and *end goal* for our Net Worth. If we aim at nothing, we hit nothing. Our gaining control of our *bottom line* each month is crucial for any gain in our *net worth*. These two figures *(progressive increase* and *end goal)* will probably be different at various times of our life.

Life changes are inevitable for most people. We don't live in the day where our grandpas and grandmas went to work for a company and stayed there 40+ years and retired with a comfortable living. Work changes (including change in companies or change in careers) are almost a given in today's society. And extreme variables like *high cost of living* changes/inflation are always a possibility. These will call for adjusting the *progressive increases* and *end goal* for our *Net Worth*.

God has given us many Truths that are relative and great to know (and implement!) for reaching our desired financial goals. Here are a couple more besides the text for this chapter:

>A prudent man forseeth the evil, and hideth himself; but
>the simple pass on, and are punished. Proverbs 27:12

It is important to know the Hebrew words for *prudent (arum)* and *simple (pethiy)*. *Arum,* one who ACTS wisely and avoids evil. *Pethiy,* one who is child-like, without knowledge, and typically ends up in a bad experience. Learn and appropriate (be prudent, *arum*) God's wisdom to avoid being *pethiy*.

If you read this book in its entirety and begin to appropriate God's Truth in your financial world, congratulations…you are becoming *arum!*

>And take thou unto thee of all food that is eaten, and thou
>shalt gather it to thee; and it shall be for food to thee, and
>for them. Genesis 6:21

Do you know the context of that verse?!? It is God speaking to Noah with instructions on preparing to fill the ark, seal off the doorways, and spend 12 months in flooded waters. God, who in other places of the Scriptures, provided manna daily from heaven and other miraculous ways of feeding His people and animals, gave Noah a typical way of provision: gather together what is provided, store up for the future need, and enjoy your preparations when the time comes you will need it. Wow! Wouldn't it have been much easier if daily God had just dropped some food and water onto the ark in some miraculous way? Well, yes. But this was a time of good old hard work and life in the real world (except for the *flood*). HOW MUCH did it take to feed Noah's family AND ALL the animals for 365+ days? Whatever, Noah did as God instructed, and all were cared for as the days went by until the water receded. THIS is GOD's WORD in a test of His people.

Listen! The *Bottom Line* is a TEST of God's Word for His people. *Living on what God provides* (and not the devil's way or the world's way) is a TEST all Saints must take into consideration and make a decision to follow, or abandon.

The Scriptures have MANY more such illustrations of God's instructions and testing. We decide whether to find out, and then whether to follow His instructions.

We should never forget to check our *bottom line* EACH MONTH…it is foundational to experiencing the desired results of *The Math of Life. Christ's Life.*

Chapter 29
Online Banking
Be thou diligent to know the state of thy flocks,
and look well to thy herds. For riches are not forever...
Proverbs 27:23-24

Who would have ever thought there would be the day when banking is done electronically by the masses? But, it is here. Online banking, also known as internet banking, web banking, or home banking, has become a common way for customers to access and use their accounts, even before and after typical "open" hours of one's financial institution.

With the discoveries in the electronic world, online banking has become the preferred method of deposits and withdrawals in a financial account. This replaces the old paper & pencil checkbooks, but the principles and actions remain the same. Income and outgo are still the key ingredients to our financial world.

Nothing changes as far as the Truths of doing the Math of Life. God's Way is still His Way. Actually, many will find it easier and more quickly accessible to carry out the transactions. And the electronic arrangement of figures can remove some of the careless errors previously made by sloppy handwriting in a paper check register.

The question still remains: HOW are online banking participants keeping track of REAL account balances? HOW (if) do they reconcile their personal accounting with the financial institution's accounting?

Therefore the major difference between paper and electronic banking is the need to learn the mechanics of the methods ascribed to the account.

- accounts can be opened in 5 minutes, applying online
- many institutions have no opening or maintenance fees
- quick and easy access, conduct a range of transactions through the institution's website
- an institution's website may vary from others, so a customer simply needs to learn their institution's methods.

In this tech savvy world the only caution I could propose is that users should remain vigilant to keep track of every penny...including using the processes of validating entries, balances, and reconciliation with their FI.

Chapter 30
Spend Every Penny You Make
or, Save Those EXTRA Dollars
A good man leaveth an inheritance to his children's children...
Proverbs 13:22a

Whoa! Wait a minute...what is THIS?

It doesn't take a genius, either mathematically or mentally, to know that the main title of this chapter *does not add up* to the Scripture text. So, why the seemingly evident contradiction?

The point I make to all that I coach with their *Spending Plan* is this: Instead of having *some money left over* at the end of the month (or, any moment during the month in one's mind), and then *foolishly* going out and spending it on frivolous things when you haven't *saved* for future purchases, PLAN to have a *purpose, place,* and *procedure* for eliminating any possibility of reckless or ridiculous spending, even to the point of diminishing the inheritance you leave to your children and children's children.

SAVE FOR YOUR FUTURE NEEDS

For instance: you have a great *Spending Plan*. But this month, for one reason or another, you spent *less* for something than what you planned for. Depending on what category that is, you either put the *balance* left in that category into a specified savings account marked for future expenses of the same kind, OR you put the amount into your general savings, emergency savings, or retirement savings. OR...you put the *left over* amount into an envelope, bucket, boot, etc. And use it for something *needed* later on.

On paper, you have *spent* the money (from your *Monthly Spending Plan*), but you have *saved* the money instead of *blowing it*.

SAVE FOR YOUR FUTURE EXTRAS

Now listen. If you have a month where the amount needed to do something in your *Spending Plan* turns out to be less than the *Spending Plan* allotted, it may be that the next month it will be more than figured. IF you have put any *extra* not spent in one month into some saving device, you will not have to go to your Emergency Fund or General Fund to cover the *extra* needed in a later month!

But here is an incredible fact: It is amazing how much money is *blown* by so many people who do not have any clue about this idea…nor do they want to *control their money instead of their money controlling them*. Think about this: Many statistics show us that more than 50% of Americans in 2023 age 65 or older *have less than $100 cash in savings*. How easy could it have been for EVERY ONE of them to have *several thousand dollars* in a savings account *just from this idea?*

SAVE FOR YOUR FUTURE LIFE

Now listen once more. Way more money is *spent* on *junk* in a person's lifetime than they typically will *save* in their lifetime. *Unbelievable!* Look no further than all the money that is *wasted* on drinking anything other than FREE water when someone goes *out* to eat! It's crazy. *Going out to eat* may have been where *crazy* began. Just from a health standpoint, it is better to drink water. But from a financial standpoint, it is just as big a *killer* to spend money on a drink that costs you!

How many times have you stopped into a GAS station and bought something to drink or a snack of some kind? How many?!? How many times have you been to a ballgame, concert, or movie, or similar activity, AND purchased drinks, popcorn, candy, and/or souvenir? How many?!? How many times have you been to a grocery store and bought a candy bar or magazine right at the checkout counter? How many!? EVERY TIME we do this adds up over the years to $1,000's we could have in our savings account *at age 65* IF we had a PLAN with a *purpose, place,* and *procedure* for eliminating any possibility of reckless or ridiculous spending, instead of saving those *extra* dollars.

I think Dave Ramsey's idea, "EVERY DOLLAR has a NAME on it BEFORE the start of each month," is one of the best PLANS to prevent the waste of dollars that either are needed later on, or could be better put to use later on. This is *spending with a purpose!* Simple planning, and good discipline, makes the *wise plan* come to fruition. *Spend every dollar on our future, not our present fleshly desires. A good man* will do this…*but a fool layeth open his folly,* said Solomon in Proverbs 13:16.

In my pastoral financial coaching, it is *unacceptable* for someone to waste hard-earned money without the *Mind of God* for the *future,* much less *His thoughts* for the *present.*

Finally, let me put this into real-life perspective: In 9 cases out of 10, I CAN THINK OF **NO EXCUSE** FOR SOMEONE IN AMERICA TO HAVE LESS THAN SEVERAL THOUSAND DOLLARS IN A SIMPLE SAVINGS ACCOUNT AT AGE 65.

NONE.

Be one who doesn't *waste* those *extra* dollars; be one who *saves* those *extra* dollars. It is *The Math of Life. Christ's Life.*

Chapter 31
God Supplies the Needs of His Saints
But my God shall supply all your need according
to His riches in glory by Christ Jesus.
Philippians 4:19

Every Saint should take the time to read the Scriptures, especially the New Testament, and meditate on certain verses where God gives us dynamic Truth for our life here on earth. I call these *Life Verses*. Philippians 4:19 is especially one of them. *Christ's Life* for our finances.

God speaking through the Apostle Paul was telling the Philippians that *his* God, Who is *our* God, WILL SUPPLY ALL OUR NEED. That alone is a dynamic big enough to settle a whole lot of issues for Saints. When it gets down to the so-called *bottom line*, there is little that can bring peace and joy more than knowing that our *need* will be supplied. But, it is imperative that we *acknowledge* and *know* that *our God* is the One Who will do this. Christianity has seemingly forgotten there is a huge difference between life, and Life. Or, in these days has seldom been taught that Life is all about *our God, not us.*

Think about it. We have GOD Who has told us that it is His *determination* to supply all we will ever need. Wow! What, in this life, do we have to be anxious about? What do we have to worry about? What do we have to be distraught about? Our GOD is going to supply all we ever need. He has taken it upon Himself to be *responsible* for the supply.

And lest we get in a tizzy thinking as to *how* in this world can He provide for ALL His children...provide ALL we need...God tells us further that He will provide this *according to His riches in glory by Christ Jesus*. Very few preachers or teachers ever mention, dwell, or emphasize this critical caveat (one definition of *caveat* is *words given to prevent misunderstanding*). Well, lest we misunderstand, God says "MY supply is unlimited...according to MY riches in glory by Christ Jesus." Break this down further. *According to His riches in glory*. Wow! Just what is the limit of *God's riches in glory*??? No limit. Unlimited. Now, look at the finish: *by Christ Jesus*. Through Christ Jesus. Never forget: *there is nothing the presence of Christ cannot provide*. And every Saint possesses Christ within...*His presence*. That brings with it *His provision*.

So, there are only three things I can think of that would prevent, hinder, or detour God's supply to His saints…

unbelief. An Unbelieving Saint is one who has been Born Again, but (this is what I call an unholy *but*) does not believe God for all that God has revealed to His Saints about life here and now. Where does *any unbelief* of God come from? In a Saint, the *Adamic natural mind* is still a residue from the *old man* who has been crucified and replaced (Holy Spirit at the Saint's New Birth/New Creation). When thinking in the *wrong* mind instead of the Mind of God in Holy Soul in Saints, a Saint can be as *unbelieving* as a *lost sinner.*

We believe in our Mind of God that God will take us to heaven one day, but *supply all our need right now?* How is that a little too far-fetched for some Saints? This *unbelief* leads to taking unscriptural actions to obtaining needs, and usually *wants*. A *want* shows discontent with what God has supplied. A *want* is a denial of our Shepherd supplying *enough*. Oh, how many Saints *love* the 23rd Psalm? But, do you remember the first line? *The LORD is my shepherd;* **I shall not want**. Huh. Sort of a slap in our face for *wanting.*

waste. This could be a major lesson for young people to learn. Many Saints have no sense of stewardship. I think this is because of little, or zero, teaching of good, practical, Scriptural financial management. I suppose this is one major reason for writing this book. If everyone 50 years or older would take just a few minutes to think back over their life, they would stagger at the memories of the *huge waste of money* for frivolous things that were nothing but a momentary happiness that faded with the next sunrise. How can one dollar spent today that is meaningless for the future compare to having nothing in our pockets at some date in the future when there is a need? And, if everyone 10-20 years of age were made to sit down, listen to, and get into a discussion of the numerous issues facing them for the next 70 years or so…how many could see the necessity of financial stewardship their entire life. Having fun, getting something to make us happy for the moment, and going & doing for some sort of *high* CANNOT take the place of responsible stewardship for the need *now* and a need in the *future*. I have been telling folks for a long time: "You have been smoking, drinking, eating, and travelling away your comfortable retirement. How does that work for you now that you are 65 and broke?" And they want me to help them out from the *hard-earned, did-without* dollars in my possession?

Need more advice from God? Try these admonitions:
> No man can serve two masters: for either he will hate the one, and love the other; or else he will hold to the one, and despise the other. Ye cannot serve God and mammon. Therefore, I say unto you, Take no thought for your life, what ye shall eat, or what ye shall drink; nor yet for your body, what ye shall put on. Is not the life more than the meat, and the body than raiment? Matthew 6:24-25

And then, after giving illustrations of how God supplies the need of the fowls of the air, the lilies of the field, the grass of the field, and asking *shall He not much more clothe you, O ye of little faith?,* Holy Spirit led Matthew to conclude with:
> Therefore take no thought, saying, What shall we eat? or, What shall we drink? or, Wherewithal shall we be clothed? For after all these things do the Gentiles seek: for your heavenly Father knoweth that you have need of all these things. But seek ye first the kingdom of God, and His righteousness; and all these things will be added unto you. Matthew 6:31-34

Wow! Take no thought (question) for all your need…but, *seek ye first the kingdom of God, and His righteousness; AND ALL THESE THINGS WILL BE ADDED UNTO YOU* (my capitalizing the last words). That leads us to the third thing I spoke of earlier:

lack of worship in Truth. Worship is *showing worth, 'worth-ship'*. If Saints were truthfully worshipping (showing worth) God, we would *hang* on every Word from God. The Scriptures would have a more significant place and impact in EVERY Saint's life. And intense study of significant verses, including seeking out the Hebrew or Greek behind the translation (including sufficient research to know the difference between the translations using *different* texts!) could lead to more BELIEVING by more

Saints. The Truths of verses like the ones I have mentioned already in this chapter (as well as the multitude in the rest of the book) are sufficient to change many Saint's minds on how they will make decisions regarding the procurement of their needs. And have an effect on the stewardship of the resources God brings their way.

Now listen to an apothegm (look that one up!) statement from the man Barbara and I first learned God's Truths on financial matters:

> Man chooses the supplier of his need. God or Satan. Truth or Deception. Obedience or Disobedience. Freedom or Bondage. Deception & Disobedience always lead to Bondage. John Morgan, Houston, Texas.

Wow! I remember first hearing those words, and can also remember the impact they made on decisions Barbara and I made to make changes from doing things the world's way (devil's influence) to God's Way.

And one more for now from Dr. Morgan,

> The devil will always say, 'If your God won't give it to you now, just sign here...I will!'

It is my hope and prayer that everyone reading these words will *choose* to do things God's Way in all financial matters! There are some points in this chapter that are straight to the point of what can keep anyone from *Living Life Debt Free - Trusting God for His Supply, and Living On It*. Be one that avoids these pitfalls. It is *The Math of Life. Christ's Life.*

Chapter 32
Pay All Your Bills On Time!
The wicked borroweth, and payeth not again...
Psalm 37:21a

God has hit the nail on the head with this verse! Only the *wicked* don't pay what they owe. And actually, that wickedness begins with borrowing in the first place. IF we NEVER borrow, we can never be guilty of *not paying back on time, or ever*. Chapter 50, *Don't Incur ANY Debt,* will speak volumes to this. And never forget *our name* as Saints is linked to God...the devil makes sure the world is cognizant of that IF we *don't pay back on time.*

First, let's look at some negative aspects of *borrowing, and not paying*. When someone *doesn't pay back on time,* the borrower has actually *lied* to the lender (the borrower *promised* to make the prescribed payments on or before the prescribed time of the lending agreement), AND the lender is now faced with some issues they did not anticipate: the *extras* they will have to deal with. They will have to pay *extra costs,* make *extra efforts,* use *extra time* to track down the delinquent borrower in order to get the *late payment*. What borrower *who doesn't pay on time* has ever given any thought to the hassle and costs to the lender?

Second, the borrower almost always incurs *extra* interest charges, and perhaps *penalties*. To incur these is about as crazy as one can get. *Late* charges are typically added to the outstanding bill when the payment is not received by the lender by a given date, increasing the total interest charges incurred. Add that to the list of *crazy* on the part of the borrower! Banks or lending institutions charge an *overdraft* fee when their depositors draw on the account with insufficient funds on deposit. Just when we were asking, "How could things get worse for the incompetent steward of God's resources?"

So, if we owe money now, what are some practical helps to insure we ALWAYS make the payments *on time*?
- establish a Monthly Spending Plan. This is first and foremost in gaining control over income and outgo. Control over spending is a **must** in making any payments due on time. (Remember chapter 24 for details on a Monthly Spending Plan)
- eliminate one current debt. Eliminating just one current debt provides additional funds (the amount we were sending that

lender) from current income to go toward other payments due. This may involve making drastic cuts in current spending until your outgo does not exceed your income. Eliminate one, then another, then another. (See chapter 51 for details on getting out of debt)
- entertain getting a 2nd income. Everyone has the time to find some way to earn some extra income. That extra income can insure making payments due on time.
- exhaust available resources. Never should anyone have *money in the bank* (in whatever form that is) and not pay a bill on time. In addition, sell whatever you have that is worth something to avoid not having any amount needed to pay a bill on time.

I have found an incredible number of people who are not paying their bills on time who have a number of assets they are not willing to part with. Whatever brought this kind of thinking into being? There can be nothing we currently have in our possession, that can be sold for a reasonable price, that is worth retaining when *our name* is becoming *wicked* by not paying what we owe on time.

> God's Spiritual Truths have more impact in our daily living when they become more of a reality than we typically have realized.

It is imperative that we take steps to get back to SOLID FINANCIAL GROUND when necessary. This MAY include selling your autos and driving older, less expensive models you can pay cash for…freeing up the current payment amounts to pay other bills being neglected, or not paid on time. This MAY include selling your house and moving to a less expensive house. This MAY include selling all your *toys* and other items that would give funds to pay off debts, which in turn will reduce your outgo, which in turn provides the necessary funds from your income to pay your remaining obligations ON TIME!

Finally, I think we should pause and think carefully ONCE AGAIN about what God has told us about *a good name*.

A good name is rather to be chosen than great riches, and loving favor rather than silver and gold. Proverbs 22:1 (review chapter 19 for more on *a good name*)

What it all boils down to is this: WHAT SORT OF NAME DO WE HAVE? Or, GREATLY DESIRE TO HAVE? And what are we willing to do to have a GOOD NAME? And how is *our name* reflecting on God's Name?

Do whatever is necessary to have a *good name* rather than that of *wicked*. It is the *Math of Life. Christ's Life.*

Chapter 33
Making Future Purchases
He that walketh with wise men shall be wise:
but a companion of fools shall be destroyed.
Proverbs 13:20

This is an awesome Life Verse, isn't it? And a lost and forgotten Way of Life for too many young people. Time and time again I hear older folks who say: "The kids won't listen or pay any attention to me. They think they know it all. The grandkids? They hardly know I exist, except to want me to buy them something." (of course, many grandparents need to own up to the fact they formed that idea in their grandkids' minds with all the gifts they have lavished upon them from early childhood).

Making a purchase of a large-ticket item is one of the most challenging endeavors for a Saint who wants to *Live debt-free*. It takes being a *wise person* to plan, decide, and exercise discipline to prepare and be able to pay CASH for future purchases. Something that can be purchased out of a monthly income figure is not that big of a deal, but something that takes multiple paychecks to purchase is a big thing. It can be difficult to face this dilemma and not succumb to the temptation of the devil: "If your God won't provide for it right now, just sign here and I will give it to you...via credit, the devil says." (Pastor John Morgan, 1979)

Well, how can we? It is simple. It is complex. But it is not complicated. And it definitely is not impossible. *Wise men* have shown God's Way.

Let me share four *ingredients* to implement in the order presented, to eventually make that future purchase with CASH, not credit. And to prove that we can walk with wise men and not have our finances destroyed like fools. This was the *only walk* for most of our elders in previous generations. It can be the *only walk* for us today.

CONTENTMENT - *Joy with one's situation*

This is a very Scriptural attribute Saints need. God can supply this *need*. This is where the Life of Christ makes a huge difference in the Life of a Saint.

Why can we not be contented? How do we get ourselves into a state of *discontentment*? Why do we have to have something *right now*? PRIDE. That's the only reason. Some family member or friend has something, and we want to keep up with them and have that same thing. We don't want to be *embarrassed* the next time we are with them. Or, we are *discontented* with what God has provided now, and we *want* whatever it is that we do not have.

Now listen, it will be impossible to start making future purchases with CASH IF we never live a life of *contentment*. I am not a big fan of *happiness* because it always involves *things* or *situations* that are temporal, or relating to our *earthly life*. And God has told us we are to what?

> If ye then be risen with Christ, seek those things which are above, where Christ sitteth on the right hand of God. Set your affections on things above, not on things on the earth. Colossians 3:1-2

We have no business setting our affections on things in this *earthly life*, and especially to the extent that it drives us to not trust God to supply our *need*, but leads us to borrow for our *wants*. What I am a fan of is *joy* (Greek *chara*), that statement of the Heart that pertains to something from God. Look at these two Scriptural references:

> ...enter thou into the joy of thy Lord. Matthew 25:21, 23

> These things have I spoken unto you, that My joy might remain in you, and that your joy might be full. John 15:11

The *joy* of my Lord is gifted to me and becomes *my joy*. And with that *joy*, I can be content in any state I am in, just like the Apostle Paul.

> Not that I speak in respect of want: for I have learned, in whatsoever state I am, therewith to be content. Philippians 4:11

It is a choice I make, to Live with Christ's *joy* as *my joy* instead of the *world's happiness* as my fixity of life.

Once I am settled into this CONTENTMENT, I can make the choice of *curtailment*.

CURTAILMENT - *Reducing our expenditures in order to save necessary funds to pay CASH*

My wife, Barbara, and I have found it incredibly easy to *curtail* our spending because of the *joy* we have in setting our affections on the things of God instead of this earthly life. And this *curtailment* has resulted in becoming financially stable on God's supply.

We are always quick to point out that our financial freedom and stability is of God, not of us. When we moved to the point of *Living Life Debt Free - Trusting God for His Supply, and Living On It*, God began to show us how He would always provide our need - no matter our circumstances, no matter our position, no matter our opposition from without.

With the peace and joy of our Lord, we began to implement the withholding of funds from frivolous or unnecessary expenditures. His Life in our finances has become a fun endeavor! We are *filled with His joy* with what He provides and then guides us to save or spend. Many of our friends think we are *extreme tightwads* because we do not spend money on things they think they cannot do without. We can do without those things. And put the money into savings.

Let me share several examples that I mention more than once in this book, but these are the most prominent of our *curtailment* activities:
- We NEVER order a drink we would have to pay for when eating out.
- We NEVER buy anything to drink or snack on when we stop for gasoline for our autos.
- And we RARELY will buy coffee when away from home, EXCEPT when driving back home late from an event or a doctor's appointment miles from home.
- And we ALMOST ALWAYS split a meal from the menu when eating out.
- Our car uses ½ as much fuel as our pickup (which is more comfortable to ride in on long trips). We drive in our car ALMOST ALWAYS when going somewhere other than a short, local drive. Listen to this figuring we just did: The car needed new tires. $500 outgo from savings. Using the car for the 4,000+ miles we know we will be driving on out-of-town trips in the next 12 months, we will save the cost of those tires (what we will pay for gasoline in the car…instead of using the truck).

Curtailment leads to multiple examples of saving money that otherwise is long gone and a definite hindrance against saving to make a future purchase.

Another thing is the act of confining our expenditures to our *Spending Plan*. The specified bounds of the pre-determined *Spending Plan* are a huge boost to curtailing our outgo and increasing our saving for future purchases. And once we began to practice CURTAILMENT, we began to choose to *complement* our *Future Purchases Savings Fund*.

COMPLEMENT – *Taking the steps to complete the supply needed*
It is important to take the time to sit down and think about the *future purchase items* you want to begin to pay CASH for, and *make a list* of these items. This is a part of your overall financial plan that needs to be developed. Notice the *Future Purchases Savings Fund* located in your 15-15-25-45 Spending Plan. All *future purchase items* will be paid for out of this fund.

The list is not complete until a *projected cost amount* has been assigned to each item. It is also important to make a *projected purchase date* a part of the list. Some items might need purchasing BEFORE the projected date (like in the case of breakdowns, etc.). That is where the *Future Purchases Savings Fund* will help make a CASH purchase instead of being caught unprepared ahead of time.

Your *future purchase items list* is not complete until you have EVERY item listed that takes more than the Monthly Expenditures of your *Monthly Spending Plan* to cover. That includes your HOME! Think about that. Paying CASH for your home. It is possible. It can be done. It will be done IF you plan your purchases and purchase according to your plan.

When you have begun to COMPLEMENT your *Future Purchases Savings Fund*, you will have arrived at the *commitment* needed to *Live Life Debt Free – Trusting God for His Supply, and Living On It*…completely.

COMMITMENT – *A life of sincere and steadfast fixity of purpose*
Most everyone has heard the illustration of the chicken and the hog *commitment* breakfast story. The chicken can be decidedly *involved* in our breakfast, but the hog must be unequivocally *committed* to our breakfast. It is one thing for a chicken to participate by laying an egg. It is quite another for the hog to commit to giving part of its body to the menu!

When you have decided and acted upon the first three *ingredients* you are already acting upon a *commitment* of binding yourself to a course of action that leads to a DEBT-FREE LIFE. That is ultimately what *Life with a Capital L* is all about. *Jesus' Life* being Lived through you in your financial Life has become COMPLETE FREEDOM. A freedom based on trust. A trust in Christ to provide ALL your need, always. And then Living on His provision.

One thing that is important to know: *this is a Spiritual as well as an intellectual and an emotional course of action.* Situations will no longer dictate to you what your spending will be. Christ will. It is the most peace YOU will ever experience. Christ's Peace. Peace of His Mind. Peace of His Emotions. Peace of His Will. Peace of His Heart. Peace of His Riches in Glory. With this type of COMMITMENT, there can never be any situation that disturbs His Peace.

When Barbara and I first embarked on a Life of Financial Freedom, we really had no idea just how providential and how peaceful this earthly life could be. *Walking in the Spirit* removes the temptations, the provocations, and the manipulations that the enemy tries to use to derail Saints with all the time. WHEN FINANCIAL PEACE IS YOURS, PEACE IN ALL OF LIFE CAN BE ENJOYED.

One final thought in all of this: I can hear many who have read this far (½-way through the book): "All this can't be FUN!" WRONG. We have been having FUN for over 40 years! Believe us. It is FUN to owe nobody nothing. It is FUN to have such PEACE that we can lay our heads on our pillows with no worries about debt, payments, or creditors. It is FUN to have such JOY in waiting and watching and participating with Christ in HIS financial Life through *our* FI accounts and pocketbooks.

Take the necessary steps to enjoy the Life of Peace. Contentment, Curtailment, Complement, and Commitment. These are *The Math of Life. Christ's Life.*

Chapter 34
Purchasing Autos
Then said the LORD unto Moses, Behold,
I will rain down bread from heaven for you;
and the people shall go out and gather a certain rate every day,
that I may prove them, whether they will walk in my law, or no.
Exodus 16:4

What is God's law on borrowing? Never do it. Never get into any debt. For food, for clothes, or for autos. Never for anything. In all of the Holy Scriptures God never asked His people to borrow for any need. God has always promised to meet any need we have. That is His Law of Living:

> For the law of the Spirit of life in Christ Jesus hath made
> me free from the law of sin and death. Romans 8:2

The context of Exodus 16:4 is the need for food. All of the children of Israel complain to Moses that they are hungry. God then speaks to Moses of how He will supply their need. But a special interesting point in the 2nd verse of chapter 16 had surfaced:

> And the whole congregation of the children of Israel
> murmured against Moses and Aaron in the wilderness.

It is never good for the people of God to murmur against God's leaders. God doesn't take too kindly of that. But in verses 6-8 God spoke through Moses and Aaron to take it to another level:

> And Moses and Aaron said unto all the children of Israel,
> At even, then ye shall know that the LORD hath brought
> you out from the land of Egypt: And in the morning, then
> ye shall see the glory of the LORD; for he heareth your
> murmurings against the LORD: and what are we, that ye
> murmur against us? And Moses said, This shall be, when
> the LORD shall give you in the evening flesh to eat, and
> in the morning bread to the full; for that the LORD
> heareth your murmurings which ye murmur against him:
> and what are we? your murmurings are not against us, but
> against the LORD.

Wow. That is an eye-opener. In verse 2, the people murmur. In verse 4, God said He will test His people to see if they believe and trust Him. In verse 8 God says the murmuring is against God, not His leaders.

Well, that was way back then. How does this apply to us today? More so, concerning our believing God and trusting Him. We have much more revelation of God and His abilities, His ways, His supply. To borrow is to not believe nor trust God.

Therefore, how do we pay cash for an auto, which can be an expensive item to purchase? The Truth (principle) is always the same. The methods can vary, but they all end in paying cash, not borrowing, to purchase any auto God provides for us.

Let me tell you how Barbara and I got onto the course of paying cash for our autos. We sold the ones we had borrowed to purchase. We then paid cash for an old, old car. It got us wherever we needed to go. Someone loaned us another vehicle while we were saving to get our 2nd vehicle. And God provided in a miraculous way through a dear Saint. Then we paid cash for an old truck to replace the old, old car we had given to a seminary neighbor couple who were in dire financial straits. And we have never borrowed money again to purchase any vehicle.

There are different methods mentioned in this book about saving for various purposes. We get to choose if one of these methods is one that God wants us to use. It could be very likely that there may be another method God will show someone, but the Truth must never be compromised.

One method I have always shared that has worked for many is this: First, sell any vehicle that has a loan against it. Second, see if someone will loan you a vehicle for a short period of time. Third, if you purchase a vehicle, only do so with cash. Begin saving toward an upgrade, saving the amount of money you were previously paying for the autos you were in debt for. Whenever God provides the opportunity and permission, repeat the third step over and over.

Will Barbara and I ever purchase a new vehicle again? We seriously doubt so. Does that mean you should never purchase a new vehicle for cash? No, it doesn't mean that. How you spend your cash is your decision. But do not be surprised if you never feel like purchasing a new auto again.

You always can pay cash for your automobiles. God will supply. It is *The Math of Life. Christ's Life.*

Chapter 35
Purchasing a Home
For which of you, intending to build a tower,
sitteth not down first, and counteth the cost,
whether he have sufficient to finish it?
Luke 14:28

Luke 14:28-30 is a special passage. There was no credit available in Jesus' day, so having cash and materials to finish the work was God's way of building. His comment in verse 29 about folks mocking or ridiculing the one unable to finish what he had started rings a bell from 40 years ago.

Pastor John Morgan always said the banks laughed at the idea most Saints had a big enough God to supply sufficiently for anyone to pay cash for most anything, and especially a house. Yet in 1979 he led Sagemont Church to get out of debt on their buildings and property, and testimonies abound of how many in the church paid off home loans in the process of *getting debt free and living on God's supply.*

In addition, I had the privilege of pastoring some who did likewise. One couple had decided before they got married to both work, live on one income, and save the other. Their savings enabled them to purchase a house for cash, and have no house mortgage, in just a few years. Think of the huge amount of interest they never paid!

It is possible to live on one income. We have been doing that for 50 years. Most of our friends call us *cheap*. We call ourselves *frugal* and *fiscally conservative*. And good at waiting on God's supply for whatever we need. We have never purchased a house that put any pressure on our finances. And always have had a kitchen, bathroom, and bedroom…lol.

The principle of *Living debt free, trusting God for His supply and Living on it* has always been our guide ever since becoming Saints. We always thank Pastor Morgan for his Financial Freedom teaching.

Every individual/couple has to decide whether they will believe God can supply the funds to pay cash for a home, or that He cannot. A decision to follow God's Way of waiting on His timing, His supply, and His leadership in making a house purchase is important also. God works miracles every day for those of His children who will believe Him, trust Him, and walk in His Ways.

OK, what to do if we are already saddled with a house mortgage? Every individual/couple could present totally different circumstances, therefore let us look at a general picture and you adjust to your own set of factors. We start with your loan balance, monthly payments, and months (years) left on the loan. Then we consider the market value of your house. If anyone has lived in a house for a few years, there typically is a good amount of *equity dollars* (difference in the price your house could sell for, and the amount of the outstanding balance on your mortgage).

This is where each individual/couple has to get direction from God on how to proceed. One option is to sell the house, use the equity dollars as a down-payment on a lessor-cost house with much smaller mortgage payments, and work to pay off the mortgage as soon as possible. Another option is to sell, invest the equity dollars, rent at a lessor monthly payment, and put as much into savings as quickly as you can. All the while asking God for His wisdom, His provision, to get you into a house without a mortgage.

Depending on a lot of circumstances it may be that someone makes it possible for you to get into a house debt-free. That has happened.

All Saints with the Mind of God indwelling can wait and listen for His wisdom, His revelation as to how to do our financial matters. Always remember: *1 + 1 = 2...usually*. But not always in God's economy. He has a way of getting 3, 5, 10, or 100 out of 1 + 1.

The main thing is to want to follow God's Truth, honor Him, trust Him, and watch how He can do even the miraculous with the dollars He allows you to be steward over. One thing for sure...God wants His children to Live debt free. Knowing that, we should be striving to be frugal, be conservative, be preservative, be content, be completely trusting our God to do what only He can do...all leading to that debt-free Life, including no house mortgage. It is possible to have a house paid for, with no mortgage. It is *The Math of Life. Christ's Life.*

Chapter 36
Grace Giving
And God is able to make all grace abound toward you;
that ye, always having all sufficiency in all things,
may abound to every good work.
2 Corinthians 9:8

"Pastor, I knew you would bring up *giving*. All pastors do."

Yes. But (a Holy *but)*...what a beautiful thought! What a beautiful experience for those who believe, trust, receive, and apply these Truths! God shares His ability and His potential in 26 words that erase any doubts whether a Saint can **enjoy** all needs met by God and **give** as God leads and performs for those who have a legitimate need. Wow!

Two things must be acknowledged before we go any further. The actuality of this verse becoming a beautiful reality in any Saint's experience is dependent upon two decisions and actions to be taken by each Saint - **abandonment** and **availability**. This is an *abandonment* of the Saint to the control and leadership of Holy Spirit, as well as making oneself *available* in all instances for His work to be done. It is where we give our consent for Him to do as He pleases. We *choose* to Live in His Soul in us as Saints. Christ's Life enacting Himself in our earthsuit is simply our choice. What follows is God's *Grace* working incredibly through such Saints.

If there is any difficulty in understanding this verse (which can affect receiving and enjoying), it is with the word *grace*. In all my speaking and writing for the last 20 years or more I have tried to clarify the Greek *charis* to its proper meaning. For some reason, many (including Scriptural scholars) have limited their definition to *God's unmerited favor*. It is that, *but much more*.

Let me ask you this, what have you or I received from God that is NOT *His unmerited favor*, that we deserved anything He has given us? Nothing. But, even a casual reading of Scripture shows us that there are instances where that definition doesn't makes any sense, nor do a verse justice for understanding and application. If anything, it sometimes is used as an excuse for not allowing or embracing something that God says HE can/will do. The Body of Christ has missed out on so much potential, so much power, so much promise, so much Life by not knowing and appropriating the totality of the *Grace of God* in the individual lives of so many Saints. And not just in *giving!*

Therefore, let me give the full meaning of *charis*, which can be found in many Greek dictionaries. Here it is: an **action** of a favor, a kindness, or a benefit that is **given** without any thought of any expectation of any of those being returned.

Yes, it is unmerited favor. But, yes, it is an **action given** by someone who doesn't expect us to return the favor. The *Grace of God* speaks of Him being the One who *acts/gives*. When we See and Believe the *Grace of God* is Him acting/giving/doing in our Life…*hooooooo-boy!*

Now, in most Scriptural cases, including our text verse, God is speaking of His *giving* an *action* to His Saints. Henceforth, we call it the *Grace of God*. IF it were Paul, or James, or Peter who were *giving* the *action*, it would be called the *grace of Paul, James, or Peter*. Got that? So, let us ALWAYS recognize, and appropriate the *Grace of God* as that which He is DOING without expecting anything in return. But, ALWAYS keep in mind and focus on *His doing, His ability, His willingness* and not just some *favor*. It is God *working* in and through every Saint that is truly God's unmerited favor.

p.s. – as a side note, many use the word *grace*, when they really mean *mercy* or *peace*. Soak on that.

So, what is GRACE GIVING in a Truthful (Life of Christ) Scriptural reality? Holy Spirit led the Apostle Paul to pen these clear Truths:
> God is able to make all **grace** (His ability and His working) abound to all Saints; Saints will always have all sufficiency in all things, and may abound to every good work.

Abound. *Perisseuo. to cause to* **super-abound** *or excel.* That is every conceivable way in which His ability or Life is needed in any way. Let your mind wander to the farthest extreme in seeing the innumerable ways in which His **Grace** could work in your finances! His Saints will ALWAYS have ALL **sufficiency** in ALL things. Once again, let your mind wrap around the Truth, *by His* **Grace***,* that you will never lack for any need you have. God is able to *supply all your need according to His riches in Christ Jesus* (Philippians 4:19).

Wonderful! We can depend on Him to provide. His Saints ALSO may **abound** to BE A PART OF/GIVE to every good work. We can depend on God to show us what are *His good works* He wants us to *abound in giving* to. Listen, this does not mean we have to give to every work that we are presented with a request, or demand/pressure, to give to. But, the great thing is that we will always be able to give *as God leads us to give.* The Truth of *tithing* and *regular giving* is adequately covered in other chapters of this book.

Grace Giving is totally just what has been defined in the last paragraph. *Grace Giving* as a practical application is how God leads EACH individual (couple, if married) Saint to give to *His good works,* but in reality God does the giving through us!

But, listen as Holy Spirit leads Paul to add more to this declaration:

> As it is written, He hath dispersed abroad; He hath given to the poor: His righteousness remaineth forever. Now He that ministereth to the sower both minister bread for your food, and multiply your seed sown, and increase the fruits of your righteousness. vs. 9-10

Notice that it is God Who does the initial giving/providing. We get to get in on His work by being His Saints. And Paul expresses a prayer that God would both provide for us as we need (our food), and multiply that which we give to other Saints in need (seed sown)…increasing the fruits of our righteous acts *(abounding to every good work)*. Awesome!

There's more!

> Being enriched in every thing to all bountifulness, which causeth through us thanksgiving to God. v. 11

Hallelujah! Our giving, even though it was **God's Grace** (He did it, not us!), CAUSES THROUGH US **thanksgiving to God**! Do you want to join me by taking off your shoes and running around the room slapping the soles of your shoes together and shouting "Hallelujah! Amen! Hallelujah!" like I am??? Amen!

And more!

> For the administration of this service not only supplieth the want of the saints, but is abundant also by many thanksgivings unto God; While by the experiment of this administration they glorify God for your professed subjection unto the gospel of Christ, and for your liberal distribution unto them, and unto all men; And by their prayer for you, which long after you for the exceeding

grace of God in you. Thanks be unto God for His unspeakable gift. vs. 12-15

There are several whole sermons in these verses! Wow! But, suffice it to say to us for now, let us look only at two phrases: *your professed* **subjection** and *the* **exceeding grace** *of God in you*. **Subjection**: *hupotage*. This is our abandonment to God. We allow Him to be **Lord** of our Life. Lord of our giving. His Life becomes truly *our Life* in abandonment. **Exceeding grace**: *huperballo charis*. This speaks of a surpassing or exceeding of God's Grace above what one might expect, perhaps reasonably expect, being cast through God's abandoned Saints. Mercy me! Thank You, LORD!

Grace Giving is the avenue God uses to prove we cannot out-give Him! Just look at the Macedonians. Read all of 2 Corinthians chapters 8 & 9…proof of God's subsequent blessings.

As a pastor, I have been privileged to know about many who have experienced *Grace Giving* in different ways. If you really want to see an amazing testimony of God in action, check out the story of our good friends, Ira T. and Judy Sansom. They have experienced *Grace Giving* (from both sides…mull on that a bit) in a magnificent way (for their story see chapter 16 in my book, *Seagulls Don't Lie!*).

Grace Giving is the *Heart of God* in Saints being allowed to give as His Heart desires. It is always *bountiful* in its giving. He is the *most bountiful* Giver there is.

Well, I hope this clarifies and specifies what many ignore, evade, or deny concerning the awesomeness of power, provision, and possibility of God working in our day by day financial world. There is Love, Joy, Peace, and Faith known (Fruit of Holy Spirit) from such profound Truth.

Let us know and experience this explicit illustration of Christ's LIFE in our finances. *Grace* is Christ's Life Lived out in us. *God is able to make all* **Grace** *abound toward you…,* that we can have plenty for everyday Living, AND GIVE abundantly to *every good work*. He is our provision for everyday Living. He is our giving abundantly to every good work. Hooooooooo-boy!

HIS GRACE IS HIS UNSPEAKABLE GIFT. I know my words do not come close to really expressing the incredible totality of *His Grace*. But, why don't you try *abandoning* to God and always being *available* to God. His *Grace* will pour forth. He is *The Math of Life. Christ's Life.*

Chapter 37
Give, Get, to Give More
*Give, and it shall be given unto you; good measure,
pressed down, and shaken together, and running over,
shall men give into your bosom. For with the same measure
that ye mete withal it shall be measured to you again.*
Luke 6:38

It always amazes me that so many Saints do not give to the Lord's work as they should when Truth shows that we *cannot out-give* the Lord! Unbelieving Saints.

I do not know of another verse that more clearly states that God will give back to us in a greater amount than we have given to Him. The LORD tells us in specific terms just how He gives. Look clearly at each premise:

good measure/same measure – a portion, a specific portion. *Good* here represents a measure that is full, as much as the container will hold.

pressed down – in Scripture days, when grain was *pressed/pushed down* into the container, the recipient knew he was getting as much as was possible.

shaken together – this imagery grants the same result as *pressed down*. Grain, or any material that can be *shaken*, that is measured in this way, additionally guarantees the maximum amount in the container.

running over – here we have an extravagant imagery of measure. It is not just the filling up of the container, but an overflowing amount.

Now, let's take a closer look at how this speaks of the LORD's giving back to those who give to Him.

When we give a *certain amount*, we give of our increase OR our possessions or substance, re: Proverbs 3:9 (that which we already have before any increase). That is our measure. When God gives back to us, He not only gives us *our portion* in return, but also a greater % or amount.

Let's take this to a more seeable picture. When I speak on this verse, I love to use an illustration with ice cream, cones, a nice scoop, and KIDS! I begin by telling a story of Barbara and me taking our daughters to a new ice cream place. They prepared each cone on an *ice table* right in front of us. The first time we went, they gave each of us a large cone FILLED INSIDE and with a HUGE SCOOP on top that *overlapped* the cone. Boy, howdy, it was terrific! Not only the flavor we each chose, but the amount they gave us.

I then bring the kids to the front and ask them if they want any ice cream. The kids are excited. The parents are nervous! So I dish up a small scoop in one cone and hand it to a kid that I have already prepped (so that they understand what I am going to do, and will not be disappointed). I then give a little larger amount to the next kid. When I get to the last one, I really press some DOWN INTO the cone, make a LARGE SCOOP, and hand it to this last kid, with a little hanging over the side of the cone. The atmosphere is dynamic! There are laughs. There are wide-eyed folks. There are some apprehensive expressions and chuckles/murmurings/etc. There is much squirming among the *other* kids. (You know how kids, even BIG kids, can get when someone GETS MORE than they have gotten!). And then, I make the application to the text.
- if we give a small portion to God, He gives us back the same, plus a little
- if we give a larger, but not great, portion to God, He gives us back likewise
- IF we give an abundance to God, He gives us back an overflowing abundant amount, that has been *pressed down* and *shaken together*

And, then I ask - which cone do you want to get from God?

> Just so you understand
> that NO KID gets less than another,
> I have an assistant make sure that the kids
> can have all they want when the service is over!

I conclude the illustration by saying this: "Do you want to know something weird? Each time we went back to that ice cream place, the servings got smaller and smaller. I was like *crazy*. The first couple of times we didn't say anything. Then one time I asked for the manager, and questioned *why* the servings were not as large as at the opening of the store. They couldn't give a satisfactory answer. We stopped going there." (ever have a similar experience with another business???)

And then I quote another verse to finish:

> Jesus Christ the same yesterday, and today, and forever.
> Hebrews 13:8

God is not in the business of diminishing returns on our giving. He does not *lessen the scoop* on us. He will always give back with *good measure, pressed down, shaken together, running over* as we have given to Him.

Now listen, the wisest of mankind, King Solomon, said it this way,

> There is that scattereth, and yet increaseth; and there is that withholdeth more than is meet, but it tendeth to poverty. The liberal soul shall be made fat: and he that watereth shall be watered also himself. Proverbs 11:24-25

Did you catch King Solomon's last words? "the liberal soul *shall be made fat:* and he that watereth *shall be watered also himself.*" Wow! That is MORE than just getting back MORE of the same measure given.

Soak on these words of wisdom, and make notes on the many ways they can be applied to your benefit.

Be sure you understand this *law* of God: giving leads to getting, to give more. Withholding leads to wanting. And the *getting* or *wanting* can often come in a different manner or mode. For instance, giving cash out of our wallet may not yield an immediate increase in cash in our wallet. But check in time to see if our *financial balance* has increased. Withhold when God tells us to give, and see if our *repair bills* increase! There are multiple ways God is working in our financial Life. What is staggering, WE are responsible for how God responds to His promise!

Now listen, this Truth is about His Life in every matter. If we are letting Him give through us out of His Life, His return gift will be huge. And the context for v.38 is in the midst of loving our enemies and how we judge others. We get back *what* we dish out in proportion to our dishing out in the first place.

Think this isn't Truth? Test it. Truth is not only preached; it is demonstrated. Be outrageous with your giving. It is *The Math of Life. Christ's Life.*

Chapter 38
Lay Up Treasures In Heaven
Lay not up for yourselves treasures upon earth,
where moth and rust doth corrupt,
and where thieves break through and steal;
But lay up for yourselves treasures in heaven,
where neither moth nor rust doth corrupt,
and where thieves do not break through nor steal.
Matthew 6:19-20

I dare say that most of us have heard the old satirical statement: "You can reach for a lot of things in a person's life, but be on guard if you reach for their pocketbook!" Some people do more to protect and preserve their belongings than they do their own life.

This is one of the most powerful statements by God showing the incredible Spiritual realm of the LIFE of Christ in our personal finances. Look at each side of this bold statement. Laying up treasures upon earth is a dangerous proposition. Laying up treasures in heaven is a safe investment. Wow!

For us *earthlings* (individuals, albeit Saints, living at present on earth) this is a challenging issue. We know we need to be good stewards of God's provision to take care of our needs now. We know that it is wise that we also use His provisions to prepare for known and unknown future needs. And here we are told that we should lay not up treasures upon the earth, but lay them up in Heaven. Sounds like a dilemma. Keep in mind, this is part of what is commonly known as *the sermon on the mount*, but it truthfully is *Christ's Life on the mount*. And His Life is IN US. We have the capacity to *see* His Life (all of chapters 5, 6, & 7) Lived out through us, more so in a seemingly extreme situation as this passage presents.

Let us look at a parallel scripture from the Gospel according to Luke 12:33:
> Sell that ye have, and give alms; provide yourselves bags which wax not old, a treasure in the heavens that faileth
> not, where no thief approacheth, neither moth corrupteth.

That really cleared things up, didn't it?!?

So, what is God telling us in layman's language for our practical understanding? A parable. A Heavenly Truth with a Heavenly meaning using an earthly illustration.

Now listen, this actually is a very uncomplicated, yet complex proclamation by our Lord concerning the handling of the resources (treasures) He places into the hands of each one of us. This is a clear guide for our stewardship.

So, let's itemize some important points:
- In Scripture days, treasures, or wealth, most often were associated with clothing and ornaments indicating a comfortable life. Therefore, *moth* and *rust* had significant meaning to the people of that day regarding the *things* they possessed. The *moth* is a small insect that finds its way to clothes and garments, and destroys them. It was common in that day for the *moth* to destroy their apparel (some of us are old enough to remember how our grandparents and parents used to put clothes in bags with mothballs, to prevent moths from eating the items while in storage!). *Rust* would eat away their metal treasures.

- In our day, treasures and wealth are more commonly thought of as gold, silver, stocks, bonds, land, etc. The connection is with these being an earthly treasure that can lose value, albeit not via *moth* or *rust* necessarily. We are to be careful where we place our treasures. There are items and locations that are known to perish. We would be incredibly blind to not know, or search to know, which are the most subject to corruption, or theft. We should know that God's *bank* is a safe place for our treasure. Our heavenly Banker has a mind like none other. He is omniscient…He offers wisdom, security, and prosperity.

With Christ's connection of these instructions to our treasures being linked to our *heart* (v.21 in Matthew, v. 34 in Luke), we can take away some pertinent Heavenly guidance for our stewardship decision-making:
- *which heart* we live out of determines our abandoning to *God's financial Way,* or not
- *possessing* earthly treasures is not a sin
- *gaining* earthly treasures God's way is not prohibited

- *what* we do with our treasure is to be an item of the *Heart* (being linked to God's purposes)
- if we have treasure *in store*, we can give it as God leads (see chapter 39, re: Proverbs 3:9-10 and chapter 43, re: 2 Corinthians 8:14; 1 John 3:17), always keeping some to be able to meet our need as well to meet a time of need for someone else in the future
- we are to Live out of Christ's *Heart* in us
- we are to *guard* His *Heart* and not turn to the *heart* of covetousness and greed and worldly mindedness
- we must first and primarily have *joy* in our Lord's Heavenly plan, particularly the eternal, before we focus on any earthly plans of our own

There are other things to consider here in these three prolific verses in Matthew and Luke, but for now just remember stewardship is more than just an earthly endeavor. How we spend or invest our treasure, and how we find pleasure in what we possess on this earth, have Heavenly repercussions.

I have a fond memory of driving down a seldom-travelled highway in East Texas back in 1989 while heading up to visit our oldest daughter, Kelly, in school at East Texas Baptist University, Marshall, Texas. As we were approaching the town of Carthage from the west, I saw some movement out of the corner of my eye. It was two young boys who had just run around the back corner of a house playing cowboys and Indians, or cops and robbers, or some similar life adventure. They were riding their *stick-horses*. One was chasing the other. I thought to myself then as I drove on…here are two young kids who probably didn't have much of the material things in life. The house was a small frame home with little shrubbery or trees around it. The garage was a small one-car structure. There was no paved driveway off the highway; just dirt separating the *driveway* from the sparsely grassed yard. Here were two young boys having a grand time with the least this world could offer in terms of materialistic toys or games. They were living life to the fullest. How many kids these days would be *content* with having a *stick-horse* and playing in the yard like those boys in 1989?

They reminded me of another story I had heard someone share a couple of years before then: An older woman once asked two young boys who were amusing themselves without any fancy gear or equipment, "Boys, are you having fun with your favorite toys...your greatest treasures?" "No, ma'am," one of the boys said. "These ain't our treasures. These are our playthings. Our treasures are in heaven." The grandmother was ecstatic that her grandsons had been listening to the preacher's message the past Sunday.

Today Kelly and her family live near Marshall, and we go that way sometimes when headed to see them. I never drive past that house without searching for two boys coming around the back corner on *stick-horses*...

I wonder how many Saints today can say these two things:
1. I have *joy* in my heart knowing that my foregoing purchasing that new _____, and giving the money to missions that God led me to give, resulted in a harvest of souls.
2. No one can *reap* such a huge dividend on any size investment like the Lord Jesus Christ!

Try laying up some treasure in Heaven… It is *The Math of Life. Christ's Life.*

Chapter 39
Honor the LORD With Your Giving
Honor the LORD with thy substance,
and with the firstfruits of all thine increase:
So shall thy barns be filled with plenty,
and thy presses shall burst out with new wine.
Proverbs 3:9-10

Let me see…God directs us to:
- give out of what we *already possess* (thy substance)
- give (at least 10%) out of *our increase* (thine increase)
- and our pocketbooks (financial net worth) will be *filled with plenty/bursting out*

Wow! What a parabolic teaching! This is another incredible illustration of how the *natural mind* can never make heads nor tails of God's Truth. Only the *Mind of Christ* in a Saint can wrap around these instructions and jump right into *trust and receive*.

When it comes to the pocketbook, many will argue or fight to keep every penny in their possession. They will not give or release one penny in any way other than of their own decisions, of whom we know many make incredulously horrific *spending* and *giving* decisions day in and day out. And, yet, God gives specific instructions to His people on stewardship, how to manage all that He has given us. And one of His grandest instructions is for us to HONOR HIM for His having showered resources upon us.

What is interesting is how few Saints really know what God has said explicitly. And how few Saints even have a thought that WHAT THEY ALREADY POSSESS is included in God's directions? Wow! Think of that…what we already possess, *thy substance*. Who does such? Who has taken out of their savings and given, sold something to give the proceeds, or placed belongings into their will…all in a manner to *honor the LORD*?

What is most sad is that very few have even looked at, pondered, considered, or taken to heart the last part of this verse. Listen to this PROMISE from God: "So shall thy barns be filled with plenty, and thy presses shall burst out with new wine." WOW! WOW! WOW! GOD PROMISES BARNS FILLED AND PRESSES BURSTING OUT. How could any ONE of God's children not want a Life like that?!?

In fact, God's promise is one that shows His desire to bring the Life of Christ into our comparatively insignificant days here on earth in an area that is most dear to each and every Saint. It is well-known that folks say it is OK to talk about numerous things, but when you reach for their pocketbook you are barking up the wrong tree!

As a preacher for so many years, I never hesitated to *preach the Word* when it came to financial matters. I learned that from my pastor, John Morgan. This whole book is about the Life from God's Word that can express Himself in so many different ways when it comes to money, things, jobs – which bring an *increase* to our *pockets* and our *substance* in our possession. I hear all the time from Saints in many locations around our country that their preachers over the years avoided speaking about tithing, and they have never heard one sermon on *giving out of something already in the bank.*

How sad. No wonder so many Saints have empty pockets, and no savings. Their *barns* don't even exist, and their *presses* are generating empty bags. Do you see the illustration showing *barns* as *substance* and *presses/new wine* as *firstfruits*? God has given some powerful Truths to share with us through life illustrations. All to point to His working in our life every day in every way. Beautiful!

So let's take a look at the practical aspects of all this.

thy substance, *what we already have in our possession.*

Without a doubt, God speaks to one of the primary premises of His position on our financial matters. God is owner. We are stewards. And this particularly includes that which we have already gained and now possess, but which is actually His and we are tending to it. This includes everything. If you want to raise the hairs on someone's neck, ask them to sell something they own or take some amount out of savings, to either pay off a debt, OR give to God's work.

Probably one of the most definitive, and hilarious, moments of my ministry came just a few years ago at a country church I was serving as Interim Pastor. The building and pews were almost 75 years old as I recall. Something was discussed about the need to have a bigger sanctuary, but how would we ever get such. I mentioned from the pulpit in a sermon on finances one Sunday that in just looking around there was the potential among the membership to tear down the existing building and build the new one PAYING CASH for the entire construction and completion, including updated and additionally needed musical instruments and sound system. I think the words I used were these: "I know without much thinking that there are enough resources available from everyone sitting in the pews this morning to…" I ended the sentence with those words on paying cash, etc. from the previous sentence. You could hear a pin drop as I paused for several seconds. Later, after the service, one sweet elderly lady (I can say that as I am up there in years!) came up to me in a hallway just off the platform. "Pastor, you don't know how close you came to being shot just now!" LOL! I wasn't aware of how close I came to being shot, but I was well aware of how close to some *hearts* I was walking! It is unbelievable how some of the most *prosperous* Saints won't part with a dime, when an elderly widow will give ALL she has. THAT speaks to the **heart** of the matter. (that says two different things, in case you didn't catch it on first reading).

firstfruits of all our increase, *a tithe-plus of all income.*

Not many topics in a local church will start an argument (er, discussion) as quickly like a mention of *the tithe*. The talk will range from *10% of the gross* to *whatever God leads you to give* (which most have meant, *nothing*). There are many who want to talk about *10% of the net*, with no clear distinction of *what net* they are talking about (certainly not the one of Simon Peter in Luke ch.5, after Jesus entered the picture). And then there is a large number who say that *God is leading me to give just a 'mite' or perhaps a 'farthing,' if anything.* Quite interesting, isn't it?

Most of us know that words have meaning, and to increase our vocabulary we want to find out and know the meaning of words. Take the word, *tithe*. The Hebrew word is *masser/massar*. That's Old Testament. The Greek word is *dekate*. That's New Testament. Both mean the tenth (1/10th). Any interested and honest look at Scripture tells us that the *tithe* is **holy** unto the LORD (God), and is to come from the *firstfruits* (first increase). *Tithe* and *firstfruits* are inseparable throughout the whole of Scripture.

The *increase* is the increase, that which comes to us which before we did not have. Not too complicated, is it? We didn't have it. God gave us an *increase*. We HONOR GOD by giving to Him at least a *tenth*. Still not complicated, is it?

What is incredible is this: After Jesus spoke of His not coming to do away with the law, but to complete it, WHY is there any argument about giving? And what amount? The final question is this: IS MY GIFT HONORING THE LORD?

Couple all this with Jesus' teaching in Luke 6:38,

> Give, and it shall be given unto you; good measure, pressed down, and shaken together, and running over, shall men give unto your bosom. For with the same measure that ye mete withal it shall be measured to you again.

Now pray tell me (all the spiritual members use this phrase frequently), WHY would any serious Saint want to keep a stranglehold on their wallet, checkbook, savings account, and all belongings when it comes to giving to God with all this testimony of God's generosity toward faithful and cheerful givers?

> Every man according as he purposeth in his heart, so let him give; not grudgingly, or of necessity: for God loveth a cheerful giver. 2 Corinthians 9:7

Wait a minute. Does *as he purposeth in his Heart* (the Christ Heart in a Saint) have anything to do with *honor the LORD*? I dare think so.

OK, we are down to:

thy barns be filled with plenty, and thy presses shall burst out with new wine

Or, *so shall* this be, our LORD says. Not, *maybe*. Not *perhaps*. Not *sometimes*. But, EVERY TIME, ALL THE TIME, when we *honor the LORD with our substance, and with the firstfruits of all our increase.* Cool. Beautiful. Glory. Grace. Well, amen! I know this is terminology that is foreign to our language and understanding on the surface, but let us take just a minute to *translate* this into 2023 common-speak: *We can make the choice by the Grace of God through us to open our Hearts, our financial resources, and our checkbook...honor the Lord by our giving, and receive from the Lord an abundance that will meet all our need and have enough left over to give to every good work.* Yes, that includes one more verse:

> And God is able to make all grace abound toward you; that ye, always having all sufficiency in all things, may abound to every good work. 2 Corinthians 9:8

Let's summarize and close out this chapter. Think about it. How could *giving* so much lead to *having* so much *if the Life of Christ* were not in control and Living in our financial world?!? Hallelujah! That is exactly what God has in mind for His Saints. Not only the LIFE of CHRIST in control of our financial world, but the LIFE of CHRIST Lived out in our financial world. All the financial promises of God wrapped up in this verse.

You and Holy Spirit can work all this out in your potential financial realm.

We *choose* a life or The Life. *Choose* The Life. It is *The Math of Life. Christ's Life.*

Chapter 40
Proving God
*Bring ye all the tithes into the storehouse,
that there maybe meat in mine house,
and prove me herewith, saith the LORD of hosts,
if I will not open the windows of heaven,
and pour you out a blessing, that there
shall not be room enough to receive it.*
Malachi 3:10

Here we have one of the clearest teachings of God about tithing, and every child of God being able to tithe, and still have plenty to live on. In fact, His abundance. This is one of the verses that displays what the LIFE of God in His Saints' financial world can be. Tithe, and watch for an outpouring in return that we won't know what to do with it!

Listen to the 2 verses before and the 2 verses following our text…

> Will a man rob God? Yet ye have robbed Me. But ye say, Wherein have we robbed Thee? In tithes and offerings. Ye are cursed with a curse: for ye have robbed Me, even this whole nation. vs. 8-9

> And I will rebuke the devourer for your sakes, and he shall not destroy the fruits of your ground; neither shall your vine cast her fruit before the time of the field, saith the LORD of hosts. And all nations shall call you blessed: for ye shall be a delightful land, saith the LORD of hosts. vs. 11-12

Now listen closely, there are many Saints today who are *robbing God* just as in the day of Malachi. How? As God says, *in tithes and offerings*. How? By not giving to God that which He has declared as *holy* (see chapter 37). And those who want to argue that *tithing* is not *for New Testament Saints*, take a look at the way God has worked in their lives. One way or another, they are *paying the price* for *robbing God*.

Very quickly, let me insert this brief picture of one couple I pastored back in the 80's and 90's. Their testimony speaks of them hearing my preaching on tithing and giving and then going home and recapping their expenses for the past year or so. Lo, and behold, they discovered that what they had *robbed God of, he had taken away in the form of unexpected expenses.* And it matched to the dollar! When they began tithing, things that had been breaking down didn't break down like before. Well, amen.

So, let's review what God has told us that we need to know and get right:

first of all, in Proverbs 3:9, God tells us that we are to *honor Him*, that is in our giving, by giving out of our *substance* (that which we already have in store) AND by giving out of our *increase* (that which God brings our way in the present moment, or future). And, God follows that in v. 10 declaring that He will make sure our *barns* (or, resources) *shall be filled with plenty,* and our *presses* (jobs/income) *shall burst out with new wine.* In other words, give out of *what we already have,* and any *increase* we get at any time in any way…and we will have plenty of work and plenty to live on, and plenty to give more.

then in Malachi, God tells us we *rob Him* when we don't give as Solomon said in Proverbs, including at least a tithe (10th) of our increase and with other offerings! We can argue all we want to, but God has laid down His *Holy Law* of honoring and giving to Him. The New Testament has no teaching to the contrary! Jesus declared so.

and, God says that HE will keep the *devourer* (the devil) from destroying our jobs, our wages, our earnings, our finances. God's power and His wisdom will take care of His belongings that He has entrusted us with as stewards.

on top of that, any nation with *God as Lord of Life* will be called *blessed* by all other nations, for that nation shall be considered *delightful.*

Now tell me, what Saint would not want all this to be proven Truth?

What is incredibly interesting is this: *God has told us to prove Him.* He says outright what He will do when we abandon to Him and let Him *show His Grace* in our finances. What better way to find out IF God's Word is Truth, IF God will honor His Word, IF God will prove to us that He will do what He says He will do **IF** we let Him Live His Life through us…and see if He proves His Word. WOW! Almighty God staking His reputation on our BELIEVING Him and TRUSTING Him for *what He has said* and *Who He is.*

If you want to see some LIFE in your financial picture, step up to the plate and take a swing at this teaching! *Living Life Debt Free - Trusting God for His Supply and Living On It* under His teaching and power is LIFE! We can prove to ourselves that OUR GOD is REAL. We can prove to ourselves that His LIFE does make a difference in our Life. We can Live Life with a Capital L. It is *The Math of Life. Christ's Life.*

p.s. Just because someone thinks the New Testament doesn't say something does not nullify a *Holy Law,* UNLESS God has clearly and specifically *changed* or *nullified* His previous Law.

Chapter 41
Give From A Willing Heart
Every man according as he purposeth in his heart,
so let him give; not grudgingly, or of necessity:
for God loveth a cheerful giver.
2 Corinthians 9:7

Here is another perfect example of a *parabolic* teaching understood and appreciated only in the Mind of God.

The context of 2 Corinthians 9:7 is in a 2 chapter, 39 verse discourse by the Apostle Paul about Saints giving financial gifts, and he mentions some being in deep poverty. Let me encourage each reader to read the entire text of 2 Corinthians chapters 8 and 9.

Just as the apostle found out, I have never known a Saint functioning in the Mind of God who didn't *want* to be a *giver*. Because it is the very Nature of Christ within every Saint to BE a *Giver*. So, why are there many who do not give at all, or give very little, when we have other teachings as well as our text expressing the Heart of God about His Saints' *Giving Hearts*?

In any discussion of activity involving the *heart* Saints must know, acknowledge, and appropriate the fact that every Saint possesses *two souls* (the *residue, natural soul* each is 1st born with, and *Christ's Soul* that every Saint is given along with Holy Spirit at the 2nd Birth/New Birth/New Creation). Now listen, *each* soul houses a mind, a set of emotions, and a will (decider). The *heart* is the combination of the thoughts of the mind, the feelings of the emotions, and the decisions of the will. Depending on *which* soul one is living out of determines the inevitable actions the person takes. Therefore, it is always important for the Saint to always differentiate *which heart* he/she is living out of. All of the time the actions show which it is.

Knowing the animosity toward God of the *residue, natural (soul) heart*, it is Truth to say that any *not giving at all, or giving very little* comes from that *residue, natural (soul) heart* all Saints still possess. Any giving *expressing the Heart of God about His Saints' Giving Hearts* represents Truth in line with *God's Heart (Soul)*, which every Saint possesses.

Every pastor knows that at least one-half or more of his members give virtually nothing, if not absolutely zero, to their church's undesignated offerings. That's correct fact. Truth. In almost *every* church. A huge issue for these churches (whether they *know* it, acknowledge it, or address it, or not) is this: WHAT is causing 50% of the members to be living out of their *residue, natural soul? That is not* the Life of Christ. Furthermore, WHY are so many churches not addressing this dilemma?

God gives us five things to ponder in this one verse…

1. as he purposeth in his heart – This is where all giving originates. In one of the Saint's *hearts*. With a decision. *Purposeth* is to choose for oneself and make a clear decision to *act* upon our intentions. The *heart* involves perceptions, thoughts, knowledge, reasonings, understandings, emotions, judgements, decisions, and action - the totality of the *soul*. Since we know all Saints have *two (2) souls,* and one of the issues all Saints face is *which* soul we are going to live out of when we *give*, we must make a decision of which one we are going to *purpose* with. That immediately gives (no pun intended!) us what our next action is going to be!

2. so let him give. – Giving is an *issue of which heart*. Think of what the *Heart of God* is when it comes to *Giving*. Wow! Think of *His Heart* Living through our earthsuit and what sort of *Giving* would be going on! It is beyond comprehension to the *natural or carnal mind*. It is an everyday experience to the *Mind of God*. We Saints who possess the *Soul of God* in our earthsuits *can* be experiencing *His Giving* each and every day!

3. not grudgingly – *Grudgingly* is sort of an ugly-sounding word, isn't it? (We will look at where this comes from and how to deal with it in the next paragraph, but listen to what is here for now). Lots of people hold grudges against other people. Sadly, many *hold a grudge against God*. That is a nasty action. It is one that defeats the idea of having the *grudge* in the first place, because it is the holder of the *grudge* that suffers the most. It is such with one who *gives grudgingly*. The word describes a person who acts out of sorrow or grief or hurt. There is something that has caused this. In the matter of giving, **it is always an issue of a Saint having a grudge with God**. This person holding the *grudge* with God is often known to be a *murmurer*. That alone is a form of *cursing God*. It is no wonder God says that we are NOT to *give grudgingly*. Once again, it is easy to see that there is ministry staring the church right in the face, and it needs to be addressed. Here is how.

Two things should occur with a *grudging giver*:

(1) the Body of Christ needs to teach WHY anyone in the body gives *grudgingly*, and that such givers should come forth and get help to get past whatever is in the past that is holding them captive to a grudge against God.
Look at this beautiful verse to start with.
> Great peace have they which love thy law: and nothing shall offend them. Psalm 119:165

Isn't that terrific! I love that verse. And I love knowing that verse and how its Truth gives me such direction in responding to God's Word AND other people, situations, circumstances. *Nothing* is supposed to *ever* offend me! Not, IF I love the law of God. And, I am a GRACE Saint!
But, listen. With 40 years of ministering I have known so many who are offended at almost everything. It's terrible. It's incredibly sad knowing many like that go to church week after week. They have been offended, blamed God (whether they realize it, or not), taken up the offense with God, have gotten no solution to their satisfaction, have gotten bitter, and now hold a grudge…against someone, some thing, and particularly God.
The Body of Christ needs to step in and minister to those holding grudges, beginning with taking a history of the lives of grudge-holders, and leading them to face everything that is holding this person captive.

(2) the Saint who knows they are giving grudgingly, **they know** they are fighting the teaching of God about giving, giving abundantly, and giving with a cheerful heart (the fifth thing in our discussion here). They need to get humble and present themselves for help *if they cannot or will not* deal with it by themselves. *The first step in church discipline is self-discipline.* Sadly, the captive most often does not know how to get released.

Listen! The issue is far greater than the money, the giving! The *seen* is indicative of the *unseen!*

This should be an unacceptable status for both the Body of Christ and individual Saints.

4. or of necessity – The Greek word *anagke*. This is an attitude that is the opposite of willingness. It is amazing that many Saints will give to what they perceive is a *necessity* (in which 90% of the times it isn't close to a *necessity*) while not giving *just to God* (as God directs all through His Word). I have seen folks, who didn't give a nickel to the Undesignated Budget Offering of the church, give a bunch of money to a Designated Offering to meet what they determine as a *necessity* of either the church or an individual, which is actually (take note!) a slap in the face to God and His plan for His Church to do His ministry. And their giving is completely opposite of what 2 Corinthians 9:7 is addressing as a *necessity…being a cheerful giver.*

All of #3 and #4 speak of a Saint living in the *wrong soul*. That's it. That's all. *Wrong soul, wrong heart* of the Saint. It is NOT the Nature of the Saint, but that same *soul/heart* that the Holy Spirit wrote about in Romans 7:14-15, 17-20:

> For we know that the law is spiritual: but I am carnal, sold under sin. For that which I do I allow not: for what I would, that do I not; but what I hate, that do I…Now then it is no more I that do it, but sin that dwelleth in me. For I know that in me, that is in my flesh, dwelleth no good thing: for to will is present with me; but how to perform that which is good I find not. For the good that I would I do not: but the evil which I would not, that I do. Now if I do that I would not, it is no more I that do it, but sin that dwelleth in me.

Do you SEE where God tells us something astounding about WHO we, as a Saint, truthfully are? Look at his words again: *Now then it is **no more I that do it**, but sin that dwelleth in me.* The *I* is the Saint. Sin is something that remains from our *unbeliever* days, a residue called *flesh*. But it is not the real *I*. A *Saint* is no longer a *sinner.*

Now here is an astounding Truth: Every Saint has one Spirit (Holy Spirit), two souls (Christ's and the *residue, natural*), and one body. The battle for every Saint, whether it be about giving or any other issue, is *which soul* are we living out of in any particular moment. And God designed us where

His Spirit does not dictate which one we choose to live out of. It is a given Truth that God does not take away our choices.

Now, let's see what happens when we operate out of Christ's Soul.

5. for God loveth a cheerful giver – The Greek for *cheerful* is *hilaros*. Ring a bell with *hilarious*? However, our typical way of describing hilarious…being overcome with laughter or mirth …is not what *hilaros* here is speaking of. Yes, it is a joyous, glad, and cheerful state of mind. But, here, in any way *hilaros* is accurately translated or defined in the English language, it describes God's Way of giving! It describes Christ's Soul in operation! A *willing* heart *willing* to give God's Way.

> This reminds me of the new Saint who was making $400/wk. The idea of giving $40 a week as a tithe was a little bit of a stretch for him. But, he wanted to be a cheerful giver. Soon he began making $600 each week. He thought God had blessed, and he cheerfully gave a $60 tithe the next Sunday. Next thing you know he got a promotion, and all of a sudden he was making $1,000/wk. On Sunday he went to the preacher and said, "Preacher, do you really think God wants me to give $100/wk as a tithe?" The preacher said, "Well, do you think God might say, 'Ok, I will just take away that promotion and move you back to the $600/wk position…you seem to be a *cheerful giver* when at that place in your life.'?" The Saint quickly learned what being a *cheerful giver* meant!

I know this chapter breaks ground for a lot of Saints so far as God's description in Scripture as to the way He has designed Saints to be in an earthsuit. BUT, with a clear picture and understanding of WHO the Saint is IN CHRIST, there can be solutions pictured as to dealing with the *inner* struggles Saints can go through when not *walking in the Spirit* (*walking in Holy Soul*).

For the sake of clear understanding and helpful guidance toward ALL Saints becoming Spirit-filled Saints, I have included at the end of this book a couple of diagrams that show WHO unbelievers and Saints are (pages 260 & 261). These diagrams show WHERE life's inner battles take place, and particularly how Saints can easily choose to *Walk in the Spirit*. It is an uncomplicated matter of choice. I have also included 2 brief writings on

On Being Born Again and *How To Be Filled With Holy Spirit* (pages 262 & 265).

So I conclude this chapter repeating the two questions:
How is it that 50% or more of all church members DO NOT give with a *willing heart?*
And why do churches put up with that figure?

Will you, dear reader – if a Saint – begin immediately, and continue, to *purpose* (choose), and *act* in *Christ's Heart* God gave you at your New Birth, to Give:
- not grudgingly,
- nor of necessity,
- (and deal with whatever has been causing you to be such),
- but, as a cheerful giver?

Be purposeful in *Christ's Heart* in you to be willing and cheerful in your giving. It is *The Math of Life. Christ's Life.*

Chapter 42
The Tithe Is Holy To God

...every devoted thing is most holy unto the LORD...
And all the tithe of the land, whether of the seed of the land,
or of the fruit of the tree, is the LORD's:
it is holy unto the LORD...
And concerning the tithe of the herd, or of the flock,
even of whatsoever passeth under the rod,
the tenth shall be holy unto the LORD.
Leviticus 27:28, 30, 32

I have briefly mentioned this idea of the *tithe* being *holy* unto God, but here we will take a more detailed look at this important Truth to God.

Very few things in the Scriptures come under scrutiny and argument among Saints as does the *tithe* of one's *increase*, no matter of what type it is. Some of those recognized as the elite of Scriptural scholars cannot agree on whether New Testament Saints are required, or at least *expected*, by God to give a tenth of their increase to God. Where do these differences come from? Some Living in the *Mind of God*...some living in the *carnal mind*.

And I don't know what your beliefs are on this subject, but let me give you some foundational fundamentals of the Holy Scriptures...

- The Holy Scriptures out of the Heart of God are the Inspired, Inerrant, and Infallible Word of God.
- Each Spiritual Word of God has a Heavenly meaning.
- God gives His Saints His Mind to know, understand, and Live by each Spiritual Word of His.
- God has told all that He is not the author of confusion (1 Corinthians 14:33).
- God has said His Saints should be functioning in One Mind, His Mind.

Therefore, there should never be any disagreements or confusion among Saints over what the Word of God says. Saints have only three responsibilities: function in the *Mind of God*, find out what God says, and believe Him.

Now, I understand a lot of the Old Testament is to be for a specific period of time or for a specific people in that day...which is not applicable for us in this time. That goes even for some of the New Testament teachings. And, I understand that a lot of the Old Testament is applicable for us in this time. I am not one of those people who ignore all OT teachings. And without a doubt the vast majority of the NT is God's Word to us in this day. In fact, what I am saying is that all of Scripture is for us in this day, but not all are teachings that apply to this day.

But, as for the *tithe*, *tithing*, and *giving*, I understand four passages give me all I need to know about whether God requires/expects me and my wife to *tithe* of all our increase He gives to us, and *how we give as God leads us to give*.

1. Leviticus 27:28, 30, 32
In the verses above in Leviticus that are our text for this chapter, God declared the *tithe* (and He gave description of what to *tithe* and the amount of the *tithe*) is HOLY UNTO HIM. Clear. Precise. Uncomplicated. Maybe parabolic, but as Saints we should easily understand and put into practical application with what our *increase* is. And it is my understanding that anything that is *holy unto the LORD* is mighty important to Him.

2. Matthew 5:17-18
> Think not that I am come to destroy the law, or the prophets: I am not come to destroy, but to fulfill. For verily I say unto you, Till heaven and earth pass, one jot or one tittle shall in no wise pass from the law, till all be fulfilled.

Jesus explicitly says the law is still with us. In a beautiful example of Jesus giving a parabolic picture of Himself fulfilling the tithe and offerings teachings, he gives us a look at the trichotomy of a Saint that will experience God carrying out His law through the earthsuit of a Saint.

3. Matthew 23:3-4
> Woe unto you, scribes and Pharisees, hypocrites! for ye pay tithe of mint and anise and cummin, and have omitted the weightier matters of the law, judgment, mercy, and faith: these ought ye to have done, and not to leave the other undone. Ye blind guides, which strain at a gnat, and swallow a camel.

Jesus didn't scold the folks for *tithing* of their mint, anise, and cummin **but for neglecting** the also important (*weightier* He called them) issues of law, judgment, mercy, and faith. He didn't tell them to *stop tithing*, or that they shouldn't keep the *tithe holy unto the Lord*. In fact, these (paying tithe of mint and anise and cummin, their increase of their *income* off these) *ought ye to have done*. He tells them to keep paying tithes of their increase (income).

4. 2 Corinthians 9:7
> Every man according as he purposeth in his heart, so let him give; not grudgingly, or of necessity: for God loveth a cheerful giver.

EVERY MAN *purposeth* in HIS HEART. I keep repeating it is important to keep in mind that Saints have *2 hearts*, and to know which one we are thinking with. Or, *should be* thinking with.

Therefore, GOD has told us "the tithe IS HOLY unto Him today" (He did not destroy His law; He fulfills His law). As for me and my house, WE WILL TITHE OF HIS INCREASE TO US…mint, anise, cummin, Social Security check, cash, fruit of the plum trees, onions-tomatoes-okra-cucumbers-squash or other vegetables of the garden, the equivalent value of such, or any other *increase* He provides. Holy is Holy.

And I know people will go on saying, "Well, the law was OT, and the NT never says that explicitly." I know. There are a multitude of other Truths that the OT Scriptures say…but no one has torn the OT out of their Scriptures to my knowledge, or stopped believing and quoting so many OT Truths… inaccurately or inappropriately out of context.

The NT passage in 2 Corinthians 9 tells us clearly that the issue TODAY is one of the *Heart*. God's Heart in every Child of God. Let me ask this: Have we ever heard a NT Saint get up and give a testimony on *tithing*, but tell everyone they don't believe in *tithing*, or regret giving the *tithe?* Have they ever said that God has spoken to their *Heart* that the *tithe* is NOT HOLY unto Him, but for *some* reason they just think it is best to *tithe?* It is always the *unbelieving non-tithers* who try to steer some Saint's giving away from the *tithe*.

Bottom-line on this: Spend time with God long enough that you *know in the Heart He has given you at your New Birth* WHAT He expects out of your giving.

Giving from *His Heart* in us IS *The Math of Life. Christ's Life.*

Chapter 43
Giving vs Loaning
And God is able to make all grace abound toward you;
that ye, always having all sufficiency in all things,
may abound to every good work.
2 Corinthians 9:8

As one who has lived *debt free* for 40+ years, I cannot imagine how it would feel to *loan* someone some money instead of *giving* to them as God leads. In fact, it would fly in the face of every Truth God has taught me about *Living Life Debt Free - Trusting God for His Supply, and Living On It.*

I would go so far as to say that it would be very difficult for a Saint who believes in *Never Borrow* or *Never Go Into Debt* (however we want to term it) to turn around and LOAN someone any amount, and place that person *in debt*. It would be very difficult to justify that for any reason.

Why would a Saint want to put someone else in bondage? in disobedience to God? in a position of stress and strain should the individual lose his ability or capacity to pay back the loan? All of this just makes no sense, and to do so is not functioning in Truth. And is really an act of betrayal of proper discipleship and stewardship.

Every Saint should be *Living Life Debt Free -Trusting God for His Supply, and Living On It.* Every Saint has a ministry of discipleship to teach other Saints proper Scriptural stewardship and trusting God's Truth.

Having said all that, is there any option for a Saint to help another Saint in a time of hardship, recovery, or any lacking. Absolutely. GIVE to the other Saint's need, IF God gives you permission and direction. No question God will at times provide one Saint's need out of another's abundance.

> But whoso hath this world's good, and seeth his brother have need, and shutteth up his bowels of compassion from him, how dwelleth the love of God in him.
> 1 John 3:17
> But if any provide not for his own, and especially for those of his house, he hath denied the faith, and is worse than an infidel. 1 Timothy 5:8

Now I love the stories God laid out for us in 2 Corinthians chapters 8 & 9. He gives some beautiful examples of giving according to what someone has, giving with a willing Mind and Heart, giving in abundance and liberally, and even giving out of poverty. All of these God says are according to the Grace of God, beyond the power of the givers themselves. The power of God's Grace. *Not one time does God tell us through any writer that we should loan money to someone else.*

That brings two important aspects to the forefront:

1. giving that is beyond the power a Saint has in himself
2. giving that is in the power of Holy Spirit (the Grace of God)

Oftentimes a Saint wants to give to another, but does not have the *power* to do it. In other words, does not have the funds to do so, or seemingly any way to *make it happen*. In this case, God makes it clear that we should not be *worried* or *distressed* if we cannot give when we do not have anything to give. God knows that. We need to KNOW that, and Live by God's Grace in the matter.

God gave us a prime example of such when the Apostle Paul was collecting some offerings for some Saints who were lacking at the present time (read the whole story in 2 Corinthians 8:1 through 9:15). Listen to this small portion of that writing...

> *(speaking of the churches of Macedonia)* And this they did, not as we hoped, but first gave their own selves to the Lord, and unto us by the will of God. Insomuch that we desired Titus, that as he had begun, so he would also finish in you the same grace also. Therefore, as ye abound in every thing, in faith, and utterance, and knowledge, and in all diligence, and in your love to us, see that ye abound in this grace also. I speak not by commandment, but by occasion of the forwardness of others, and to prove the sincerity of your love. For ye know the grace of our Lord Jesus Christ, that, though He was rich, yet for your sakes He became poor, that ye through His poverty might be rich. And herein I give my advice: for this is expedient for you, who have begun before, not only to do, but also to be forward a year ago. Now therefore perform the doing of it; that as there was a readiness to will, so there may be a performance also out of that which ye have. For if there be first a willing mind, it is accepted according to that a

man hath, and not according to that he hath not. For I mean not that other men be eased, and ye burdened: But by an equality, that now at this time your abundance may be a supply for their want, that their abundance also may be a supply for your want; that there may be equality: As it is written, He that had gathered much had nothing over; and he that had gathered little had no lack. 2 Corinthians 8:5-15

There are other times we *have the power to give, an abundance to give,* and we may give, but God may direct us to *give more*. In this case, God will always make it possible to give whatever He has directed us to give. This is exactly what Christ's Life in our finances is all about. It is His ability, His resources, His *riches in Christ Jesus* that God wants us to draw upon through His Life.

And there can be times when we *do not have the power to give (resources in hand)* and yet the Mind of God is telling us to *give*. I know of one instance in a church where a family wanted to participate in a special offering, but had nothing to give. The man of the home went to the pastor and said such. The pastor suggested they commit to God to believe Him for their participation, acknowledge to God their desire to participate but they had nothing to give. They *signed up to participate*. Guess what God did? He brought an inheritance totally unexpected, even totally unaware of the possibility. And the family gave ALL of the inheritance as their commitment to participate would call for. Wow. Remember what Jesus said,

The things which are impossible with men are possible with God. Luke 18:27

When we are abandoned to God in our financial life, He can make it abruptly visible for His supply to be realized. I have heard testimony after testimony of God doing something that folks never dreamed was possible, but once they committed and abandoned, God showed HIS SUPPLY for the moment and received recognition of His glory and power and provision! He gave *miraculous* amounts through these committed and abandoned Saints.

Now those last words are a powerful example of *giving in the power of Holy Spirit* (the *Grace* of God). The willing mind, liberality, and obedience of the Macedonian Saints in Paul's report led to their being able to give *beyond their power.* Whose power was it? God's. But listen, *what they did first* led to all that followed: *first gave their own selves to the Lord, and unto us by the will of God* (2 Corinthians 8:5). Do you get that? They *gave themselves* first to the Lord, *then* they gave to Paul by the *will of God*. WOW! AMEN!

Abandonment to God gives Him the one through whom He will shower His resources and Grace.

So, that brings us to the question and application of all this Truth: Giving to a loved one, or another Saint, instead of loaning to them. First we give ourselves to God. Next He directs our paths (to whom, when, and how much). Then He opens the windows of Heaven, if need be, for us to give as He has directed. THIS is the epitome and most beautiful illustration of our text verse:
God is able to make all grace abound toward you – His Grace is His work performed in our life, making it His Life doing the performing.
that ye, always having all sufficiency in all things – a testimony of Philippians 4:19, and His provision to meet all our need in all things.
(that ye) *may abound to every good work.* – what is *every good work*? That which God *announces* to our Hearts, and provides and directs for us to participate in.

Let me close this chapter by encouraging you to read how God provided for George Mueller to build orphanages, send missionaries all over the world, and print materials to be sent all over the world. He was committed to *never borrowing* any money. He was committed to *giving, and not lending.* God puts it in the Hearts of Saints to GIVE, who know He would not approve any LENDING.

Do you think God is *able* to do today as He did in the church at Macedonia in Paul's day?
Sagemont Church, Houston, Texas…same thing beginning in 1979.
Anchor Baptist Church, Houston, Texas…same thing in the 1990's.
R. G. LeTourneau…same thing in mission endeavors all over the world.

Over and over again, God proves *The Math of Life, His Life,* in His Saints' financial math. Well, amen! So, be a GIVER (not a LENDER)…it IS *The Math of Life. Christ's Life.*

Chapter 44
Pay Yourself 2nd
And this they did…
first gave their own selves to the Lord,
and unto us by the will of God.
2 Corinthians 8:5

The world is always trying to control our money, steal our money, or at least direct where & how we spend our money. That is what advertising is all about! Yes, there are times we gain an advantage of knowing of truthfully great sales. BUT, most of the time it is to the world's advantage against our dollars.

There is also an idea that has deceived us forever. *You deserve this. You deserve a break today. You deserve to treat yourself to (name the item). You have worked hard…it is OK to reward yourself.* That always costs us our money! To which they cry, *Sucker!*

Back in the 1970's I was blessed to meet and be friends with a banker a couple of years younger than me. He possessed a lot of worldly wisdom regarding building personal assets and net worth. I will never forget an illustration he gave me one time while we were playing tennis at an indoor club in Friendswood, Texas: *Pay yourself first*, he said. He gave one short illustration:

> "Lee, you work long hours and work hard at your job. You make good money. There are many times you figure that it would be nice, be easy, and be very enjoyable to just *go out* to eat or for entertainment. In fact, you might get to the point you do this often. You can have all sorts of reasons that seem practical as to why you do this. You have listened to all the reasons the world has told you. So you and Barbara go out. You can afford to do so. When you wake up in the morning, how do you feel? What has all that *going out* done for you? Do you need to once again do what you did last night?" (Then, finally, he asked this question) "WHO HAS YOUR MONEY?"
>
> "Yes, you earned it. Yes, you worked hard. Yes, you spent many hours doing so. But, who has your money now?

THEY do. Whomever you spent your hard-earned dollars with, THEY have it. How much did you pay yourself of those $$$ you worked so hard for? Who ended up with your money?"

His advice was, *Pay yourself 1st*. Always. Always taking something off the top and putting it to work in some sort of savings or investment for ourselves. Accumulation and compounding was the way to end up with the nest egg we really wanted to have.

I don't know about you, but Barbara and I *want to keep some of the money we earn* to be put into one of our accounts before we give it to someone else! So, Barbara and I were able to start making some great decisions with our dollars that led to our *bottom line* becoming greater in terms of our *net worth*. A lot of the things this banker friend told me that day…we still do!

HOWEVER, when we were Born Again in 1980, GOD showed us a change in our priorities of dispersing dollars. God became # 1. It became *Pay God 1st, pay ourselves 2nd, and then pay others 3rd*. Since 1980, we have ALWAYS *paid God 1st* with our tithe of His increase to us, plus additional offerings, plus giving some out of our existing substance. Notice in Proverbs 3:10-11 that it says,

> Honor the LORD with thy substance *(that which you already have)*, and with the first fruits of all thine increase *(your income):* so shall thy barns be filled with plenty, and thy presses shall burst out with new wine. (see chapter 39)

Here are some examples of how we started *paying ourselves* after giving to God…We determined an amount to put into *our savings* right after writing our gifts to God. Then we started figuring ways we could *pay ourselves* by altering our spending habits.

Check out these illustrations of *paying ourselves 2nd*:
- *Drinking free water when eating out, no paid-for drinks.*

Think about this. Tea or coffee today costs $1.50, $2.00, $2.50, or more, at any restaurant. It is not a matter of whether we can afford that or not. It is stewardship. THINK of how many dollars we could still have in OUR pockets in a lifetime IF we put that amount of money into a CAN when we get home after eating out?!? Drink water, and put the cost of tea or coffee or a soft drink into savings.

- *Sharing a meal if we eat out.*

One thing we enjoy doing is scouring a menu and finding a *value-deal:* enough food that we will enjoy and for both of us to *get full*…at a great price. Sharing a meal when eating out, we rarely order more than *one* item. And we rarely, if ever, leave the eating place still hungry. And guess what…we don't over eat!

Here's an example: at one Mexican restaurant, we always order the Taco Dinner. It consists of 3 tacos, rice, beans, a little guacamole, some pic de gallo, and all the chips and salsa we want. And, of course, the free water. We order the soft tacos, not the crispy ones. They put twice as much meat in the soft ones! We enjoy the meal and get full for $8.95.

p.s. They have great salsas. We usually go to a Mexican restaurant only if we like their salsa!

Another example: we have one restaurant we go to every once in a while that has a plate with one main entry plus some sides. The price is around $12. But…if we want a plate with a double main entry, it costs $2 more. Bargain! And plenty for the two of us!

One more example: A new favorite Mexican place has $1 tacos on Wednesdays, if we select corn tortillas. My preacher friend, Dee Daniel, introduced me to this place. Funny thing is, they pile the meat on top of two tortillas that are on top of one another. We remove the meat, onions, and cilantro, then separate the tortillas, and put the meat, onions, and cilantro on both…plenty for each!

Two for the price of one! Get this: they give FREE grilled onions, FREE grilled potatoes, FREE chips & salsa, a FREE small bowl of guacamole, sliced jalapenos, and some pico de gallo…plus some grilled jalapenos…ALL FREE!

- *Eat like this,* and put the savings (from typical spending by folks eating out) in *your savings.*
- *Eat at home!* The cooking is great. The cook is more beautiful! You know who has handled the food. You fix what you want, in the amount you want, the exact way you want it, and save some money.

NOW DO YOU REALLY WANT to *pay yourself 2nd*, and SAVE MONEY? Figure out how much it would have cost to *eat out*, subtract what it cost to *eat at home*, and put the difference into SAVINGS!

Do the same shopping for food. Use coupons, look for *2 for 1* pricing, etc. THEN note the *savings* on your checkout ticket...and put your *savings* INTO SAVINGS! How convenient, most grocery stores today TELL you how much you *saved* by shopping at their store with *their card!*

Eating clubs. What? Well, when teaching a financial freedom class I ask the participants to bring a report to class about some place they eat out at...and how they *scour* the menu and find a *bargain meal* (like the ones I have mentioned above). The class participants love it! They begin to see how they *pay themselves* by using these ideas, and putting the money they save into some savings account. You could start a *club* like this with any group!

OK. I know. You're saying, "This couple is crazy!" YOU'RE RIGHT! We are crazy about being the best stewards of God's resources He sends our way. We are crazy about living like no one else right now, so we can live like no one else later! (that is a play on words of a favorite saying of Dave Ramsey that I like so much).

Listen, the three key ingredients of this chapter are this:
- pay God first!
- pay Yourself 2nd
- pay everyone else afterwards

Unquestionably, this process begins by joining Hearts with the Macedonians whom God speaks of in 2 Corinthians 8:5. Giving **ourselves** totally (100%) to God, then Giving to Him FIRST the $$$'s as He teaches, THEN giving to ourselves 2nd...BEFORE we ever give one dollar to a 3rd party. Always.

By the way, as I am writing this, I just remembered: It's Wednesday, $1 Taco Night! See ya there! It is *The Math of Life. Christ's Life.*

Chapter 45
A Channel For Another's Need
Therefore, as ye abound in every thing, in faith,
and utterance, and knowledge, and in all diligence,
and in your love to us,
see that ye abound in this grace also.
2 Corinthians 8:7

Wow! What a complete encouragement carrying the weight of a direct command. Holy Spirit, speaking through the Apostle Paul, wrote to the Corinthians MANY things in this chapter about their financial matters with a specific attention to their concern and care for other brethren. If I haven't already said so in this book, we must ALWAYS keep in mind when hearing, reading, or proclaiming Scripture that Holy Spirit is the Author. The individuals are just the pensmen or spoke-persons.

Something that is a simple idea to wrap our minds around, Holy Spirit led Paul to speak abundantly about various aspects of our sharing with our brethren of the faith in their time of want/need. It is a beautiful discourse that carries a dramatic impact upon our financial planning.

First, let me address this idea with a term we use now. *Benevolence*. That is an English word that appears only 1 time in the New Testament, and that having nothing to do with finances, but the marriage fellowship between husband and wife (1 Corinthians 7:3). Meaning *good will*. Interesting. Today Saints use it as having *good will* to those with a perceived need, specifically financial. Many churches today have what they call a Benevolence Fund.

Therein lies one of the difficulties addressing this chapter's topic in just a short *chapter*. I recall vividly two illustrations from my first full-time ministry position: Bus Minister & Minister of Evangelism at Sagemont Church in Houston, TX.

On one Sunday I was asked by a bus captain to go visit a family near the church that had some *financial needs*, specifically some beds for the 3 girls riding that captain's bus each week. Upon arriving at the home I discovered this *need* was truthfully a negligence on the part of the parents, that is, *4 parents* living in the same house. All four had jobs. The biological father owned a business that was doing OK. (Yes, the father was living there with his girlfriend. And the mother was living there with her boyfriend. This also included a dog inside the house that was almost as big as a horse.)

Was it a *benevolent need*? No. Information always helps when making these choices/taking any action. Did we provide the beds and bedding the three girls needed? Yes. God led us to do so.

Second illustration: each Thanksgiving our church helped out families who may not have been able to provide a good meal for the family on Thanksgiving Day. Our bus ministry got involved easily. We had *many* possible families to take a basket to. As my wife and I entered this one apartment of a family whose name was given to the church, we found the entire family watching a program on a TV bigger than any I had ever seen (this was in 1983!). Very quickly we determined this was a place where the gifts from the church were not as *needed* as had been presented.

Was it a *benevolent need*? No. Information always helps when making these choices/taking any action. Did we help? Yes, but in a limited manner, as God led.

Also for consideration, what is helping the *poor* vs aiding the *broke*? Information always helps. Review chapter 19!
AND YET, our Lord has given us the command to give out of our abundance (*as ye abound in everything*) and willing Heart to *brethren* who are less fortunate than us at the time.
Having said all this, let us look quickly at a few verses I think deserve our attention in this matter of being *A Channel for Another's Need*...
> Moreover, brethren, we do you to wit (that's *we want you to know* or *we make known unto you* for non-KJV folks) of the grace of God bestowed on the churches of Macedonia; How that in a great trial of affliction the abundance of their joy and their deep poverty abounded unto the riches of their liberality. For to their power, I bear record, yea, and beyond their power they were willing of themselves; Praying us with much entreaty that we would receive the gift, and take upon us the fellowship of the ministering to the saints. 2 Corinthians 8:1-4

Beautiful! In proposing the taking of a collection for the poor saints at Jerusalem, God makes sure the church at Corinth (and ultimately a couple of other places) knows the saints at Macedonia were having a difficult time of their own, and yet their joy midst their deep poverty *abounded unto the riches of their liberality*. Hello! The ones in a *great trial of affliction along with their deep poverty* gave liberally. Amen! And then God makes sure we get introduced to the *Way* they did this: *to their power...and beyond their power*. **That IS the Grace** of God.

> And this they did, not as we had hoped, but first gave their own selves to the Lord, and unto us by the will of God. 8:5

God tells us they didn't do it the way we often think at first. First they *gave their own selves to the Lord.* THAT is abandonment to God. Total abandonment is the only way to see the *Grace of God* become a reality in our life, where His working through us is known to all. The Greek for *will* is a word that means *heart*. The Macedonians were in tune with the *Heart of God* in the matter, and it resulted in their liberal Giving by the will (Heart) of God. As I have said for years, "We cannot out-give our God." How would it be possible?

That brings us to our text verse...

> Therefore, as ye abound in every thing, in faith, and utterance, and knowledge, and in all diligence, and in your love to us, see that ye abound in this grace also. 8:7

Do you see it??? *Therefore, as ye abound in...see that ye abound in this grace also...***in this grace also.** When we know and understand *Grace* to be *God's working through us,* we begin to see how *liberal giving* for *other's needs* is a distinct possibility and can be a realistic actuality, no matter our financial circumstances.

Before I close this chapter, let me bring in three other thoughts. **One,** God makes it clear that **brethren** are our primary responsibility to help. Matthew 25:34-40 is a passage showing that when we meet the needs of *one of the least of these My* **brethren**, *ye have done it unto Me* (Jesus). And in 1 John 3:17, God tells us *But whoso hath this world's good, and seeth his* **brother** *have need, and shutteth up his bowels of compassion from him, how dwelleth the love of God in him?* (bold print in verses is my emphasis).

Two, there are many who have what I call *bleeding hearts*. They cannot see *anyone* (covering the whole spectrum of life) having a *need*, without thinking *the church* HAS to help ALL. Has anyone seen a tree growing on the church property with dollar bills budding out from the limbs? EVERY dollar *the church* has to give benevolently comes from OFFERINGS made by the members who give out of their *abundance*. The same is true for Saints giving out of their own pockets instead of through the church. Be careful when presenting *needs* to *the church*.

And, **three**, our pastor, John Morgan (Sagemont Church, Houston, TX) gave what I always used as a truth to teach the churches I pastored. "Give to God through the church, not directly to a brethren's need. God gets ALL the praise and recognition! And, we do not have to deflect such, nor does the recipient can ever feel obligated (or, perhaps feel embarrassed) to us." That has been a great way that exemplifies the Grace giving to meet the needs of the brethren in Jerusalem in our text in 2 Corinthians 8.

ALL things are possible with God, including Giving liberally and abundantly to the need of brethren through His Grace working in our lives. Confirm a truthful *need*, then *abound in this Grace also*. It is *The Math of Life. Christ's Life.*

Chapter 46
Start Saving By Age 12
He becometh poor that dealeth with a slack hand:
but the hand of the diligent maketh rich.
He that gathereth in summer is a wise son:
but he that sleepeth in harvest is a son that causeth shame.
Proverbs 10:4-5

I had my 1st savings account at age 14, about 1 week before turning 15. Bill & Lillian Hinson (friends of our family – see Ch. 5 of my book, *Seagulls Don't Lie!*) gave me a savings account with a small amount to start saving for the future, as a graduation gift from Jr. High School (in 1960, we didn't enter High School until the 10th grade). I began to learn what it meant to plan on putting something into *savings* from that early age. Actually, I am still learning (and being reminded of the many things learned the previous 60+ years!) WHY *saving* is a wise thing to do, now at age 78.

Who…Do you remember opening your **1st savings account**, or maybe someone else opened it for you?

What…was the initial amount deposited?

When…did you open it?…how old were you?

Perhaps this is the biggest question:

Why…did you open the account?

> "The key to a great story is not *who, what,* or *when*…but **why**."
> from James Bond movie…*Tomorrow Never Dies*

So what I want to explore is WHY to have a savings account, and WHY to start at an early age…like 12 years old. *Although it is never too late to start saving.*

Here are 5 good reasons!

1st, establishing a savings account at an early age, and consistently and regularly adding to your savings, leads you to following one of God's prime financial principles: Proverbs 21:20,

> There is treasure to be desired and oil in the dwelling of the wise; but a foolish man spendeth it up.

That's WHY. The only way to have the treasure and oil in your dwelling that God speaks of, and not *spendeth it up,* is to BE WISE and have a *place* to put some *away* and *add to* your accumulation on a regular basis. But don't miss God's *warning: A foolish man spendeth it up.*

It is amazing how a country founded by Saints on God's Truth can today be operating so far from that Truth. Every year we hear more and more about how so many Americans are reaching age 65 and have little or nothing in savings. (and then they want those who are working, or have saved, to pay for *everything* for them…free food, free housing, free health care…the list goes on and on). Sorry, but I find it difficult to have any empathy for those who have *spent their retirement* through the years as they lived to age 65 or older. And they defy another of God's principles: *family* is our primary *caretaker.* DON'T BE one of those who reach age 65 and have no *treasure to be desired and oil in the dwelling of the wise.*

Have you ever stopped to think that IF an individual places $1 into savings (can, bag, sack, savings account) every day from age 15 to age 65 – that individual would have $18,250 in their savings…not counting any interest that could have been earned. $1/day. And someone wants someone else to help them because they have zero at age 65???

Listen to this. One of my grandmothers, (Maurine McDowell) was a nurse. She served in the Women's Army Corps in WW II. She probably never made more than $300/month her entire life. She had $20,000 in savings when she died at age 91. She loved U.S. Savings Bonds.

2nd, typically around the age of 12, boys and girls can begin to earn some money. That's the best time to start saving. **That's WHY.** I say typically because at that age different jobs are available (like mowing lawns, babysitting, doing all sorts of errands, etc.). IF a young kid is taught two things: (1) tithing, and (2) saving, when making their first dollar, their financial life will be more fruitful and fulfilling. I have yet to find someone *walking in the Spirit* who will say otherwise.

3rd, establishing a savings account, and consistently and regularly adding to your savings, establishes one of life's best financial principles: *pay yourself before giving your money to someone else.* **That's WHY.** *Be diligent.*

Now, ever since I became a Saint in 1980, I have held to *pay God first, then pay myself*. But, I still *pay myself* before I pay someone else, other than God! (a MUST: for a detailed expansion of this principle, re-read chapter 44)

4th, everyone simply knows that IF a young person begins to save at an early age, and *consistently* saves, the balance in the account at a later age will be greater. **That's WHY**. Start early, start being *consistent,* end up reaping what you have sown.

5th, establishing a savings account at an early age, and consistently and regularly adding to your savings, shows you have Lived on *knowing* (mind) and *deciding* (will) to do the Godly thing, as opposed to letting your *feelings, impulses, wants,* or *pride* (emotions) misdirect your handling of your finances. **That's WHY**. Dave Ramsey (www.daveramsey.com) has always stated that one's emotions can keep them from saving anything, when they know they should be saving or have the desire to do so. Wow!

Well, there may be more, much more, that could be said about starting to save money early in life, and continuing to save until the end of life, but this is enough Truth for most to help anyone in their family to get started by age 12! (that's assuming most reading this are older than 12).

But, wait, what about **IF** you are older & haven't started? WHY should you start NOW? That's easy. NOW is the time to start IF you haven't already done so. No age is *too late* to START! **That's WHY.**

Teach kids to start early, add consistently, do not withdraw, and do not end up at age 65 like 50% or more of our country's population. It is *The Math of Life. Christ's Life.*

Chapter 47
A Living Savings Fund Is A Must
There is treasure to be desired and oil in the dwelling
of the wise; but a foolish man spendeth it up.
Proverbs 21:20

What is a **Living Savings Fund** for? Well...how many of you think you will need or want to replace:
- a television?
- a dishwasher?
- a hot water heater?
- a computer?
- a lawn mower?
- a different cell phone?
- etc., etc., etc.

or, want to go/do something like:
- a vacation?
- a family gathering?
- a special event?

It takes **saving money each month** for a certain period of time to have the funds needed to make that replacement purchase or special trip without having to borrow the money! (you can go back and check out chapter 24 for how a *Living Savings Fund* fits into a *Monthly Spending Plan*)

We know that borrowing is a *no-no*! Charging ANY amount on a credit card IS *borrowing* (where you don't intend to pay the full balance at the end of the month from either your checking or some savings account)!

The amount(s) put into the *Living Savings Fund* is a 2-fold task:
- a determined amount is deposited
- this amount comes out of the Monthly Spending Plan

There you have it: the basics of this MUST *Living Savings Fund*. The big question is this: WILL YOU DO IT?!?

1st – You think about all the *items* or *events* you need or want to save for.
2nd – Once you have a beginning list, you then determine the *amounts* needed for the things on your list. That includes either an estimate of the

total amount they will each cost, or perhaps you have a good idea of an exact figure.

3rd – You must figure and determine *when* you expect to expend the money.

4th – Once you have figured this for **ALL items** and **events** you have listed, you then get a grand total of the amounts needed.

5th – Next comes decision time:
- Take into consideration the likelihood of the date in the future that you will need to spend the amount on the things you are saving for.
- Divide your grand total by a guesstimate of the total number of months when all items need to be replaced.
- Evaluate all your figuring. This gives you a plan with a monthly amount that eventually will provide you money in savings to pay for whatever, whenever you want/need to make that expenditure.

Let me give you an example: Let us say we figure the following...
- clothes & shoes - $500
- television - $600
- dishwasher - $600
- hot water heater - $1,300
- computer   - $1,200
- household items (light bulbs, broom, garbage can, etc. – small items) - $100
- weed-eater - $150
- chain saw - $400
- (you name it...) - $150

Those add up to $5,000 that will be needed over (let's say a period of the next 84 months/7 years). $5,000 divided by 84 = $60/month we must put into our *Living Savings Fund*.
- ADJUST THIS EXAMPLE to fit what you think you will need.
- Remember, you have a list. Use this fund ONLY to purchase with CASH any item from this list.

Now listen, assuming that we don't HAVE TO HAVE a new water heater within the next seven years, nor a new dishwasher, nor a new TV, we will have enough money in our LSF account to pay CASH for all these things when we need them.

Here is a real winner: KEEP PUTTING THIS MONEY ASIDE even after the 84 months, even IF you haven't had to replace the water heater, dishwasher, or TV. Perhaps look at this as a continuing *every 7 year plan* with adjustments made as you see fit. You will continue to build your LSF account for CASH PURCHASES, and be able to handle an *emergency* if there is something you hadn't figured in the first place!

Step out and be wise as Solomon says with your planning and saving.

Use a *Living Savings Fund*...it is *The Math of Life. Christ's Life.*

Chapter 48
An Emergency Fund Is A Must
And let them gather all the food of those good years that come,
and lay up corn under the hand of Pharoah,
and let them keep food in the cities.
And that food shall be for store to the land
against the seven years of famine,
which shall be in the land of Egypt;
that the land perish not through the famine.
Genesis 41:35-36

God knew there was going to be an *emergency* in the land, a seven-year famine He was to bring upon all people. He had a plan, and a purpose. And in His plan, He provided an *emergency fund* that would be used to bring Him praise and recognition…and establish Joseph over the land of Egypt under Pharoah, plus ultimately bring Joseph and his family back into fellowship. This was a plan for the ages.

In our day, it is not uncommon to hear someone speak of having a *financial crisis,* a *major* loss occurring in their financial world, and then the eventual questions come. "How are we going to pay our bills, like the electric or water or house payment?!? How are we going to replace what we lost?!?" Sound familiar? Well, in every family's financial life there can come a time when an unexpected *emergency* arises. Perhaps, it is the emergency of losing a job, making a job change without any income until that next 1st paycheck, or hospital stays for injuries or surgeries that include a loss of income. The big question is: *How do we pay for these things,* **and** *our ongoing regular expenses during such an emergency?* Cash or Credit?

Well, with our commitments to *Living Life Debt Free - Trusting God for His Supply, and Living On It*, and NEVER *borrowing to pay for something,* that means an EMERGENCY FUND is a MUST. Three things to consider:
1. Just as in the days of the famine in Egypt, an *emergency* fund is preparation ahead of time for what may lie ahead.
2. Always keep in mind: Your *emergency* WILL NOT have caught GOD by surprise! He knows it is coming. He has promised to supply our need (Philippians 4:19). But, how?
3. The only variable possible is whether *we have figured and taken action* **ahead of time** *for such a situation.* (just like Joseph in Genesis 41).

PLAN FOR EMERGENCIES. THIS is the first savings fund we should *fund*. Period. Be ready for the emergency of a loss of income.

A sudden emergency can eat at our financial well-being every month unless we begin to set aside funds from our *Monthly income*.

Therefore, it is a simple thing to include this *Emergency Fund* in our **initial** *Monthly Spending Plan* until we have a pre-determined amount accumulated. So, the question is *what amount do we need to have in our Emergency Fund?*

Most financial planners give a recommended figure equaling *six months of our take-home pay*. *Take-home pay* is the amount of our pay AFTER the income tax(es) and Social Security/Medicare amounts have been deducted from our Gross Income.

Gross Monthly Salary/Income	$ 5,000.00
Income Tax	750.00
SS/Medicare	400.00
Take-home Pay	$ 3,850.00

Why do we figure *take-home pay* in our *Emergency Fund* calculations? This is the monthly amount we have been using to figure our *Monthly Spending Plan* after taxes have been considered.

When the amount we need to keep in the *Emergency Fund* has been reached, then we can allocate the monthly deposit we have been making to that fund for another line-item expenditure or savings.

> IF we also have any amounts taken out
> of our paycheck other than taxes, we must
> be sure to consider them as part of
> our *need* per month in our *Emergency Fund*.

Well, if we don't have a job, no income, we don't pay any Income Tax or Social Security or Medicare payments those months, therefore, we only need the remainder (take-home pay amount) to live on while we are searching for a new job. And, even then, we could get by with less using some financial ingenuity in the pinch!

Let us think of our *example* of a family with a gross monthly income of $5,000. Take home pay is $3,850. OK, 6 X $3,850 = $23,100. When $23,100 has been saved into the *special savings account* called *Emergency Fund*, then the monthly amount deposited to reach that total can be used for another *Monthly Spending Plan* item...a good way to build the *Living Savings Fund (LSF)*. We have six months of *emergency* living funds readily available to carry us through to the next paycheck if ever needed!

So, we must figure the monthly amount to include in our *Monthly Spending Plan* that will have to be set aside in the *Emergency Fund*. How do we do that? Same principles and procedures as we used to prepare our *Living Savings Fund*.

We have the total amount needed. Now we need to take a look at our *Monthly Spending Plan* and figure two things: what amount could we comfortably set aside without stressing our *living off the rest* figures, and how many months do we figure on doing this. It is best if we can *stretch* and get the amount saved as soon as feasible.

This might be a great time, and personal commitment, to get a 2nd job temporarily or find some other way to fund our *Emergency Fund*.

Getting started is always more difficult
than maintaining good stewardship.

Two things must be known and kept in mind:
1. The *Emergency Fund* is primarily set aside **for** IF and WHEN we may have a job loss, temporary loss of income, or change jobs without any income during that time, or in the event of a major catastrophe.
2. The monies in this fund *are not to be used* for any other purchase or expenditure.

Do we think something like this could *never* happen to us? Think again! Think of all the folks who have had an *emergency* because of Covid-19. An *Emergency Fund* has been a blessing for those who had planned and executed ahead of this catastrophe.

I know of families prior to Covid-19 that had to deal with other catastrophes. With the incredible *natural* tragedies that thousands (perhaps a few million) experienced in recent times (Hurricane Harvey, Hurricane Ike, Hurricane Sandy, various tornadoes across the country, forest fires across the western United States), with *no advance warning* over a couple of weeks in most cases, *and are likely to happen again sometime,* an Emergency Fund is a MUST for any kind of financial preparation. For such an event can bring a halt or a severe strain to our regular income/monthly spending plan.

Here's some more good news also: in any such emergency, there are kind-hearted, generous folks whom God may send alongside to provide in different ways that ease the financial burden of a true emergency. Be it family, or neighbors, or friends from wherever, God will supply your need. It is our responsibility to know that He can and will supply our need IN ADVANCE as well as the PRESENT. **Do we really think God would not give us opportunity to set aside necessary funds for an emergency He knows is about to hit us?** Come on. As a friend used to always say, "I may have been born at night, but it wasn't last night." Yes! We need to *know* and *prepare now* for a time that could come upon us. And, if it never happens…well, amen.

Be diligent to be prepared with what God brings your way…it is *The Math of Life. Christ's Life.*

Chapter 49
Typical Savings of Americans
How long wilt thou sleep, O sluggard?
when wilt thou arise out of thy sleep?
Proverbs 6:9

There are so many words expounded upon every year about the savings rates, savings plans, lack of savings, and several other aspects of the *typical savings of Americans*. But, in the end, the only thing that really matters is what one grandmother said many, many years ago: "The proof is in the pudding!" Yep, HOW MUCH money do you and I have in our savings account(s) total? That's where the pudding is. And the *proof* is the figure telling of our total amount saved.

In this chapter, I want to present several quotes from recent years. All are facts. Some are comparisons of one year to another year. And some are evidence of just how tasty the pudding is for a few people, and for most there is no pudding in the fridge.

Looking At Recent Years

According to many sources (internet search) in 2016: Most Americans were unable to cover a $1,000 cash need. That includes: 67% of those earning between $50,000 to $100,000/year; 38% of those earning more than $100,000/year.

Think about those facts for a moment. It is staggering just how few have $1,000 CASH on hand. But, to me, it is even more staggering how many are in that category who make $50,000 to $100,000 per year. Wow! How could that be? AND THEN... look at the staggering number of 38% who earn MORE than $100,000 each year who DID NOT have access to $1,000 CASH. Incredible! Almost beyond belief. What are these people thinking?!?

And we must ask ourselves: am I one of those mentioned in any of these categories?

In another search, several give this more specific perspective:
- 69% of all Americans have less than $1,000 in savings

- 44% of all Americans making $100,000 to 150,000/year have less than, or easily available, $1,000 in savings.
- 29% of all Americans making $150,000+/year have less than, or easily available, $1,000 in savings.

All financial experts tell us that we must try to save between 12-15% of our annual salary every year. Of all the developed nations around the world, the United States is near the bottom today for the rate of those saving anything.

 I found figures from 2017 showing once again the pitiful number of all Americans with LESS THAN $1,000 CASH on hand. And still, 44% (yes, 44%) of Americans making $100,000 to $150,000 a year did not have that small amount of savings on hand. Is it *good news* that of those making OVER $150,000 a year, ONLY 29% of them did not have at least $1,000 CASH on hand???

 But, perhaps, the *reason*: by 2016, in the last 50 years, the *savings rate* had dropped dramatically. More Americans making more, less Americans saving anything. The personal savings rate = personal savings as a percentage of disposable personal income. What a financial fiasco for the typical American. *Make and spend* seems to be most Americans financial plan.

 Oh, wait a minute…what about in 2018?

> Bankrate said "61% of all Americans have less than $1,000 in savings in Jan 2018. And, more than 1/3rd of households had a major unplanned expense *(emergency!)* in 2017. With half of those costing at least $2,500." Their survey also found that "34% of Americans don't have a dime" in their savings account. IF they even have a savings account!

(I looked and looked for OTHER surveys/reports, but everybody seemed satisfied with quoting Bankrate)

And, what about the savings rate in 2022? July, 2022 = 2.7%. Things look better in 2023. February, 4.5%. Many financial experts say this is because of the effects of Covid, layoffs, drastic lifestyle changes…that many have seen how they could get by with less, and save more of their income once the jobs came back.

Well, we see the dilemma. But two questions persist.

Why? Why do so few have so little or no savings? Why are they thinking like they are thinking? Here is my simple practical answer: almost everyone is living on credit. Loans and credit cards instead of paying with cash.

All available cash is going to make debt payments. Therefore, there is no cash to put into savings. Credit has robbed the minds of nearly all from *Living Life Debt Free – Trusting God for His Supply, and Living On It*. Credit and pride are kissing cousins. More people have become dependent on the god of credit than the supply and stewardship of Almighty God.

What? What are they going to do when the *emergency* DOES COME? What are they going to *pay* with? What do they think is the reason *why* they don't have any savings? Or, are they even *thinking* about that? What are they going to do when they reach *retirement*?

Let me finish this perhaps discouraging chapter with some encouraging ideas for those who may do none of the other things I've mentioned…
- start by putting *$1 each day* into a can in your closet (or, some place *safe*)
- try aiming to have at least $5,000 in that CAN, or a savings account, by age 40. That calls for doing step 1 every day for 14 years, so you could start at age 26 and have the $5,000 by age 40. If you are over 26, but less than 40, re-figure a *daily amount* to have $5,000 by 40.
- try aiming to have at least $25,000 in savings by age 50. After age 40, every person should have some things paid for, and *extra* money to put into savings. That means you would only have to save $2,000/year (about an extra $165/month you put into the CAN) from age 40 to age 50 to have that $25,000 figure.
- try aiming to have at least $75,000 in saving by age 60. That calls for $5,000 each year ($400/month) saved that next 10 years. But, again, that should not be difficult for folks that age.
- try aiming to have at least $100,000+ in savings by age 65. That calls for saving at the same rate as the previous 10 years.

You may be saying, "HOW ON GOD'S GREEN EARTH do you think I could do this?!?" Well, re-read chapters 24-28, and 41-46 to see how easy that would be. The question is never *how could I* but always *will I*.

Let me remind everyone who calls on the Name of the LORD: we are accountable to God for what we do with everything He gives us in this life, and that includes money. To save some of His gifts to us shows we also believe in being good stewards for all the possibilities of unexpected bills as well as the future called *later life*. Every one of us knows that being prepared for the latter years is a good thing.

As an idea of how each of us can be better off than _____% of those who reach age 65 with little or nothing in savings…

> How many of us waste $5/day? Think about this. So, IF we were to put that $5/day into a can, after 30 years (age 20-50, 30-60, 40-70) we would have $54,750. Do the math. Try $10/day for 30 years…$109,500.
>
> How many blow $250/month? I can think of several ways. $250/month – 30 years - $90,000.
>
> If we save the wasted $10/day and blown $250/month – 30 years - we have $254,250 in our CAN! That is not counting any interest or growth if we invest the money. Just think of the *Devastation of Depreciation* (Ch. 54) to start with.
>
> Think that cannot be done? My mind quickly moves to a book I read many years ago: *The Millionaire Next Door*. Multiple stories of Americans who did this sort of thing way back when…

So, let's be good stewards. Let's be faithful to not spend all that comes our way, but put some aside. Let's be found faithful to be prepared at all times. And let's be one of those our LORD speaks these words to: "Well done, thou good and faithful steward." It is *The Math of Life. Christ's Life*.

Chapter 50
Don't Incur ANY Debt
Living Life Debt Free, trusting God for His supply and Living on it.
Be not thou one of them that strike hands,
or of them that are sureties for debts.
If thou hast nothing to pay,
why should he take away thy bed from under thee?
Proverbs 22:26-27

I mentioned in the first chapter that in this book, the **Spiritual** will always take precedence over the so-called **practical**. There are other verses from God's Word that confirm to me all I need to know that God *never intends for His children to borrow to pay for anything*. Let me give two or three more, and then show you why Barbara and I adopted our controlling premise for financial matters *(Living Life Debt Free: Trusting God for His Supply, and Living On It)*.

> No man can serve two masters: for either he will hate the one, and love the other; or else he will hold to the one, and despise the other. Ye cannot serve God and mammon.
> Matthew 6:24

> The rich ruleth over the poor, and the borrower is servant to the lender.
> Proverbs 22:7

> But my God shall supply all your need according to His riches in glory by Christ Jesus. Philippians 4:19

There are four principles in our text and these other three verses that give us clear teaching of God's prohibition against trusting the devil's supply (borrowing/debt) as opposed to trusting God's supply.

First, God tells us in our text verse that we should NEVER sign a note of indebtedness for ourselves and certainly NEVER co-sign a note/loan for anyone. Co-signing is becoming a surety for a debt. We will look more in depth at this forbiddance in Chapter 52. Nothing ever matters how you and I think or figure…only what God says.

Second, God tells us that it is impossible to serve two masters, and that we cannot serve God and mammon. Mammon is a comprehensive word in the financial world which includes any and all kinds of:
- **earnings** – salaries, commissions, bonuses, etc.
- **gains** - an inheritance, stock dividends, interest earned, stock price gain, property value increase, etc.
- **possessions** - cash on hand, property, jewelry, other valuables, etc.

The *god of mammon*, materialism, and material values have gotten a stronghold in many lives today, including those of Saints. Who is master of our financial life? That is God's question to us. Pastor John Morgan (Sagemont Church, Houston, Texas) has a favorite saying that speaks to this point: *The devil will always say, 'If your God won't give it to you now, just sign here. I will!'* We choose who rules when it comes to making purchases, paying cash, or going into debt. Re-read Chapter 8.

Third, God tells us explicitly that anyone who borrows to pay for something (whether that be a product or something like a share of stock) has become indebted to the lender, a servant to the lender.

We won't (can't) get into any debt, and become a servant to a lender, IF we don't borrow! The term *debt service* gives us a clear statement of the positions assumed by the lender and borrower. This servant position is untenable for a Saint. There is no way to Scripturally defend or occupy being a servant to a lender. Remember this: Saints can have only one Master, and He is God.

Fourth, God tells us there can be absolutely no reason for a Saint to borrow (go into debt, become a *borrower*) for the most practical reason under heaven: our God will supply all our need, with sufficient supply, and through a capable Provider (study Philippians 4:19, chapter 31 and several other references in this book closely and thoroughly).

God goes so far as to describe *His supply* in an extreme Spiritual way: *according to His riches in glory by Christ Jesus*. Which of us Saints believe for even one second that *His riches in glory by Christ Jesus* is not guarantee enough for whatever we need. **Whatever** we need! God is able to bring to our pockets whatever amount for whatever we need. Tell me then, WHY would a Saint EVER consider borrowing/going into debt to pay for something? A part of the mind change which Romans 12:2 is talking about is for Saints to begin and continue operating out of the New Mind we Saints have been given at our New Birth. Christ's Mind would never make a decision to ever borrow, but to Live in financial freedom.

If we have an inadequate supply for an action we are thinking of taking, then that action is not a *need*. It is in reality a *desire, a matter of pride*. To borrow any amount of money would violate at least four (4) distinct Scriptural principles:

1. Proverbs 22:26, signing a note of indebtedness when God says to never do such.
2. Matthew 6:24 & Proverbs 22:7, serving another master besides God.
3. Psalm 23:1, not being content with our Shepherd's supply. Not being content with His meeting our *need*, but (an unholy *but*) *wanting* more.
4. Philippians 4:19, simply *not trusting God to be able to supply our need*.

> To borrow is to cease trusting in God's supply,
> and turning to trust in the world's/devil's supply.

I believe only an Unbelieving Saint, or deliberately disobedient Saint, would consider (much less actually take the action) borrowing/going into debt for any reason. Borrowing defies the Power of God to provide for His children for any need at any time (and at the correct time!) in His child's life. As my wife and I have lived debt-free for over 40 years, we have become more and more convicted that God's **timing** in providing a need for one of His children is as important a consideration as any in this matter of not borrowing/going into debt. And what Saint wants to be known as challenging God's power and wisdom, or resisting boldly and openly their Heavenly Father?

I thank the Lord for giving Barbara and me the conviction (not preference) to determine that we would not borrow/go into debt for anything. First of all, when we were Born Again God gave us His Mind to See, Understand, and Make decisions as He would. It was back in 1980 when we first heard Pastor John Morgan's *Financial Freedom Seminar* instructions giving us the scriptural basis of paying CASH for everything that we adopted the premise:

Living Life Debt Free -Trusting God for His Supply, and Living On It.

Let me conclude this chapter by encouraging you to seek out the advice on *Getting Out of Debt*, if you want to Live Debt Free. Chapter 51 is an excellent tool for getting rid of any debt bondage. And as I mention there, I have never had anyone I couldn't show how to get out of debt in 1 year or less.

It is where Living Life debt free – Trusting God for His supply, and Living on it *begins.*

Be determined (convicted) to NOT incur (become subject to) any debt. It IS *The Math of Life. Christ's Life.*

Chapter 51
Getting Out of Debt
*But Jesus beheld them, and said unto them,
With men this is impossible;
but with God all things are possible.
Matthew 19:26*

*I am not a financial advisor.
I am not certified or licensed to give financial advice.
I am a pastor showing some mathematical illustrations.
You will have to do your own figuring IF YOU choose
to use the methods illustrated.*

I have long said, "I can show anyone how to get out of debt in one year or less." And I have not yet been proven wrong. However, I think the Lord spared us from a huge challenge (although I would have LOVED to see Him perform a miracle for those folks) several years back when I had a couple who came to talk about their personal finances. They had right at $70,000 in credit card debt with very little assets or income to fight the battle. They left without undertaking the endeavor because they disagreed with my teaching what the Scriptures had to say about *tithing*.

Oh, well. Let me say once more, "I do believe I can show anyone how to get out of debt in one year or less." And I always follow that up with this: "It will take making some difficult choices and taking VERY difficult actions for some folks."

What is staggering is to see just how many people have so much debt and really have no clue as to WHY they got into that deep of a hole! A man I worked with one time said they just thought the best way to operate today was charge as much as you can, enjoy as much as you can, and someday you can take care of what you owe…whatever that amount is. Wow!

The incredible lack of *personal financial teaching* is a bane upon America that has led to horrific personal debt amounts, pitiful personal savings amounts, and contributed to unbridled use of credit which has had dramatic impact on the high cost of everything. And the same is true for our city, county, state, and federal governments. It doesn't take a well-informed 3rd grader long to tell us that *the borrower is servant to the lender,* and being a servant is not a good job, except *unto the LORD.*

But with the ease of obtaining credit cards, and the abundance of them available to one person (at the same time), along with the lack of personal financial teaching and lack of personal discipline and responsibility, we find way too many people with Rocky Mountain High debt balances. Someone once said, "Getting into debt is as easy as getting down an ice-covered mountain. Getting out of debt is just as difficult as climbing that same mountain."

The good news is this: Getting out of debt CAN BE DONE.

And it can be done with relative ease. What I want to present in this book is my *preferred* way of coaching someone to get rid of their debt. There are many *ways,* and most are *good* ways. I invite folks to use a way that breeds success by having just one victory as soon as possible. The whole perspective of *winning* leads to *wanting more wins.* And with *more wins,* becoming a *champion* (DEBT FREE!) is a driving force. So, let's see how this works easier for more folks with a greater success rate than other *ways.*

The following is a sample chart **(step 1)** to use in filling out your current indebtedness according to the amounts owed to each creditor, listing each in an order *starting* with the one to whom you owe the *least amount.* Next would be the creditor to whom you owe the *next smallest amount.* Keep listing your creditors in that order. You have to know *where* you *are* before looking to *how* you can get to *where* you want to go. (I have given an idea of such a listing by putting names and amounts, as an *example* for clarification of the plan).

Remember, this plan works to get rid of the debt with the least amount of an outstanding balance. A *win.* Then the next step is to get rid of the debt with the smallest outstanding balance left on your chart. *win #2.* This continues forward from the *least* outstanding balance left after each *win.*

Here is an important point: you can also aid in reducing the amount of time to get completely out of debt by making some extraordinarily difficult and emotional choices. These will be mentioned as we go along. Prepare yourself to see some challenging thoughts.

Creditor's Chart

Company	Balance Due	Term	Interest Rate	Mo. Payment
Personal Loan	1,000		0%	100
Credit Card #1	2,400		16.50%	250
Credit Card #2	5,000		16.50%	300
Auto #1	14,000 *	36 mos.	6%	425
Auto #2	20,000 *	36 mos.	6%	600
Home Mortg.	120,000 *	30 yrs.	5.20%	660
Total	162,400			2,335

*assumes current balances no matter when the loans originated

The process of paying off all indebtedness begins **(step 2)** with gathering as much CASH as you can to start with. This would include:
- money in checking accounts
- money in savings accounts
- money in your billfold
- money in a home safe
- money in a sack/can in your closet (or, other *hiding* places)

It is very unlikely that the total amount you have gathered (or, know where it can easily be reached) is adequate to pay off ALL your creditors. OK…let's do a little evaluation **(step 3)**:
1. just HOW FAST do you want to get out of debt completely?
2. just HOW WILLING are you to take some *drastic* actions to aid in debt reduction?

3. just HOW EMOTIONAL are you going to get if SELLING some of your possessions is a part of those *drastic* actions? Make a list of some possessions that could be turned into cash easily, and then begin to sell them.

IF...you are desiring to get out of indebtedness AS SOON AS POSSIBLE, and have been willing to deal with your *emotions* (perhaps even with the aid of your spouse, a friend, or financial coach), then this next chart will help you see how to use available CASH to steadily remove your debt.

Are you ready to START? **Step 4** begins with using the *Debt Retirement Sheet* to start paying off your creditors in the order they are listed, from top to bottom, of the chart. The process involves first paying off the creditor to whom you owe the least amount. Then you continue to pay off the next, then the next, etc.

There are a couple of other steps that speed up the process to financial freedom IF you are willing to take the difficult steps shown. Without taking these steps it could be years before you are debt free.

This sheet lists the creditors from the Creditor's Chart, the amounts of debt outstanding, and the monthly payment plan. This is just one of the ways to get out of debt quickly. But, it works!

This plan is dependent upon you doing some serious thinking, serious figuring (and writing down the figures), some serious decisions, and some serious action. There is no way to sugarcoat this challenge. But these actions are not much of a hill for a Saint to climb.

> I can do all things through Christ which strengtheneth me.
> Philippians 4:13

Just remember this is a parabolic saying (Heavenly Truth with a Heavenly meaning) telling Saints that God can do anything He calls us to do. If God has called you to Live Debt Free, then He will provide the thoughts, the decisions, and the power to carry this through. And you will know it has been Him when you reach the time where you are Debt Free and *living like no one else*.

Debt Retirement Sheet

	personal loan 1,000 bal 100/mo	credit card #1 2,400 bal 250/mo	credit card #2 5,000 bal 300/mo	auto loan #1 14,000 bal 425/mo	auto loan #2 20,000 bal 600/mo	house mortgage 120,000 bal 660/mo 30 yrs	total monthly pymts 2,335/mo
mo 1	465	60	125	425	600	660	2,335
mo 2	535	415	125	0	600	660	2,335
mo 3	0	1,550	125		0	660	2,335
mo 4		375	1,300			660	2,335
mo 5		0	1,675			660	2,335
mo 6			1,650			685	2,335
mo 7			0			2,335	2,810
mo 8						2,335	2,335
mo 9						2,335	2,335
mo 10						2,335	2,335
mo 11						2,335	2,335
mo 12						2,335	2,335
	1,000	2,400	5,000	425	1,200	17,995	

outstanding debt total @ beginning = 162,400
monthly debt retirement payments total 2,335 entire time
All this assumes current debt balances no matter when loans originated.

mortgage loan balance after month 6 = 116,015
mortgage loan balance after month 12 = 102,005

If re-finance house mortgage to 15 yrs somehow and continue to pay 2,335/mo., the house can be paid off in a little more than 3.5 years!

Before we go any further, the secret to all this (if you want to call it that) is this: how serious are you about *getting out of debt, Living Debt Free, Trusting God for His Supply and Living On It?*

A major premise must be decided upon.

You will not add any more debt to your Creditor's Chart!

Ok, let's work the sheet. Notice in Month 1, you will send the Credit Cards the minimum payment amount instead of what you have been doing. You take the difference and add that to the regular payment you have been making on your Personal Loan. You have the same total outlay for debt for the month as before you started working this plan.

You continue this until the Personal Loan is paid off. Then you follow the same process until the Credit Card with the least balance is paid off. And then the next Credit Card. Soon you have only the two auto loans and house mortgage. Wow!

> The balances shown in the Debt Retirement Sheet will not be as exact as shown…interest charges each month reduce the amount going to the principal balance. BUT, IF you find extra money in any way (extra work, selling personal items, etc.) and send that money along with the payments shown to the item with the *least* balance, the debt is gone in about the same time.

From here you continue to work the process.

Ok, here is an astounding thought. Sell the two autos. Ask God to bring replacement autos at really inexpensive prices. Perhaps even a loaner auto from a family member or friend. This worked wonders for us.

Two things happened in our life. We no longer needed a NEW vehicle to drive. A good vehicle that gets us from point A to point B is now our ride. And when we had the cash to obtain a vehicle that better fit our needs, we were able to give a vehicle to someone who desired to get out of debt.

I know what you are thinking. These are some difficult thoughts to mull over. Yes, they are. But, they are God's Way. Which way do you choose to live. On the devil's supply, or God's?

And I know something else you are thinking. What about the mortgage of your home? Well, God has an answer.

1. Sell your home and use the equity as a down-payment to procure a *downgrade* for the time being. Or, rent one. With the lessor monthly mortgage/rent payment on the different home, along with all the money you WERE making payments with to the loan now paid off, you can build toward eliminating any mortgage or adding to your home savings.
2. Repeat the process a time or two.
3. In the not too distant future you can move back to a home like you used to have…if that is God's leading.
4. And when you begin to trust God for His supply, He will work wonders in this matter. Back in 1990 we could have never dreamed of the way God worked to get rid of our home mortgage and provide a great home for us, for the next 30+ years (and remember, we had an income less than ½ of what we used to have). And we have, and will, only pay cash for any home we live in from now on.

Perhaps you don't want to sell your home, but pay off the mortgage as soon as you can. Here are some practical steps to paying off your home mortgage after all other debt is gone…
- secure a lower finance rate without re-finance charges.
- reduce the number of years the home is financed (30 to 15, 15 to 5).
- continue to find additional monies to add to your house payments.
- continue to find ways to reduce monthly living expenses and add that to your payments.

Believe me. These are all possible. We did them.

Barbara and I had a completely different life before we first learned of living debt free. New autos, a boat, and many other worldly things. Since the introduction to living debt free and choosing to do so, we also have had a change in income. We have never made an annual income equivalent to even ½ what we were making before. We have never made an annual income equivalent to most middle-class incomes. This has not stopped us in trusting God and Living on His supply.

Without a shadow of any doubt, getting DEBT FREE and LIVING DEBT FREE is a work of God in the Life of a Saint. It is all about Living

Life (the Life of Christ) debt free – Trusting God for His supply, and Living on it.

Be one to accept His challenge! It is *The Math of Life. Christ's Life.*

Keep in mind...none of these ideas or illustrations are from a certified financial planner/advisor. Just from a pastor with years of experience working with folks wanting to get out of debt. It would be wise to verify all this with a legally authorized person who believes in living debt free.

Chapter 52
Never Co-Sign For Another!
A man void of understanding striketh hands,
and becometh surety in the presence of his friend.
Proverbs 17:18

Be not thou one of them that strike hands,
or of them that are sureties for debts.
Proverbs 22:26

I mentioned this briefly back in chapter 50.
Here we will go into more detail.

Up front this promises to be one of the shortest chapters in this whole book. This is a simple Truth that really shouldn't need rehearsing. But, you know families…

I say *families*, because 99% of CO-SIGNING takes place in a family situation, doesn't it? (that's a good number, isn't it?). The vast majority of the time this involves a parent co-signing for a child for one of two primary reasons:
1. the child has not established any, or good enough, credit to get their own loan
2. the child has bad enough credit to not be able to get their own loan

How is it that any Saintly parent can ignore, deny, or out-and-out disobey God in this matter? The underlying Truth is this: the one who co-signs *(becomes surety)* IS the primary one who is making the loan (the *borrower*). And we know that no one is to borrow to purchase a *need,* much less a *want,* as per God's instructions.

Listen.
Emotions can run Rocky Mountain high
when discussing this.
Blood runs thicker than water.
Families are closer than friends.
It can be very difficult to see a child
or a sibling doing without.

It can be extremely challenging to say *No* to a loved one. But each of us have to decide if we *believe* and *trust* God.

> Let us look at more verses before we go on…
> My son, if thou be surety for thy friend, if thou has stricken thy hand with a stranger, Thou art snared with the words of thy mouth, thou art taken with the words of thy mouth. Do this now, my son, and deliver thyself, when thou art come into the hand of thy friend; go, humble thyself, and make sure thy friend. Give not sleep to thine eyes, nor slumber to thine eyelids. Deliver thyself as a roe from the hand of the hunter, and as a bird from the hand of the fowler. Proverbs 6:1-5

He that is surety for a stranger shall smart for it: and he that hateth suretyship is sure. Proverbs 11:15

The thought comes to my mind that God did not see it necessary to say too much about co-signing when it comes to family. Why? Because He always raised the family to another level of care-giving and life.

> But if any provide not for his own, and especially for those of his own house, he hath denied the faith, and is worse than an infidel. 1 Timothy 5:8

But, is there a difference between providing for *needs,* and co-signing (or, *providing)* for *wants?* Absolutely. Much of the co-signing for a child that I have seen is where the younger has not gotten a job, or has not saved, and *wants* something like a car – perhaps even saying they *need* it. IF they *need* one to get to and from a job, then they have wasted years of saving to get what they could PAY for (with CASH) by the time they either had a driver's license or have reached the *work force age.* By not teaching *tithing* and *saving* at an early age, the parents have raised a child to be in position to either cause the parents to disobey God, or the child to disobey God.

What about the situation of a child with bad credit? What a question! They disobeyed God for borrowing and going into debt in the first place. They didn't take steps to protect a *good name* (chapter 19). Many times disgracing a *family name.* They also disgraced the *Name of their God.*

Here is a prime situation for the child to learn to Live (in the Life of Christ) by paying CASH ONLY for everything, including saving to get that auto. Co-signing for one with bad credit is like asking for an opportunity to make more payments...the financial institution will soon come looking for your pocketbook! As my grandma used to say, "The proof is in the pudding!"

And, actually, God makes it clear...don't co-sign a loan with ANYONE.

There are a couple other verses I will leave you with...
> Take his garment that is surety for a stranger: and take a pledge of him for a strange woman. Proverbs 20:16

> Take his garment that is surety for a stranger, and take a pledge of him for a strange woman. Proverbs 27:13

I've often heard it said that when God repeats Himself it is because *He really means it*. Well, maybe so. And if that is Truth, He has given a stern warning against being a surety for a loan, with a certain penalty. The Hebrew for *surety* is *arab*, meaning to mix together as in a braid, to intermingle as a guarantee in a business dealing. The Hebrew for *pledge* is *chaval*, meaning to bind. Every scholar I have ever researched speaks of a judge issuing an edict to remove the garments (belongings) of one who is crazy enough to be a surety for another...especially a *strange woman*.

Well, that's enough said. We can close with DON'T DO IT!

The bottom line in any financial matters with the Life of Christ in charge will result in plenty, enough to Live on, and Give as He directs...not having to *sign* or *co-sign!*

This is *The Math of Life. Christ's Life.*

Chapter 53
The Emotional Hooks of Money
The Spirit of the Lord is upon me,
because He hath anointed me…
to preach deliverance to the captives…
to set at liberty them that are bruised.
Luke 4:18

This is an important chapter. It deals with that which gets little attention from Saints, and far less capable help. And yet, it is a driving force that entraps far too many Saints in the error of their ways. Emotions can easily be the hook of the devil.

When Barbara and I were first married, she had a good friend she would go shopping with. As was the case of so many young couples back in that day (late 1960's), money was *tight*, and buying things that were not necessary for everyday life was an unusual happening. However, this friend had a hook. It grabbed her and gave her a *jerk* every time they went shopping.

Barbara and I were talking about it one day. She told me that this friend just could not head toward home without buying something. Could not. There was a force (a hook) inside her that controlled her to the extent that she found it impossible to go out shopping without buying something. That *something* was always something that was NOT a necessary item for everyday living.

What was that hook? Well, it was several years later that another minister showed me that the devil is the author of setting the hook in people to do things that they would not otherwise do. And not only would they not otherwise do, but they could not get by without doing such. That hook is *one or more emotions. Emotional* hooks do much damage.

Let me also mention that in all the past years of ministering I have found MANY to have some sort of *emotional* hook that has jerked on them repeatedly and gotten them to do things they did not really want to do. This includes all sorts of issues. But for now, this is evident in the financial lives of many Saints. It is sad to say that very few have ever been given God's path to freedom. That is what we want to discuss in this chapter.

Once we know and understand this hook, we then can turn to God for deliverance from the devil's hooks.

It is incumbent upon those who just can't seem to control themselves when shopping, spending and incurring more debt without wanting to, that they acknowledge this hook and step forward toward freedom. These people KNOW they need to stop spending/stop incurring more debt/get out of debt, but they have never been given God's *path* to victory. Well, it is in these pages.

Before you think I am just speaking off the top of my head, let me share a couple of thoughts that these recognized financial experts and counselors have spoken:

> **Dave Ramsey**, "What I have learned is that personal finance is 20% head knowledge and 80% behavior." Dave Ramsey has argued that debtors need to *feel* a sense of accomplishment with multiple small wins, as opposed to one large win, in order to be motivated to move forward in their debt-reduction goals. And Dave has said much about the *emotional* hooks that control people when it comes to making financial decisions or taking financial actions.
>
> **Suze Orman** has noted that fear, shame, and anger are the most common *emotions* surrounding money.

If you think we are exempt from any emotional attachment to money, stop to think of the last time someone asked you to reach for your wallet. Or, how did you *feel* the last time you were down to your last penny? Ever *feel* any fear, panic, anger, even depression when you saw that you didn't have enough cash (or, credit) to cover a bill you owed?

It has been said that sometimes our feelings towards money are so strong that we start to hate money because we believe that money is the cause of all of our problems. Hate IS a strong emotion. But, sadly, it is another emotion concerning money that is truthfully the cause of all our problems.

> For the love of money is the root of all evil: which while some coveted after, they have erred from the faith, and pierced themselves through with many sorrows. 1 Timothy 6:10 (see chapter 12. *The Love of Money*, for much more on this, along with other mentions in this book).

The LOVE of money, not the hate of it, is the cause. *Hate* of money comes after our *love of money* has brought on our problems. Amazing! What an incredible picture of life and finances *without* the LIFE of CHRIST! Debt goes hand-in-hand with *greed*, another emotional hook.

Now listen, just as Jesus was quoted in Luke 4:18, He is Life. He is the One Who can *preach* deliverance…and *deliver* deliverance…to anyone held captive by a hook of the devil when it comes to financial bondage of any kind! This Truth is crucial.

Listen to the following for God's guidance, power, and deliverance from this bondage:

> Be careful for nothing; but in everything by prayer and supplication with thanksgiving let your requests be made known unto God. And the peace of God, which passeth understanding, shall keep your hearts and minds through Christ Jesus. Philippians 4:6-7
>
> For to be carnally minded is death; but to be spiritually minded is life and peace. Romans 8:6
>
> Search me, O God, and know my heart: try me, and know my thoughts: And see if there be any wicked way in me, and lead me in the way of everlasting. Psalm 139:23-24
>
> Trust in the LORD with all thine heart; and lean not unto thine own understanding. In all thy ways acknowledge him, and he shall direct thy paths. Proverbs 3:5-6
>
> Thou wilt keep him in perfect peace, whose mind is stayed on thee: because he trusteth in thee. Trust ye in the LORD forever: for in the LORD JEHOVAH is everlasting strength. Isaiah 26:3-4

Now all of that is powerful…very powerful. It is the Word of God. Soak (meditate, mull) on His Words and see how His Spirit will open to you His resources from Heaven. But, in addition, let me suggest some steps that I have found resourceful and have brought great peace in my own life, as well as many I have shared this with:

- ask Holy Spirit for a fresh *cleansing* with the Blood of Christ. (1 John 1:7)

- tell Holy Spirit you want to be free from any *emotional* hooks the devil may have in you. Luke 4:18
- make a list of those that come to His Mind in you (ask Holy spirit to bring them forward).
- ask Him to remove them, take them away, to *wash* them away with Christ's Blood. 1 John 1:7-9
- ask Holy Spirit to heal any memories of these hooks, their *effects*, their *bondage* in you. Psalm 147:3
- thank Him for doing so.
- then ask Holy Spirit to completely prohibit all those *emotional* hooks from coming back and taunting you.
- thank Him for doing so.
- praise Holy Spirit for delivering you from the past controls (hooks) of the enemy and for the victory He has now given you.
- My friend, David Ruby (when proof-reading this for me) added this wonderful *footnote:* When the old hook comes back at you (and it will for a time), praise God that He has taken the hook. Thank Him every time the hook comes to mind that He HAS it and is dealing with it!

After 40 years of ministry, I have found many who *know/knew* Scripture, but were not *free*. But, when they called out to Him Who is sent to set the captives *free*, using these steps, they were *set free immediately*.

We Saints KNOW and BELIEVE in the Power of the Blood of Christ and Holy Spirit! Enjoy your new freedom in Christ, His Life in the Math of your financial life. *The Math of Life. Christ's Life.*

Chapter 54
The Devastation of Depreciation
Lay not up for yourselves treasures upon earth,
where moth and rust doth corrupt...
Matthew 6:19

Matthew 6:19 was used in chapter 38 on *Lay Up Treasures In Heaven* as it being contrary to 6:20 stating that title. But here, we look at it for the impact this verse's content shows us relative to what can take place with our resources and finances on earth. And looking at the *devastation of depreciation* should give us some insight that when we consider the impact, we can make much wiser decisions on purchases, insurance, and a number of other issues. I cannot think of two better earthly illustrations for *depreciation* than *moths* and *rust*. For one who has lived the better part of my life near the Gulf Coast of Texas, I would add *salt water* to the picture if there were a verse mentioning it. Or, salt on the roads in icy climates.

To make this idea of *depreciation* more understandable and perhaps more dramatic, let us also know it as *a drop in value* of whatever we possess. Nobody likes a *drop in value* of anything we have. With some things it is completely unavoidable. With some things it can be *managed* (slowed, or even eliminated).

So, let me begin with some uncomplicated practical ideas:
- it can be a good idea to sit down and list *large ticket* items you have purchased in the past that cost more than $5,000. That is column one.
- In column two, list the purchase price you paid (estimate?).
- Column three can show each item as to whether it will, or will not, depreciate (lose any value as time goes by).
- Column four can show the VALUE (worth) of the item NOW.
- In column 5, figure the % of depreciation (drop in value) from what you originally paid for the item and what it is worth today.

With the above list you have made, this gives you an idea going forward of just how your money is *working for you*, or *leaving you*. The idea that your money is *leaving you* should make you sit up and take note. HOW MUCH is *leaving you* each year WILL really make you sit up and take note!

For instance, consider the following example:

Purchasing a new automobile. The depreciation of the value of an automobile is roughly 20% the first year. Then 15% each year thereafter for the next 4 years. That totals to about 60% of the original cost by the end of year 5. Many will say, "Who wants to drive a 5 year old automobile. What does that feel like?" OK. Two scenarios. (1) if you buy a new vehicle and drive it for 5 years...how do you feel driving your now 5 year old auto? (2) if you just cannot drive a 5 year old auto, let's figure you purchase a new vehicle for $40,000 and you trade it in after 3 years. 20%, 15%, 15% depreciation. At the end of year three, a $23,000 retail value approximately. The dealer will give you the wholesale value at trade-in. That is about 60% of what the auto will sell for at the time. $23,000 x .60 = $14,000. Let's see...the $40,000 new car is worth $14,000 to you at trade-in (it doesn't matter what the dealer shows you he is giving you on paper...these are the real dollars behind the scene). $14,000 is about 35% of the original purchase price 3 years before.

How does that make you feel? That presents us with another real consideration: the *emotional cost* of money *leaving you*, or of you *doing without* something. This can be a part of the *emotional hooks of money* (ch.53) or *emotional stress* surrounding financial items. *This factor* is very rarely ever considered even though we *all know* it is real. We can all agree that life on earth was never *intended* to be one of *fun and games, vacations, get-a-ways*, and *buying, buying, buying, spending, spending, spending*. But many have bought the lies of the devil, and *these are the realities of too many people*.

Let me tell you the feeling my wife and I have had for 40 years: driving a comfortable, dependable vehicle that is paid for. Keeping in mind the main goal is to get from point A to point B, period. And with timely maintenance like oil changes, etc. a vehicle can last a long time and it feels good driving along with no payments. We currently have a 2003 GMC pickup...20 years old. We would not hesitate to drive 1,000, 2,000, or more miles on a trip today. We also have a 2006 Toyota car...17 years old. We went on a 1,700 mile trip 2 years ago. And regularly make 400-500 mile trips at least 4-5 times a year. Maintenance other than oil changes, etc.? Average about $500-750/yr. total for the two vehicles including new tires. Feels good.

Purchase of a new boat? Use the same percentages...what do you think of that? How does that make you feel?

When is the last time you took into consideration the idea of *real money leaving you* when you purchased a large ticket item like a refrigerator, stove, or lawnmower brand new, then walked out of the store and thought, "I just paid $1,000 for _____, and now that I have it home it is worth maybe one-half (1/2) that much." Oh, it is nice to have that new item at home, but is it worth ½ of your money *leaving you* the same day? What if you paid $25,000 or $50,000 for a new vehicle (let's pretend…IN CASH), and you drive it home and think, "This is a great vehicle I paid $_____ for, and it is worth 3/4th that much now that I have gotten it home." How does that make you *feel*? Does the *feeling* of having that new vehicle justify (satisfy) the *feeling* of it being worth ¾ what you paid for it the day you handed over YOUR CASH and drove it home? What if you thought of it this way: *someone just STOLE $6,250 from me*. How would that make you *feel*? Or, *someone just stole $12,500 from me*? How about that?!? THAT IS THE DEVASTATION OF DEPRECIATION.

Am I saying *Don't ever buy a new vehicle?* No. But, let's at least be honest with ourselves and know that whatever we pay for the vehicle, it will be worth about 75-80% of that amount when we drive it home from the dealership. It is our choice. It affects our *net worth*.

On the other hand, a house and land can appreciate in value. CAN appreciate. Not always. I know of three huge illustrations that speak to the fact that land and houses do not always appreciate in value. And I will not share them to keep from embarrassing some folks. One other, I can readily share.

One church I pastored, the church family was able to purchase some land for a cost of about 10% of what the land had been selling for 5 years before. Timing, and sometimes factors that are beyond anyone's control, can make a difference in the value of something.

What I am speaking of in this chapter is something that we should all be keeping in mind when we make any purchase. Whether it is money that we spend on **eating** (which is *gone*) or on **clothes** (which for all practical purposes is *gone*) or on a **trip** or any **entertainment** (*gone*) or on a **vehicle** (much of which is *gone*) or a **house/land** (can be an investment…gain in value…preserve the value of our money spent), we just need to know that at the end of the year, our *net worth* (see chapter 27) is affected by *depreciation*. And that is important. It is *devastating* 99% of the time.

So, how do we bring Christ's Life into this chapter? Easy. *Lord, would it be good stewardship for me to purchase _____?* Easy.

> Trust in the LORD with all thine heart; and lean not unto thine own understanding. In all thy ways acknowledge him, and he shall direct thy paths. Proverbs 3:5-6

Also, ask the Lord to bring His great depreciated values to you, in His timing, when you need something. Well, amen. THAT can be the Grace of God. It can be *The Math of Life. Christ's Life.*

Chapter 55
Bondage – The Result of Greed
*For what shall it profit a man, if he
shall gain the whole world, and lose his own soul.*
Mark 8:36

It is interesting that life took me on a path of being around wealthy people when I was young and playing golf. I began a life of watching, seeing, and hearing the disdainful heart issue of *greed* grab hold of people who experience a taste of something they have never had, or perhaps were born into it, and *wanting more*. Or, those who simply have a *craving* for that which others have.

Our LORD has some harsh words for *greedy* people. And words of warning for those who might entertain any thought of *greedy* gain.

> But they that will be rich fall into temptation and a snare, and into many foolish and hurtful lusts, which drown men in destruction and perdition. 1 Timothy 6:9

> He that is greedy of gain troubleth his own house… Proverbs 15:27

> For the wicked boasteth of his heart's desire, and blesseth the covetous, whom the LORD abhorreth. The wicked, through the pride of his countenance, will not seek after God: God is not in all his thoughts. Psalm 10:3-4

> He that hasteth to be rich hath an evil eye, and considereth not that poverty shall come upon him. Proverbs 28:22

> The desire of the slothful killeth him; for his hands refuse to labor. He coveteth greedily all the day long: but the righteous giveth and spareth not. Proverbs 21:25-26

> My son, if sinners entice thee, consent thou not. If they say, Come with us, let us lay wait for blood, let us lurk privily for the innocent without cause: Let us swallow

them up alive as the grave; and whole, as those that go down into the pit: We shall find all precious substance, we shall fill our houses with spoil: Cast in thy lot among us; let us all have one purse: My son, walk not thou in the way with them; refrain thy foot from their path: For their feet run to evil, and make haste to shed blood…So are the ways of every one that is greedy of gain; which taketh away the life of the owners thereof. Proverbs 1:10-16, 18

Jesus said unto them, Take heed, and beware of covetousness: for a man's life consisteth not in the abundance of the things which he possesseth. Luke 12:15

Greed leads to debt/bondage. Greek: *pleonexia* – a strong desire for getting or having more. It is a stronger word than *philarguria*, which is the word for *love* in 1 Timothy 6:10. Thieves and extortioners are ones who practice *pleonexia*. When one can't be satisfied with what the Lord provides, he must turn to what the devil will yield. And that takes borrowing, if not thievery. And we know to borrow is to go into debt, and to go into debt is to go into bondage. *Debt and bondage go hand-in-hand with greed.*

Pastor John Morgan gives a terrific definition of *bondage* in his Financial Freedom Seminar: *When even the smallest or seemingly most insignificant area of our financial life hinders or obstructs God's will in our life, we enter into financial bondage.* Let me summarize the tenets of *actions* or *mindsets* Dr. Morgan gave back in 1980 for being in *financial bondage*:

- trusting in my possessions more than I trust in God
- putting my desires above God's desires
- having a burning desire to get rich quick
- having to put off paying bills that are due
- compromising my beliefs as a Saint
- failing to honor moral obligations
- failing to make investments for future needs
- making my wife work to provide for basic family needs
- buying depreciating items on credit
- not giving from a willing heart

For many, greed is a *natural man's heart issue* that overrides the contentment that *Christ's Heart* directs. Don't ever forget that Saints have 2 spiritual hearts: the one first born with *(natural heart)* and the One given *(Christ's Heart)* when we were Born Again. *Saints* can fall prey to a *greedy heart* just as well as a *sinner*. When greed is present, it leads to trusting the devil's supply rather than God's supply. Way too many Saints have folded and given in to Pastor Morgan's warning: *Beware when the devil says, 'If your God won't give it to you right now, I will. Just sign right here.'*

Remember, God's Way is Living Life debt free – Trusting God for His supply, and Living on it.

Be content with God's provision…it is *The Math of Life. Christ's Life.*

Chapter 56
Investing For the Long Term
But this I say, He which soweth sparingly shall reap also sparingly; and he which soweth bountifully shall reap also bountifully.
2 Corinthians 9:6

I am not a licensed or registered financial planner. I give my input here as a pastor who believes in the Word of God and His teaching of God's financial Way, and one who has tried to help his church members get a grip on planning for the future, especially their later years. DO NOT take my opinions as any sort of guarantee of a plan for financial increase, but just as the sharing of personal experiences and Scriptural Truth.

Based on statistics I have shared in a couple of other chapters in this book about the savings habits and amounts people are saving these days, the idea of investing period (short-term or long-term) could not be something too many are interested in. HOWEVER, everyone should be.

Particularly when I see a statistic like *only 30-40% of Americans have more than $500 in savings at age 65 or older*. I wonder how we have failed as a society to teach and instill in our citizens the *need* and *necessity* to *think long-term* and *save/invest for the future*. Each individual (or couple) that lives to be 65 years old (retirement age for many) will have to be prepared in some way to be financially able to LIVE.

And, as one couple who has been thinking about this for over 50 years, we don't have much empathy for anyone who has *spent their retirement* during the same amount of time. It is my calculation that every person/couple makes over 150,000 spending decisions in a life-span of 65 years (recognizing this really means the last 40 or so years of that lifetime). Every dollar spent on anything other than a *life necessity* is a dollar that could have been saved and invested safely with the retirement years in mind.

Stop and think for a minute what the parents of kids in the 1800's would think today if they could see how little teaching and training of children is done by parents of today relative to gaining, spending, or saving. Not to mention the tremendous waste they would see. They would be so shocked they might not be able to handle it.

God gave us a beautiful illustration of *planting (saving to grow for a season in need)* in our text verse. To *sow* is to plant with the idea of reaping a *harvest*. To *sow sparingly* will reap a *sparse harvest*. That is one that will prove to be deficient, limited, and inadequate for what is needed. The Greek for *soweth* is *speiro* which carries with it the idea of scattering seed. Most expert financial advisors tell folks to *scatter seed*, spread our dollars, into more than one basket or one place. Also, anyone with their thinking cap on would know that the MORE *seed* they scatter, the BIGGER *harvest/return* they could expect to have. Which leads to the questions of how much, how often, and where?

Some of the particulars needed to answer those questions demand that you seek the counsel of a licensed, competent, and experienced professional advisor/investment person. And it is always best to find one who has a *successful track record* of bringing positive growth results to their clients.

However, for the sake of uncomplicated, unlicensed financial advice, let me suggest the following practical steps we have found to be productive and lucrative:

HOW MUCH? Simple answer: *invest as much as you can*. God has said, *sow in bountiful numbers*. Bountiful sowing yields a bountiful harvest. Anyone who has tried growing a garden of any size knows this principle. And one of the easiest crops to grow in warm states is that of okra. One plant can yield quite a few fruit of the vine in one season, but several plants can yield a harvest that puts much/adequate fruit on the table for a couple or family of six for a whole year. The couple usually finds itself trying to give okra away!

If it is your desire to have an adequate retirement fund, then it is typically a necessity that you sow bountifully. A few dollars a year typically will not reap a bountiful return/adequate retirement monies. It matters not whether this is sown in a company retirement plan or your individual retirement plan, the AMOUNT is an imperative consideration.

Be honest with yourself. Check the scoreboard often. It may be that you find a few years down the road that it would be best if you increase how much you are putting into that retirement fund. As any old athlete knows (that's someone who remembers the cheer yells back in the 1950's), *Watermelon, watermelon, watermelon rind. Look at the scoreboard and see who's behind!* Let us never hear those yells being screamed at us at any time in our *saving life*.

HOW OFTEN? That question is like asking a fishing guide this, *How often should I put my bait in the water? As often as you want* to have an opportunity to catch something! Do you want to catch a *return* and growth of your retirement fund? I suggest you put some amount into the fund *as often as you can!* But, it is practical to have a plan of at least once/month putting a *regular amount* into your fund. It is 3rd grade math that *much x often = (will yield) more*. In all my years of pastoring, I found it comfortable for most members to commit to a particular amount out of the paycheck on the 15th of the month. They paid their major bills out of the paycheck on the 1st of the month, then used *arbitrary* funds from the paycheck in the middle of the month to invest for short-term and long-term accounts.

But once again, don't forget that simple 3rd grade admonition. And never forget that blasted scoreboard!

WHERE? *Where* is where the experts come in. I am no expert. And I am probably a little more cautious than many experts. So I have no answers or words of advice about *where* other than to say:
- ask several people if they will share with whom they trust and invest
- read, watch, listen…materials abound with *advice*
- speak to your family (parents especially) and close friends as to what has succeeded for them
- and, be sure to ask someone who has shown to be astute and successful in their investments

Let me expand our 3rd grade equation to a much higher level: *much often in the best spot (or, a great spot) always yields more.*

Now, this chapter really doesn't provide *any expertise* or *precise directions* particularly, just *practicality*. But if you get nothing else out of these words, I hope you have been *sold* on these:

Much often in the best spot (or, a great spot) always yields more.
Keep looking at the SCOREBOARD!

If you are not doing at least these, you best get started no matter what age you are! Things add up, and age does have a way of catching up with us all. In the end, your SCORECARD will be all that matters. Choose to be a bountiful sower. It is *The Math of Life. Christ's Life.*

Chapter 57
The Importance and Need For Insurance
And that food shall be for store to the land against the seven years of famine, which shall be in the land of Egypt; that the land perish not through the famine.
Genesis 41:36

I am not a licensed insurance agent. I give my input here as a pastor who has dealt with all sorts of insurance issues involving the churches I pastored or church members and their families. DO NOT take anything I say as Absolute Truth or a Legal Opinion except for the Scriptural Truth given. I write this chapter on the basis of knowing many who either had incorrect insurance coverage, inadequate insurance coverage, or NO insurance coverage when a dramatic financial event occurred in their life.

The first Financial Insurance Plan ever. The complete story is way too long to print in this chapter. But, do take the time to go to Genesis, chapter 41, and see God's Plan for an event that the people would have not expected, and would have been caught empty-handed *if not for a plan* in case of a *disastrous event*.

Insurance is all about risk. It is making sure we are protected in the event of a disaster. Insurance is the pooling together of resources from a number of participants for when one or more of the insureds (a participant in the pooling who is doing their required share) has a need arise to repair or replace a loss from a destructive event. In most cases these would be considered a *dramatic financial event*.

It is interesting that in one way or another I have been a part of (or, know someone who has had it happen) a *dramatic financial event* occurring. In fact, just taking a moment to evaluate, I am not sure that there is anyone who doesn't have this happen in their lifetime. Each event involves a *dramatic impact,* as least in the eyes of the victim.

So, what do we do about that? Be prepared in the event such a *dramatic financial event* comes our way. Even when we might least, or would never, expect it.

INSURANCE can be the answer. But, the real answer is *correct, adequate, and dependable insurance coverage*. So, in addition to giving a synopsis of the Genesis account, and giving brief testimonies or recaps of known personal tragedies, I will address the three categories of insurance I just mentioned.

First, let's start with the Genesis story. The story actually starts several chapters before with Joseph, one of the sons of Jacob/Israel, being *sold* into slavery by his other brothers. He was taken to Egypt, and all sorts of bad things happen to him with the result being he is put in prison. The Pharoah has a bad dream. Joseph is the only one who has an answer. That's where chapter 41 begins. God gives Joseph the interpretation of Pharoah's dream. It is a dream of what was about to take place in the land regarding *7 years of great plenty* (v.29) to be followed by *7 years of famine* (v.30). Joseph goes on to tell Pharoah that *all the plenty will be forgotten in the land of Egypt; and the famine shall consume the land* (v.30).

Joseph then tells Pharoah that a man discreet and wise should be selected and put in charge over the land of Egypt, with a plan to prepare for the 14 years to follow. It results in Pharoah selecting Joseph to be that man (v.37-41). Our text (v.36) is what this Insurance Plan was initiated for. Adequate knowledge, responsible preparation, and the necessary action gave the people of Egypt enough food during the *7 years of great plenty* to meet their daily need AND to set aside enough to INSURE they would have enough during the *7 years of famine*...food that would have otherwise not been available.

Our family has had a couple of *dramatic financial events* come our way. One was the theft of one of our automobiles from right in front of our home. It turns out it was a particular make that was popular for thieves to strip the parts and resell. We had no idea of such a *business*. It also turned out that we were prepared because we had *correct, adequate, and dependable insurance*. Our insurance premiums had provided coverage that paid what the auto was worth and was enough to replace it. But we never thought for one minute that we would have a car stolen from us in front of our home!

We have family members that on more than one occasion have had property damaged by storm winds and flooding. One of the events happened in a manner that no one could have imagined possible. Insurance coverage provided adequate funds in one case I know of, and *not having insurance* left one family member having to pay thousands of dollars out of pocket. And it really was simply because it was an event that no one would ever dream could happen. Sometimes the importance and need is something that has to be imagined. There are coverages for these type things.

So, how do we do adequate research, determine just what knowledge we should possess to make a wise decision, and take the appropriate action to obtain the correct, adequate, and dependable insurance coverage? Ask financially responsible family and friends. Seek info from reputable financial advisors. And another good way is to have an experienced, knowledgeable, and trustworthy insurance agent to give counsel to be insured correctly and adequately.

CORRECT COVERAGE – Inquire, inquire, inquire. Even with years of experience (having purchased coverage for 50 years), my wife and I still ask questions over and over of insurance agents as to whether they think we have *correct* coverage for the items we want covered. AND, we ask other family members, friends, and anyone we think might yield some expertise or experience. Bankers can be of great help. Business owners can be of great help also. Financial magazines or newsletters, plus financial TV or internet programs/posts are a good way to learn more. We feel we can never have too much info to help us make sure we are *correctly* covered in case a loss may occur.

I cannot tell anyone what is the correct coverage for them. *Every* different person's need will be different from someone else's. That doesn't mean all these resources can't give us some good advice or bring something to our attention that we didn't know. But I am telling you how we do all we can to make sure we have correct coverage for us. I am advising you to do due diligence in determining *correct coverage* for you! And your insurance agent should be an important part of your planning.

ADEQUATE COVERAGE – Basically, the same approach as with *correct coverage* should be undertaken. The numbers are pretty uncomplicated to determine. We must know *how much* our coverage will PAY us when a loss occurs. That figure in comparison to what we have lost goes a long way in determining whether we feel we have *adequate coverage*. Keep in mind…deductibles and co-pays also play a big part in deciding what coverage to purchase. A competent insurance agent should be a big help with this.

DEPENDABLE COVERAGE – In many states, the companies that are licensed to sell coverage in a particular state are financially backed by the state itself. My wife and I look for a PERSON to purchase coverage from as much as we want to have confidence in the COMPANY we get the coverage from. Personal contact and a business-like relationship with the agent is most important to us.

Before we end this chapter, let me address a couple of Truths that we must not ignore:

Too many people waste what God has given in advance that would meet their need later on. This frivolous, unnecessary, unthoughtful, unplanned, undisciplined spending is the ruin of way too many Saints who otherwise should be faithful stewards of all that God provides. Spending money on correct and adequate insurance can be a very wise action.

God has promised to *supply our need*, and that can include an abundance ahead of the time a later need arises. God knows what the future holds. We MUST take the matter of faithful stewardship, including preparation for future needs, in a serious way. Preparation for future needs can include correct and adequate insurance coverage.

Finally, we have often heard people say, "We are *insurance poor*," referring to the several premiums they pay for various coverages. *Insurance poor?* Ask those who didn't have any insurance (or, had inadequate coverages) when their *dramatic financial event* occurred in their life. Be prepared. It is *The Math of Life. Christ's Life.*

Chapter 58
Is A Will Worth Anything?
A good man leaveth an inheritance to his children's children...
Proverbs 13:22a

I am NOT an attorney. I give NO legal advice. I give my input here as a pastor who has dealt with all sorts of issues involving church members and their families at the death of a loved one. DO NOT take anything I say as Absolute Truth or a Legal Opinion. I write this chapter on the basis of knowing many who either had no will, had an inadequate will, or had an invalid will.

I have been constantly amazed at the number of people, Saints included, that have no will. WHY would anyone not have a will? It is the *only* way one can tell how they want their belongings and other financial assets dispersed upon death.

Many think that one's spouse's interest in community property just automatically goes to the surviving spouse. What I have seen is that it doesn't necessarily. What many people do not know...the state of the deceased's residence *has a will* for those who die without a will. And it often disperses property quite differently than most would like to happen.

And it is widely acknowledged among legal and financial experts that a *will* is the device that gives YOU the power to determine who gets your assets when you die. If you have particular items or amounts that you want to go to particular persons, then you state these in a will. Die without a will, and your state in which you reside will likely determine who gets what. And this is without any input or argument for what you wish, or what your heirs want or need.

What a tragedy! What a tragedy that can be avoided by one simple action: *prepare your will*. If money is a problem, office supply stores typically have printed, blank, generic wills available at little cost. It will be a simple form for those who don't have complicated situations, but this will do for the vast majority of people. Besides, it is better than *no will*.

I live in Texas, and research shows *the will* that Texas has for those who die without their own will. For everyone's benefit, each *must* go to their state's resources to see just what their *state will* says and dictates. Just this education alone should certainly spur everyone to get their *own will* immediately! And, know this: state laws CAN and DO change over the years (Texas law *had* changed since I last researched it!).

Two big questions come to my mind immediately upon thinking about this issue:

- If I have a will, is it *up to date*? One attorney we have used for family purposes previously told us that he finds wills in general being outdated due to court decisions. For instance, someone challenges a will in a family, and the court rules one way or another. That ruling, if applicable in your state or territory *could* render *your* current will invalid to one extent or another. Just a thought to make sure you know of this possibility.

- Are my preparations for disposal of property upon my death in accordance with God's desires? IF God says *a good man leaveth an inheritance to his children's children*, then it is important to *plan* for such! And how many have ever thought of leaving an inheritance to their grandchildren?!? And why is this important?

God has much to say about the issues concerning the family. Don't ever forget, God created the family *before* any other institution. That ought to give us great concern that we find out, know, and implement God's wishes regarding family.

Now, let me give just a couple of *special* situations that everyone might want to know about and consider:

- I know of a situation where a couple had *more* than one child. They desired to have their estate pass to *each* child, or their heirs, in equal shares. They also had one of their children who passed BEFORE the parents did (they were still alive at the time I knew them). They credit the Lord for giving them the thought to have their wills changed to include the children of the deceased child. IF they had not done this, ONLY the living child would have received ALL of their estate upon the parents' death. But, what if you or I did not think of this? Are our wills worded so as to make sure that ALL grandchildren would be considered? This is good stewardship of an estate honoring God's Word in Proverbs 13:22. Well, amen.

- I know of a situation where a person was considering purchasing a piece of property. It turned out that one child of a deceased father was wanting *his share* of his father's estate *right now*. Interestingly, there was a surviving spouse. BUT, it turns out the deceased spouse had passed without a will. Their state law directed that under such situations the estate was to be divided ½ to the surviving spouse, equal shares of the remaining half to the living children. And, when the one child took the issue to court, the judge ruled that the property had to be sold within a short period of time and proceeds distributed as state law dictated. As you might imagine, all sorts of battles, hardships, and other issues arose from that settlement. Is not having a will good stewardship of your estate? (One thing most would never think of: the sale price, under such a court-ordered short amount of time, was greatly affected. Another issue of stewardship.)

One other thought that is relevant for consideration: dispersal of property is based upon *living heirs*. You might immediately think, *Why is that worth thinking about?* Consider a family, husband and wife, plus two adult kids. Well, let's say the couple and one of their kids are riding in an automobile together (or, a situation that is not that uncommon…riding on a small airplane together – or, any situation that involves multiple family deaths) and all 3 are killed in an accident. The law being the law *will determine* to the best of the authorities' ability the exact time of *each* individual's death. Are you beginning to get the picture? It is important to *plan* for *untimely* deaths of family members, *and* the order of deaths. For instance, if the father, mother, and one child are killed in the same accident, that leaves just the one child still living as the typical inheritor of the parents' estate. Would you want your other child's family/particularly their kids (your grandkids)…if they are married and have kids…*left out* of your estate dispersal? That could happen. It may not be *likely*, but it could happen. A simple inclusion in your will can cover any such situations. This is where a good attorney is very valuable.

So, all of this is a great example of the necessity and importance of having the Life of Christ (which includes the Mind of Christ) in our estate planning. Just the one example of the couple who credit the Mind of Christ bringing to Mind the need to change their wills after their one child's death is something that ought to encourage us to seek the Lord for

His Mind on all issues and possibilities, seek Scriptural advice and counsel, and seek the best legal protection of that estate that He has given us to be His stewards. All of these things are important to God. Let us make them important to us. Plan for the future. It is *The Math of Life. Christ's Life.*

Chapter 59
Funny & Fake Money

All the labor of man is for his mouth,
and yet the appetite is not filled.
For what hath the wise more than the fool?
what hath the poor, that knoweth to walk before the living?
Better is the sight of the eyes than the wandering of the desire:
this is also vanity and vexation of spirit.
Ecclesiastes 6:7-9

Many Saints treat *real* financial situations as if they were playing the game of Monopoly. Grab a handful of *fake* money, roll the dice, and have a good time. Today, the vast majority of people have added a billfold full of *credit cards* to throw around like they are a whole bunch of some kind of *free* money, and increase the ways to go have a good time.

Well, there is nothing *funny* about the deceitful loaning of *fake money* to some unsuspecting or uneducated borrower. There is nothing *funny* about *credit card bills*. *Charging* with a *credit card* is *fake* money - a *loan,* and not a gift tree. And for many, the idea that money grows on trees is not far-fetched.

This is as *fake, faux,* and *fraudulent* as anything can be. Not *funny*.

The devil is always about counterfeit, lies, and the like. He is the father of lies. As my pastor, John Morgan, said back in 1980, *The devil sneaks up next to you and says, 'If your God will not give you what you want, sign here and I will.'* And almost everyone has bought into that deception. Credit doesn't give you anything…except bondage and less purchasing power. The proof is in that pudding. Actually, the real proof is in the *INCOME/OUTGO PICTURE* (see diagram on next page).

Take a look at the diagram of the *INCOME/OUTGO PICTURE,* the *rectangular box,* and all the *spending boxes* to get a good idea of your potential *cash flow*. As you can see, ALL the dollars that come your way in any manner are *funneled* down into the *rectangular-shaped box* indicating your total receipts. These are the actual, *real* dollars you should be figuring on having to allocate and spend for whatever you choose to spend them on. But, whatever the total is, that should be your limit of spending.

diagram of "the INCOME/OUTGO PICTURE"
of my financial seminar

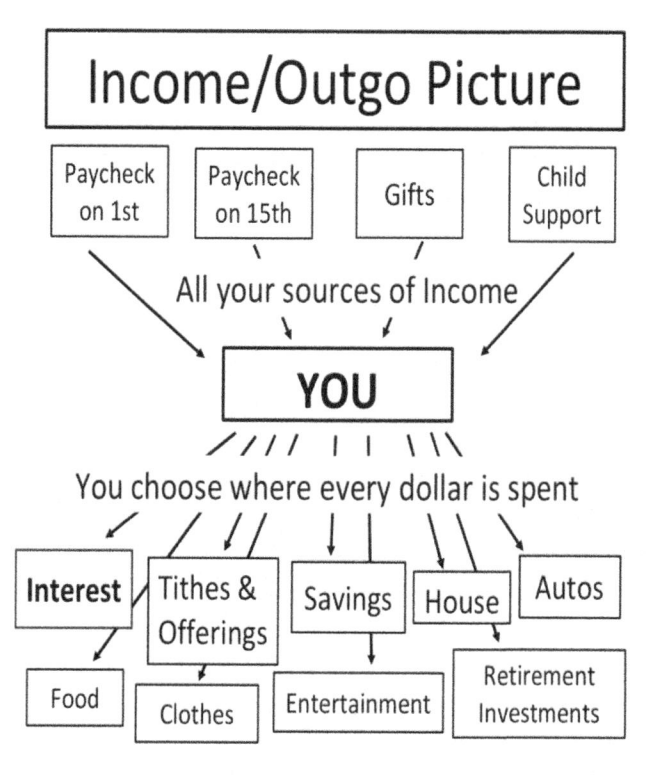

Income/Outgo Picture

- Paycheck on 1st
- Paycheck on 15th
- Gifts
- Child Support

All your sources of Income

↓

YOU

You choose where every dollar is spent

- Interest
- Tithes & Offerings
- Savings
- House
- Autos
- Food
- Clothes
- Entertainment
- Retirement Investments

EVERY DOLLAR YOU "SPEND" ON **INTEREST**
IS ONE DOLLAR LESS TO SPEND ON EVERYTHING ELSE!!!

This picture is a stark truth that should shock you.
You have been taught credit and debt increase your
Standard of living...
But, in reality, they reduce it!
Credit and **Debt** are NOT your friends!

237

The smaller *spending boxes* are all the particular items or ways in which your money is actually spent. You should have some boxes for necessities like tithes & giving, savings, housing, food, some clothing, medical, transportation, etc. Then you need some boxes that may be more preferences than necessities, like entertainment, travel, etc. You decide how many and the name of each and every box you want (refer to your *Monthly Spending Plan* for a good start). Give yourself plenty of room... size of worksheet and number of boxes. BUT, make sure you notice the box called INTEREST. It consists of your hard-earned dollars that give you no benefit or pleasure whatsoever. And realize that all $$$'s that go into the INTEREST box *cannot* be spent on anything else you choose. A total *loss* & *waste* of funds.

Create your own INCOME/OUTGO PICTURE. Make a drawing for your income and outgo. Be as general in your labeling of the boxes as possible. But, you get the idea. Do it for each month. That is easy to do. Use the *Income/Outgo Statement* from Chapter 28 to show the actual dollars *spent* into each box category. Seeing the chart filled out will enhance what you have compiled on the statement. Every way you can make this *income/outgo cash flow* become more REAL to you will help you see what your *financial life* is truthfully like. Seeing the Truth is a great step toward getting control of your money, instead of your money controlling you.

You choose where every dollar is spent.
Every dollar you *spend* on interest
is one dollar less to spend on everything else!
Using credit lowers your standard of living.

These are real Truths. Truths that can MAKE you free. It is *The Math of Life. Christ's Life.*

Chapter 60
Pay CASH for EVERYTHING
For which of you, intending to build a tower, sitteth not down first,
and counteth the cost, whether he have sufficient to finish it?
Lest haply, after he hath laid the foundation, and is not able to finish it, all that behold it begin to mock him, Saying,
This man began to build, and was not able to finish.
Luke 14:28-30

Don't ever make any purchase, especially a large-ticket purchase, before you are CONVICTED of paying CASH for everything. And notice the parabolism in *sitteth not down first*...And then know what your purchase's total cost will be, and counting your coins to see if you have enough to make that purchase without going into any debt. See how easy it is to *know God's will about making all purchases!*

Debt is bondage. Debt insults our GOD Who has told us He will supply all our need. The devil is the author of debt.

One of the greatest teachings Barbara and I ever heard from Pastor John Morgan when we first started Living financially God's Way was this: *Cash a check before going shopping. Don't enter a store without the CASH! Get $1 bills BEFORE you go shopping!* When checking out, start plopping down the $1 bills, one at a time. Then, and only then, will you really see how much something costs. Ladies, try buying a dress of *$40* (remember, this was in 1980!) laying $1 down, then another, then another, then another, then another, then another...40 in total. Guys, do the same for that new fishing rod, or set of golf clubs, etc. (use 2023 amounts for current thinking!)

THAT is how you find out and realize exactly *how much* you are spending on any given purchase. *Imagine doing this for something over $1,000!*

Now listen, this helps with gaining victory over the emotions of charging something so easily, forgetting that somehow someday that *charge* will have to be paid. Laying down ALL those $1 bills is so much more difficult than just signing your name, but (and this is a Holy *but*) you walk out of the store owing nobody anything!

Every time I have given one of my *Family Financial Fun Workshops*, I bring $3,000 or $4,000 in *one dollar bills*. Preferably new, uncirculated ones. You should see the kids' eyes and exclamations at the pile of $1 bills poured out on the table at the front of the gathering. And then, step by step, using my *15-15-25-45 Plan* and corresponding detailed outlines, I put the allocated amounts into little stacks all over the table around the initial pile. Of course, everyone can see the original pile representing a family's *gross income* (including pre-income tax, etc.) dwindling fast. Then, after ALL expenditures and planned savings amounts have been stacked, what remains is the amount we have to *do with as we please.* (p.s. adjust *gross income amount* to fit the typical family for the illustration. Barbara and I actually DID this with our two teenage daughters in 1986).

Now listen, carefully. I ask the folks in attendance to give me a typical expenditure amount (house payment/rent, auto payments, total of groceries for the month, utility bills, etc., etc.). *I have never had a workshop where there was anything left in the pile to put $1 into any savings, much less spend on "whatever we please."* In **every case**, the people are *spending* MORE than they are making each month. OUTGO IS EXCEEDING INCOME. How? Credit.

And they are just giving me the monthly payment amounts! Not the total of amounts *charged* via credit. And much to the dismay of most, they have to admit that not only is their *outgo exceeding their income*, but they have INCREASING DEBT mounting each month!

Again, how does this happen? *Only one way.* **Charging** so much of what is *spent*. Without any *Monthly Spending Plan* AND a conviction and commitment to *pay cash only*, it is incredibly easy to *buy* more than we actually have the CASH to truthfully *pay* for. In fact, here is a truth we must readily admit: **Charging** is **not** truthfully **buying** anything. It is *borrowing*, NOT *buying*. The lender still *owns* the item.

We only BUY something
when we have given our CASH
for the item obtained.

(that would include making the *last payment* to clear any debt)

Words have accurate meanings. We cannot get honest with ourselves about our financial dealings until we get honest with ourselves about the words we use.

Millions of Saints are only *kidding themselves* (God calls it *deceiving* ourselves) when they tell everyone about the new car/truck they *bought*. They signed a *loan (debt-obligation-bondage)* that allowed them to drive the vehicle home. The next month they have to make new decisions on how to *spend* their *take-home pay* with this new high-dollar check that has to be written to the loan institution occupying a large chunk of that original *pile* we discussed in the Funnel illustration (p. 237). Or else, the lending institution comes calling to repossess the vehicle. Nice *purchase*, wasn't it!

So, for a simple summary:
- Make a monthly Spending Plan (chapter 24). Make sure you have a *monthly* plan!
- Make sure you are committed to every dollar having a *name* on it as your plan dictates to you, and only spending each dollar for what the *name* dictates.
- Charging is NOT *buying*. It is *borrowing*. *None* of *your dollars* have been *spent* as yet when you *charge* a purchase.
- If you have been listening to satan instead of God, take the time to go to God's altar and get a Word from Him regarding your financial stewardship.

This can be summarized with our favorite saying: Living Life debt free – Trusting God for His supply, and Living on it.

Be convicted and committed to PAYING CASH ONLY for ALL purchases. It is *The Math of Life. Christ's Life.*

Chapter 61
Prepare For the Expected
Go to the ant, thou sluggard; consider her ways, and be wise:
Which having no guide, overseer, or ruler,
Provideth her meat in the summer,
and gathereth her food in the harvest.
Proverbs 6:6-8

    I love God's story through King Solomon about the tiny, oftentimes aggravating ant. As obnoxious as they can be, just look at how intelligent and diligent they are in their own little world. They are most often busy. They are most often attentive. They are most often aggressive. And they are always preparing for the days to come. They expect the expected to happen.
    Every person's financial planning should take into consideration the things we KNOW are to be *expected* expenses whether…

- right now,
- in the near future,
- or, even sometime *down the road*.

What is amazing is how little knowledge is being passed on to each generation about what to expect. Some of this is because of the lack of teaching and training by parents and grandparents of previous generations, or perhaps because too many people have just come to rely on CREDIT to get by.

To be forewarned is to be forearmed.

    What I will not cover in this chapter are the items that are basic to everyone's financial picture like church offerings, groceries, clothing, mortgage payment, utilities, auto payments and fuel, various insurance premiums, and other regular expenditures. Those we covered in chapter 24 looking at how to prepare a typical Monthly Spending Plan. (or chapter 23 on *Your Spending Plan Portrays Your Priorities*).
    What I would like to open many eyes to in this chapter is a list of the *probable* items that most should *expect* to encounter. It is a staggering number of somewhat insignificant items that WILL impact almost every household. I use the word *insignificant* speaking of several items that are

everyday items people typically do not talk about and plan for. See how many of these YOU have planned for in your financial stewardship:

__ house cleaning/maintenance	__ auto inspections
__ cleaning & laundry	__ auto license plates
__ eating out	__ auto oil changes
__ babysitting / child care	__ auto toll fees
__ recreation	__ auto parking fees
__ trips & vacations	__ auto maintenance
__ beauty & barber shops	__ birthday gifts
__ toiletry & cosmetics	__ anniversary gifts
__ bathroom supplies	__ Christmas gifts
__ child #1 school books	__ computer expenses
__ child #2 school books	__ cell phone expenses
__ child #1 school materials	__ yard maintenance
__ child #2 school materials	__ specialist doctors
__ movie/video rentals	__ special medicines
__ driver's license renewals	__ pets – MANY costs!

It is incredible, isn't it! The list keeps growing and growing… The *drain* on finances can be unbelievable!

Add to the above list a more detailed description and cost figuring for all the different types of *recreation* or *school sports* and *clubs* that family members can enter into. These could add up to a large amount of money that should be *expected*, but devastating to the family Monthly Spending Plan, if not accounted for somewhere in the family's financial picture.

Add to the above list all the different variables of *medical* expenses. Expect them at some time or another. Prescription costs are going to be a part of every family's outgo. Expect them. Plan ahead for them. Just because we don't know the exact amounts does not mean we should not be setting aside money for them. There will be times when *specialist* doctors will be seen. The basic cost for an office visit to a *specialist* can be 2 to 3 times more than for a PCP/general practitioner. Expect them. Plan ahead for them.

And all these items should not be a part of your Emergency Fund spending. These are TO BE EXPECTED costs for every family.

Now, think about REPLACEMENT COSTS for:

__ auto tires   __ household furniture

__ auto parts   __ household appliances

__ lawn mowers   __ personal cell phones

__ lawn furniture   __ personal computers

__ plants & trees   __ other personal electronics

These we covered in chapters 47 and 48 on *A Living Savings Fund Is A Must* and *An Emergency Fund Is A Must*. But they are initially handled through the Monthly Spending Plan. Understanding all these funds and planning are critical in being prepared for the expected (that most do NOT expect!).

Are you beginning to consider the UNTHOUGHT-OF *miscellaneous* expenditures that are a drain on our finances? Now listen, apart from those listed as *Replacement Costs,* these are to be provided for in the use of your Monthly Spending Plan.

These are the proverbial *1,000 ways* our money *disappears*. BUT, with the following STEWARDSHIP DISCIPLINES we can be prepared for ALL the ways, AND to not have to go into debt when the *need* arises.
- think and search out for knowledge on what to EXPECT
- ask family and friends about costs they least planned for
- incorporate the info we gather into our Monthly Spending Plan
- make sure we are setting funds aside for all the *to be expected* expenses

Living Life debt free – Trusting God for His supply, and Living on it.

Be diligent to prepare for all these *to be expected* expenses. It is *The Math of Life. Christ's Life.*

Chapter 62
Prepare For the Unexpected
Watch therefore: for ye know not
what hour your Lord doth come.
Matthew 24:42

This may look like a crazy verse to use for a financial truth, but just as Jesus told His disciples to *keep watch* for they knew not when He might come (for the rapture), *we must be vigilant with the resources God has given us* that we might be ready when *the unexpected* drain on those resources might come. In fact, it is most interesting that Jesus used an earthly illustration of *finances* to emphasize His warning:

> But know this, that if the goodman of the house had known in what watch the thief would come, he would have watched, and would not have suffered his house to broken up. Matthew 24:43

What everyone has to be aware of is the possibility of the *unexpected* coming in a moment that we least think possible, with the devastating amounts that do happen to some folks. So, what we are to do is to have a *designated account* where we put monies aside for these costs that come without our knowing they were going to come. We've talked about this already. Remember the *Emergency Fund*.

It is ONLY for *emergencies* that come at us in the least expected moments. Folks like John Morgan (Financial Freedom Seminar, 1979) suggest an amount be saved up in the *Emergency Fund* that equals about six (6) months' of our salary (or, monthly income). I agree.

But (can be a Holy *but*), then, *what if* something more than a *job loss*, or *smaller tragedy*, occurs?

Let's take a look at three time periods in our life where these *unexpected costs* may arise, and some of the actual possible causes…

in the present or near future

The testimony of many a person is that *if I had known, or even thought it could happen…* they would have prepared ahead of time for the *unknown* and *unexpected expenses* that they faced. And sometimes, those *unexpected expenses* can really be *large*.

Let me give a list of some that my wife and I have encountered, and that others I have pastored have faced:
- a medical incident or accident that immediately initiates large amounts of bills to be paid...trips to the Emergency Room or unexpected surgeries.
- multiple doctor visits to specialists that cost more per office visit (can involve travel costs, and overnight stays).
- perhaps multiple tests that involve extra money for co-pays, etc.
- one or more hospital stays that can involve travel costs, overnight stays (for a family member), and perhaps large co-pays.
- special medicines that are tremendously expensive.
- vehicle repairs...depending on what it is, it can be a very expensive cost.
- premature death expenses...which include more than just the cost of a casket.
- the breakdown of expensive household appliances, or equipment...plumbing or electrical breakdowns.
- AND THE LIST COULD GO ON AND ON...

in our mid-life years

As we grow older, there are certainly more of the doctor, hospital, and other medical care costs that many families face. And virtually they are all at an unexpected time! But what are some of the others???
- family needs that are not expected...like emergencies that arise with the kids and their families.
- care for emergencies in parents' lives.
- relocation and moving expenses.
- house repairs
- legal costs for you or family members
- AND THE LIST COULD GO ON AND ON...

in our senior years

(think ahead, ask parents and grandparents, research financial advisors who have experience)
- much more unexpected medical bills and costs.
- multiple doctor visits to specialists that cost more per office visit, can involve travel costs, and overnight stays often occur.
- multiple tests that involve extra money for co-pays, etc. will likely occur.
- one or more hospital stays that can involve travel costs, overnight stays, and perhaps large co-pays are very likely to occur.
- care for a *dependent* child, or grandchild (starts the cycle all over of costs involved in *rearing kids*).
- more legal costs for you or family members
- AND THE LIST COULD GO ON AND ON…

Now before you get depressed…realize two important truths about all this:
1. many of these *unexpected* financial drains **should be EXPECTED**
2. with a little interest in and recognition of these possibilities, some minor action early on can prevent stress and strain in the event these *unexpected* expenses occur

It is a sad testimony of too many people who have WASTED a dollar here and a dollar there that ended up without ANY dollars in the bank when the *unexpected* expense showed up. How have so many gotten to the mindset that *the future will take care of itself?* The Mind and Life of Christ has never taught that. God's Word is chock full of instances where God told His people to BE PREPARED for the future.

The whole idea of SALVATION and the NEW BIRTH is testimony to God's teaching of BEING PREPARED. No one can just believe that *whatever comes my way, God will take care of me.* Philippians 4:19 is NOT a promise of God's provision when one has WASTED the provision given ahead of the need, of being an *unfaithful steward by not preparing ahead.* Remember Joseph and *the 7 years of plenty?*

How much should anyone have in their various savings funds? Each individual will have to decide the amounts. But it should at least be a few thousand dollars. In the end, a good rule to follow is this: *Make more. Save more. Live free.* Or, as Dave Ramsey has said, *Live like no one else, so that later on you can LIVE LIKE NO ONE ELSE.*

Living Life debt free – Trusting God for His supply, and Living on it.

Be different. Prepare for the *unexpected.* It is *The Math of Life. Christ's Life.*

Chapter 63
Wise Counsel Provides Protection
Where no counsel is, the people fall:
but in the multitude of counselors there is safety.
Proverbs 11:14

Solomon, whom God called the wisest man to ever live, always spoke of counsel that is the *Wisdom of God*. When he says *multitude of counselors*, he is not telling us to seek out a whole bunch, all with *different wisdom*, but many who walk in the *Wisdom of God* and can share that with us. These, in multitude of counsel, *confirm* and *solidify* what God has said.

This is where the *safety (protection)* comes of which Solomon spoke. People of God, walking with God, trusting God completely can provide counsel of the Word of God which is the Wisdom of God. This can include all aspects of God's Truth about finances, jobs, and record keeping.

There's an old song that went: *I've been looking for love in all the wrong places.* Wow. What a discovery and admission. I wonder how many have said, *I have been seeking advice about making financial decisions in all the wrong places…with all the wrong people.* Quite a common endeavor for too many. How many reached this discovery and admission?

The question is: will these
finally seek *counsel* and *Wisdom* from God?

One of the tragedies of many younger people today is not seeking counsel from older folks who have walked with God for years and have much Wisdom of God to share. It was my privilege growing up to be given opportunity to be around some very wise older people who gave me multiple truths to make great decisions with.

And keep in mind that the Holy Scriptures have an amazing number of verses speaking about financial matters? I have a list of over 300 such verses.

But, the big thing is not the *volume* of information we have, but the *quality* of the information.

So, it is not just *how many counselors do I have*, but *who are the counselors?* God says so, doesn't He? *Wisdom*. And what kind of *wisdom* are they dispersing? Every financial counselor, teacher, discipler can be categorized as giving *worldly wisdom* or *God's Wisdom*. It's not the *person*, but the *counsel*. And God has plenty to say about the difference between *worldly wisdom* and *His Wisdom*.

> Because the foolishness of God is wiser than men, and the weakness of God is stronger than men. 1 Corinthians 1:25

> The Jews require a sign, and the Greeks seek after wisdom. 1 Corinthians 1:22

It is interesting to note that the Greek word for *sign* is *semeion*. It refers to the Jews wanting a miracle signifying some sort of spiritual reason, end, or purpose. Truth in and of itself was not sufficient for them. The Greek word for *wisdom* is *sophia*. It can mean knowledge or moral insight, a skill, or some sort of wise management. However, the learning and so-called *wisdom* among the Greeks and Romans in Jesus' day was a definitive effort to pull and lead the minds and mentality of the people as far from Divine Truth as possible. This is why Holy Spirit led the Apostle Paul to speak and pen words with an uncomplicated message of the Gospel. And they *were* the Words of God! *God gives us an uncomplicated message for our financial world.*

What are some of the more basic verses regarding the Wisdom of God on financial matters?

> The thoughts of the diligent tend only to plenteousness; but of every one that is hasty only to want. Proverbs 21:5

> Through wisdom is a house builded; and by understanding it is established: and by knowledge shall the chambers be filled with all precious and pleasant riches.
> Proverbs 24:3-4

> For which of you, intending to build a tower, sitteth not down first, and counteth the cost, whether he have sufficient to finish it? Lest haply, after he hath laid the

foundation, and is not able to finish it, all that behold it begin to mock him, Saying, This man begin to build, and was not able to finish. Luke 14:28-30

Better is a little with righteousness than great revenues without right. Proverbs 16:8

A man's heart deviseth his way: but the LORD directeth his steps. Proverbs 16:9

Trust in the LORD with all thine heart; and lean not unto thine own understanding. In all thy ways acknowledge Him, and He shall direct thy paths. Proverbs 3:5-6

After reading about God and His wisdom, it leads me to say this: "Am I going to trust the wisdom of man (the smartest of whom might have an IQ of 150 or so) or the Wisdom of God, whose IQ is something like 100 kazillion and counting!"

One thing we need is more Saints showing and teaching God's Wisdom.

When all is said and done, it is up to each of us to determine whether we will believe someone giving out *worldly wisdom* or someone showing us the *Wisdom of God*. Do I trust someone telling me the *world's ways*, or do I trust someone telling me *God's Ways*? If we want LIFE in our financial thinking, we must choose the *Wisdom of God*. It is *The Math of Life. Christ's Life*.

Chapter 64
I Can't Afford Not To...
Length of days is in her right hand;
and in her left hand riches and honor.
Proverbs 3:16

For those of us who were living in the 1970's, we remember inflation affecting prices like most had never experienced, and really haven't again UNTIL NOW! Prices go up on almost everything overnight. And the next night. And the next night.

In the 1970's that brought about a sales pitch with the words, *You can't afford to pass up this deal. There will be a price increase tomorrow!* And with credit readily available, many bought, and told friends: *I can't afford not to...* And truth was, prices DID go up the next day. And didn't come down. Are we looking at déjà vu? Oh, my goodness. What a time to be thinking of all the points in this book!

Well, let me show some wisdom that was made available to us 3,000 years ago, and is just as relevant TODAY as it was then:

> My son, forget not My law; but let thine heart keep My commandments: For length of days, and long life, and peace, shall they add to thee. Let not mercy and truth forsake thee: bind them about thy neck; write them upon the table of thine heart: So shalt thou find favor and good understanding in the sight of God and man.
> Proverbs 3:1-4

> Happy is the man that findeth wisdom, and the man that getteth understanding. For the merchandise of it is better than the merchandise of silver, and the gain thereof than fine gold. She is more precious than rubies: and all the things thou canst desire are not compared unto her. Length of days is in her right hand; and in her left hand riches and honor. Her ways are ways of pleasantness, and all her paths are peace. She is a tree of life to them that lay hold upon her: and happy is every one that retaineth her.
> Proverbs 3:13-18

It would do us well to stop and meditate and soak on Solomon's words of wisdom from around 1,000 B.C. In these words from the 3rd chapter of Proverbs, we find a huge number of principles that could guide us in many ways in life, including our financial life. *But there is one verse in particular that I want us to take a moment and digest:* verse18. Notice the phrase *She is a tree of life.*

Recognize those words: *tree of life*? This phrase appears only 10 times in the Holy Scriptures. Genesis 2:9; 3:22, 24. Proverbs 3:18; 11:30; 13:12; 15:4. Revelation 2:7; 22:2, 14. It has great significance. Most of us know the story in Genesis about this tree, but look at the appearance at the last in Revelation ch.22:

> And he showed me a pure river of water of life, clear as crystal, proceeding out of the throne of God and of the Lamb. In the midst of the street of it, and on either side of the river, was there the tree of life, which bare twelve manner of fruits, and yielded her fruit every month: and the leaves of the tree for the healing of the nations. 22:1-2
>
> Blessed are they that do his commandments, that they may have right to the tree of life, and may enter in through the gates into the city. 22:14

These words, *tree of life*, are speaking of Jesus. And *Jesus' Life* can bring His *fruit,* His *wisdom,* His *healing,* His *ways,* and His *works* to our Life including our *financial life*. WE CAN'T AFFORD NOT TO *know His wisdom and His ways* in order to abandon to Him and get in on *His works* in our finances.

God's Word is chock full of the *Life of Christ* speaking to His wisdom, His ways, and His works He enacts when His people follow His Words. How can we who are Saints and possess the Word of God, coupled with the *Mind of Christ*, AFFORD NOT TO *seek to find* all the wise counsel God has given us in His Word? WE CAN'T AFFORD NOT TO! Why would we listen to the *world's* ideas and ways?

I don't know about you, but I CAN'T AFFORD NOT TO *follow the direction of God* as He has given in ALL the verses shown in this book.

Listen to God. Do as He says. It is *The Math of Life. Christ's Life.*

Chapter 65
Superlative Quotes
that Give Guidance
...and a few other good sayings
The way of a fool is right in his own eyes:
but he that hearkeneth unto counsel is wise.
Proverbs 12:15

The heart of having this chapter is founded upon King Solomon's wisdom given around 3,000 years ago...here are two more of his best pieces of counsel:

Without counsel purposes are disappointed: but in the
multitude of counselors they are established.
Proverbs 15:22

Where no counsel is, the people fall: but in the multitude
of counselors there is safety. Proverbs 11:14

It is my joy to share a handful of quotes I have gathered over the years from folks I have had the pleasure and privilege to see, read, & hear give their learning and experience for others like you and me to have and to use. This is in no way a complete record of all the quotes I have and cherish from some of the more prominent advisors I have gleaned from over the years. But, it's a good start.

Counsel from wise people has made a wonderful difference in our life. The source of all these quotes comes from attending conferences, listening to TV-radio-and CD's (of these people), and reading various books and workbooks (from them). I enjoy taking notes of great sayings that give great advice, and especially from folks who have learned, connected with, and put into practice the Wisdom of God.

Enjoy! And take to Heart as many as God impresses upon you!
Carly Fiorina
Examine every dollar,
Cut many dollars,
Move any dollar.

Ron Blue

Getting into debt is as easy as getting down an ice-covered mountain. Getting out of debt is just as difficult as climbing that same mountain.

Dave Ramsey

Every dollar should have a NAME on it BEFORE the start of every month.

Live like no one else, so that later you can live like no one else.

You must gain control over your money, or the lack of it will forever control you.

Financial peace isn't the acquisition of stuff. It's learning to live on less than you make, so you can give money back and have money to invest. You can't win until you do this.

If you give kids money without knowledge, you curse them. If you give kids knowledge without money, they will find the money. If you give kids both money and knowledge, you bless them and empower them.

John Morgan

When your outgo exceeds your income, your upkeep becomes your downfall.

Financial Freedom is:
- Freedom from financial debt
- Freedom from financial worry
- Freedom from financial selfishness
- Freedom to obey God financially

All needs are purposed of God to be supplied for a spiritual growth experience. Money is a physical medium of exchange used of God in the supplying of our needs. Therefore, God's ultimate purpose of money is spiritual growth through His faith plan of supplying all need.

God wants to grow us spiritually by growing our faith, by our having needs and trusting God by believing Him to supply all of our needs.

There are other great quotes from folks who just had a knack for saying something about money or finances or life that really strike a chord with our pocketbook, whether humorous or ingenious. Let these few one-liners bless your heart one by one…

Ayn Rand
Money is only a tool. It will take you wherever you wish, but it will not replace you as the driver.

Benjamin Franklin
An investment in knowledge pays the best interest.

David Feherty
It is how you deal with failure that determines how you achieve success.

Dale Carnegie
Develop success from failures. Discouragement and failure are two of the surest stepping stones to success.

Donald Trump
As long as you're going to be thinking anyway, think big.
Sometimes your best investments are the ones you do not make.
Exploit your passion.
I have made the tough decisions, always with an eye toward the bottom line.
I learn from the past, but plan for the future by exclusively focusing on the present. That's where the fun is.

Eleanor Roosevelt
He who loses money, loses much; He who loses a friend, loses much more; He who loses faith, loses all.

Epictetus
Wealth consists not in having great possessions, but in having few wants.

Henry Ford
It's not the employer who pays the wages. Employers only handle the money. It's the customer who pays the wages.

Jim Rohn
Formal education will make you a living; self-education will make you a fortune.

John Wayne
Courage is being scared to death, but saddling up anyway.

Jonathan Winters
If your ship doesn't come in, swim out to meet it!

P.T. Barnum
Money is a terrible master but an excellent servant.

Robert Kiyosaki
It's not how much money you make, but how much money you keep, how hard it works for you, and how many generations you keep it for.

Thomas Edison
Opportunity is missed by most people because it is dressed in overalls and looks like work.
I have not failed. I've just found 10,000 ways that won't work.

Thomas Jefferson
Never spend your money before you have it.

Will Rogers
Too many people spend money they earned…to buy things they don't want…to impress people that they don't like.

Winston Churchill
We make a living by what we get, but we make a life by what we give.
Success is walking from failure to failure with no loss of enthusiasm.

Yogi Berra
A nickel ain't worth a dime anymore.

Now, listen, the vast majority of these quotes are some sort of APPLICATION of one of God's Truths. I would never want myself or you to hold a *man's* words in greater esteem or preference over God's. God Himself has warned us of such:
> The LORD bringeth the counsel of the heathen to naught:
> He maketh the devices of the people of none effect. The
> counsel of the LORD standeth forever, the thoughts of
> His heart to all generations. Psalm 33:10-11

So, I certainly don't consider any of the people I have included in this chapter as a *heathen*, but they are not God either. Yet, we can take the applications of knowledge and experience of *man* (their counsel) in this chapter with a word of caution: choose God's Words over any *man's* when there is a conflict.

And these last words apply to any of my words in this entire book, or others referenced and quoted:

ONLY GOD BRINGS HIS LIFE to our financial life…it is *The Math of Life. Christ's Life.*

SINNER
Not a Christian
(called lost man, unbeliever, unregenerated, unrighteous man)

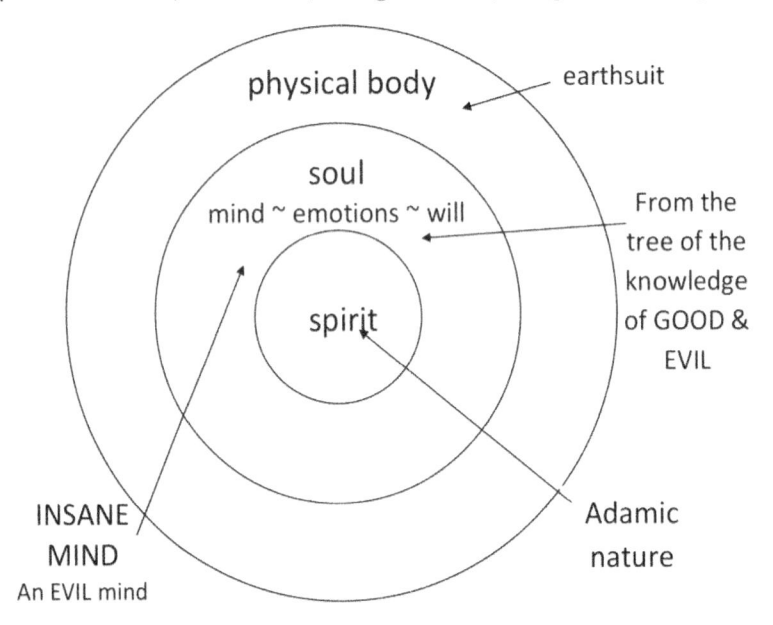

- physical body — earthsuit
- soul
  mind ~ emotions ~ will
- spirit

From the tree of the knowledge of GOOD & EVIL

INSANE MIND
An EVIL mind

Adamic nature

This diagram pictures the "Adamic nature" of sinners since the Fall, that which all are physically born with. ALL earthly beings are physically born with this spiritual nature (spirit) and soul. Notice both are with a "small" letter, indicating the absence of Holy Spirit and Christ's Soul.

SINNER
humanism (man is god)
pride (me, not Christ)
self-righteousness
complexity
unbelief
distrust
lies

BORN AGAIN SAINT
The Christian

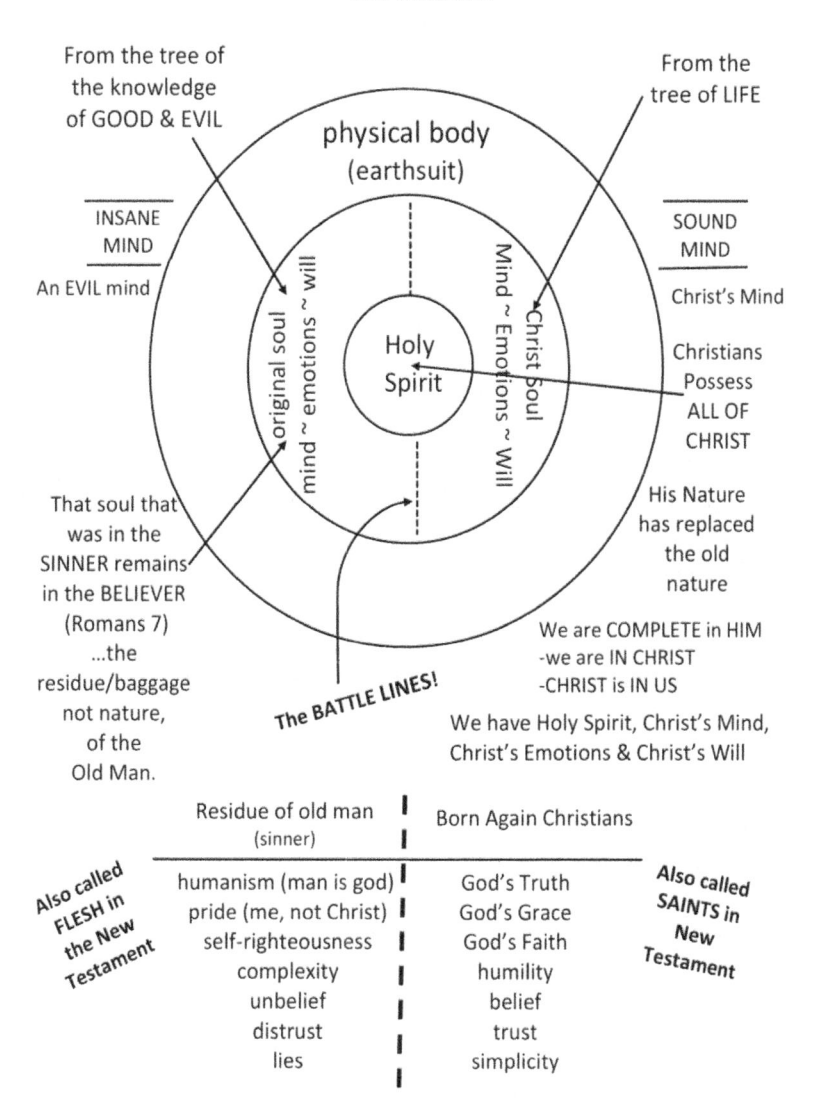

From the tree of the knowledge of GOOD & EVIL

From the tree of LIFE

physical body (earthsuit)

INSANE MIND

An EVIL mind

SOUND MIND

Christ's Mind

original soul
mind ~ emotions ~ will

Christ Soul
Mind ~ Emotions ~ Will

Holy Spirit

Christians Possess ALL OF CHRIST

That soul that was in the SINNER remains in the BELIEVER (Romans 7) …the residue/baggage not nature, of the Old Man.

His Nature has replaced the old nature

We are COMPLETE in HIM
- we are IN CHRIST
- CHRIST is IN US

The BATTLE LINES!

We have Holy Spirit, Christ's Mind, Christ's Emotions & Christ's Will

Residue of old man (sinner)	Born Again Christians
humanism (man is god)	God's Truth
pride (me, not Christ)	God's Grace
self-righteousness	God's Faith
complexity	humility
unbelief	belief
distrust	trust
lies	simplicity

Also called FLESH in the New Testament

Also called SAINTS in New Testament

On Being Born Again

> Jesus answered and said unto him, Verily, verily, I say unto thee,
> Except a man be born again, he cannot see the kingdom of God.
> Nicodemus saith unto him, How can a man be born when he is old?
> Can he enter the second time into his mother's womb, and be born?
> Jesus answered, Verily, verily, I say unto thee, Except a man
> be born of water and of the Spirit, he cannot enter into
> the kingdom of God. That which is born of the flesh is flesh;
> and that which is born of the Spirit is spirit.
> Marvel not that I said unto thee, Ye must be born again.
> John 3:3-7

God's Way of His Salvation

Our Lord Jesus Christ made some very definitive statements about *becoming* a Saint (Christian) and *receiving* Eternal Life. Read the text verses (and John 1:11-12; 14:6 and Ephesians 2:8-9 below) carefully, and my further comments, and then if you need more explanation or answers to some questions please contact me or someone you know who can give you God's wisdom and answers:

> Jesus saith unto him, I am the way, the truth, and the life:
> no man cometh unto the Father, but by Me. John 14:6

> He came unto His own, and His own received Him not.
> But as many as received Him, to them gave He power to
> become the sons of God, even to them that believe on His
> name. John 1:11-12

> For by grace are ye saved through faith; and that not of
> yourselves: it is the gift of God: Not of works, lest any man
> should boast. Ephesians 2:8-9

Within these four passages is *God's Way of His salvation* from our being a sinner. Many other scriptures show *God's Way* to *Eternal Life* (Jesus) also. God tells us of our need for His salvation; that everyone will die the physical death, and then face the judgment of God. Some people call this salvation being *saved*. There is Truth in that, but I like to make it clear and complete that a *New Spiritual Birth* more definitely describes *becoming* a Saint (Christian) and *knowing* you have become one.

So, let me share Truth shown four ways in the verses above: *God's salvation* is…
- only through the Lord Jesus Christ (by His Grace) and His blood shed on His Cross.
- only through a new Supernatural Spiritual Birth…a Holy Spirit accomplished Spiritual Birth (this is being *Born Again)*.
- only as a gift of God. A gift cannot be earned, cannot be worked for, cannot be achieved by any of our efforts…just *received*.
- it is a must…no way around it. Jesus pronounced it. Jesus provided for it.

This is the New Birth (being Born Again). This New Birth is *God's Way* of salvation. Think about this: *birth brings life*. The Spiritual Birth brings forth the Spiritual Life. Saints have it now, and it continues with God after the physical life is over. That is Eternal Life.

Now, here is mankind's basic dilemma…anyone who has not been *Supernaturally Spiritually Born Again* thinks the way to Heaven is a path of *good works*. However, God's standard is perfection. Jesus Himself was perfect. And God says:

> But as He which hath called you is holy, so be ye holy in all manner of conversation (behavior); Because it is written, Be ye holy; for I am holy. 1 Peter 1:15-16

Are you perfect? Are you holy? Does a sinner live up to that? Does a Saint live up to that? Well, we all know the Truth is that a sinner living a perfect life is impossible. But God sent His perfect Son to be the perfect substitutionary, all-sufficient atoning sacrifice for all sinners' sin at His Cross of Calvary. And to give us the opportunity to BE Holy in God's Eyes. You may not understand that, but it is God's Truth.

Full forgiveness of one's sin can only come through a sinner confessing their sin, asking God for His forgiveness, receiving His Grace (His payment) by trusting in the Lord Jesus Christ and His death and shedding of His blood for that perfect sacrifice for one's sin. Then the new Saint is *perfect*. Being made *Holy* in God's eyes. That is known as *receiving Christ*.

The *perfection* in a Saint is Holy Spirit and His Soul. A Saint with Holy Spirit functioning out of Holy Soul will yield *perfection*.

Now good works do matter for a Saint (Christian), but only after salvation, not to escape God's righteous judgment. Even after salvation, any good Spiritual works are of God through a Saint, His Grace.

> For we are His workmanship, created in Christ Jesus
> unto good works, which God hath before ordained
> that we should walk in them. Ephesians 2:10

Is there a *perfect* prayer to pray for God's forgiveness and gift of *Eternal Life*? Perhaps. But God knows a repentant heart and a sinner's desire for *trusting Christ* for His salvation and His forgiveness. The following will help you with a *righteous prayer* if that is your desire:

> *Dear Lord Jesus Christ, I thank You for dying upon Your Cross for me, a guilty sinner, shedding Your blood to pay the penalty for my sin. I ask You, Lord Jesus, to have mercy on me. I believe You are the Way, the Truth, and the Life. And there is no other. I desire to be Supernaturally Spiritually Born Again. I deny and cease from any self-effort to save myself. I can't save myself. I call on Your mercy. I trust Your payment for my sin, and accept, and receive You gladly, as my Savior.*
>
> *Thank You for cleansing me and forgiving me of all my sin – past, present, and future. I believe, and by Your Holy Spirit now Living in me, KNOW I am redeemed, and You will never leave me nor forsake me. You are Lord Jesus Christ my Savior, my Lord, my God, my Life – forever! Amen.*

Just as you are *Born Again* by God's Grace when you trust in the Lord Jesus Christ and His payment, you are kept by God's Grace for all Eternity. Enjoy God's Mercy, His Love, His Grace NOW and for all Eternity as a *Born Again* child of God, one who once WAS a sinner but is NOW a HOLY Saint (Christian).

On Being Spirit-filled

> And be not drunk with wine, wherein is excess;
> but be filled with the Spirit.
> Ephesians 5:18

God's Way of Be-being Filled

I remember being shown and told about Christians needing to be Spirit-filled soon after being Born Again in 1980. But I also remember asking two questions: why? or how? I never got a good answer.

The answers varied from *because God says so* to *you know*, to *you just get filled*, to *it is something God does for us*, or *it is how we are to live the Christian life*. So, I went on my merry way. Never getting any more, always searching for a clearer, more complete description of *being Spirit-filled*. And HOW to *be filled with Holy Spirit*. In fact, I later learned that the Greek means to *be being Spirit-filled*. A 24/7/52 filling.

Oh, I also remember being told that I should beware of *getting too much of the Spirit*. That was a no-no in the circles I was in. You know, the Charismatics and Assemblies were *out-on-a-limb* with this, and I needed to avoid that. So, here again I went on searching in my merry way.

In fact, in my first pastorate I had a sweet older lady who would come up to me at the back door of the sanctuary on a Sunday where I had mentioned Holy Spirit more than once, and she would tell me, "You are getting Him, Pastor!" Well, I knew who she watched on TV and sent money to. I did not put much merit in her exaltation.

But, one day as I was focusing on Galatians Chapter 5, *walking in the flesh* vs *walking in the Spirit*, God started bringing me His Truth that led to me having the proper knowledge of this whole thing. So, let me see if I can give someone who has the same, or similar, questions some clarity…

- to be *filled with Holy Spirit* is to *be being filled* with the Life of the Lord Jesus Christ. The result? The manifestation of Christ's Life in our earthsuit through Christ's Spirit and Christ's Soul in us.
- the *how* is simply to *abandon* OUR strength and flesh to Holy Spirit, *ask* Him to fill us, *believe* and *trust* that He has. This is a *Spiritual* transaction that cannot be explained or understood in any other way. It is *His Way*, not man's way.

- the best reason *why* is because God has told us this is *His Way* of *Life as a Christian*. That encompasses all God tells us in the *New Testament, His Way* of the *New Covenant*.
- to *walk in the Spirit* is to *walk in dependence on the Spirit*. Our weakness leads to dependence. Our strength (a characteristic of pride and flesh) leads to independence.

If a *Saint* (every Christian is a *Saint*) is at any time NOT *filled with Holy Spirit* that means his earthsuit (the housing of our Spirit and 2 souls) is *abandoned* in some part to his *flesh* (the control of his *carnal soul*). Out of *that heart* will flow something in animosity to God.

Now here is something that is not on this subject explicitly, but can be of help: God tells us in *2nd Corinthians 5:16-17*:

> Wherefore henceforth know we no man after the flesh: yea, though we have known Christ after the flesh, yet now henceforth know we him no more. Therefore if any man be in Christ, he is a new creature: old things are passed away; behold, all things are become new.

Did you get that? We are to *know no man after the flesh* (the earthsuit). What else is there? *Know all men after their spirit.* HOW? By our new Creation in the Holy Spirit of God. Separate the physical from the spiritual. Know every person whether they are a new Creation, Born Again, or not. As far as knowing Christians, we must know also *which soul* they are *living* out of at any moment.

The *Good News* is that *being Spirit-filled* is not a complicated or difficult challenge. It is quite the opposite. *God's Way* is always the *easy Way* for us. God does all the work! We just have to do one thing: Believe, Trust, and Receive: BE BEING SPIRIT-FILLED! 24/7/52.

Scripture References

verse	page #	verse	page #
Genesis		**Psalms**	
2:9	254	37:21	132
2:15	72	62:12	74
2:15-17	76	90:10	24
3:1-7	14	119:130	45
3:22,24	254	119:165	165
6:21	122	139:23-24	215
22:1-2,14	255	147:3	216
41:35-36	190	**Proverbs**	
41:36	228	1:10-16,18	221
Exodus		3:1-4	253
16:2	140	3:5-6	215,219,252
16:4	140	3:9-10	51,94,153,155,161
16:6-8	140	3:10-11	177
Leviticus		3:13-18	253
27:28,30,32	169,170	3:16	253
Deuteronomy		3:18	254
8:17	64	3:33	42
8:18	64	6:1-5	211
8:19-20	66	6:6-8	242
Joshua		6:6-11	74,90
24:15	45	6:9	194
2 Chronicles		9:9	42
12:6	42	10:4-5	184
Psalms		10:6	42
5:10	12	11:1	42
10:3-4	221	11:9	42
23:1	11,55,89,113,200	11:14	250,255
23:1-3	11	11:15	211
33:10-11	259	11:24-25	150

Scripture References (cont'd)

verse	page #	verse	page #
Proverbs		Proverbs	
11:30	254	22:26-27	198
12:15	26,90,255	24:3-4	251
13:11	62	27:7	91
13:12	254	27:12	122
13:18-20	90	27:13	212
13:20	135	27:23	112
13:22	125,233	27:23-24	115,124
15:4	254	27:24-27	113
15:21-22	26	28:19	90
15:22	255	28:20	62
15:27	221	28:22	61,221
16:8	252	29:14	91
16:9	252	Ecclesiastes	
16:11	42	6:7-9	236
17:18	210	Isaiah	
19:24	90	26:3-4	215
20:4	74	Daniel	
20:7	42	1:1-6:28	43
20:11	74	Habakkuk	
20:13	74	2:4	41
20.16	212	Malachi	
21:5	99,251	3:8-12	51,160
21:6	62	3:10	160
21:20	89,119,184,187	Matthew	
21:25-26	221	6:19	94,217
22:1	82	6:19-20	94,151
22:6	22, 24	6:20	94
22:7	198,200	6:21	93,95,152
22:26	200,210	6:22	61

Scripture References (cont'd)

verse	page #	verse	page #
Matthew		**Luke**	
6:24	49,198,200	17:7-9	69
6:24-25	130	17:10	69
6:31-34	130	18:27	174
6:33	96	**John**	
10:29-31	77	1:11-12	262
chapter 13	23	3:3	262
19:26	29,202	3:5-7	262
23:3-4	170	3:16	45,86
24:42	246	6.63	27
24:43	246	8:32	35
25:21,23	136	8:32,36	17
25:34-40	182	8:44	14
Mark		12:24	31
8:36	221	chs 14-17	18
9:23	29	14:6	262
10:27	29	15:15	11
Luke		16:33	18
4:18	213,216	**Romans**	
chapter 5	157	7:14-15, 17-20	166
6:38	51,148,158	8:2	140
12:13-21	66	8:6	215
12:15	222	8:31	12
12:33	151	12:2	199
12:34	152	**1 Corinthians**	
12:42-44	45	1:22	251
14:28	142	1:25	251
14:28-30	142,239,251	2:14	18,24
16:10	31,68		
16:10-13	49		

Scripture References (cont'd)

verse	page #
1 Corinthians	
2:16	18
7:3	180
14:33	169
2 Corinthians	
5:16-17	266
5:18	107
chs 8 & 9	147,163,172
8:1 - 9:15	173
8:1-4	181
8:5	175,176,181
8:5-15	174
8:7	180,182
8:14	153
chapter 9	66,171
9:6	224
9:6-8	170
9:7	158,163,167
9:8	144,159,172
9:9-10	146
9:11	146
9:12-15	146
Galatians	
chapter 5	265
Ephesians	
2:8-9	264
2:10	264
2:20	29-30
5:18	265

verse	page #
Philippians	
4:4-9	54
4:6-7	215
4:11	55,136
4:13	55,205
4:18	55
4:19	55,89,128,145,175, 190,198,199,200
Colossians	
3:1-2	136
2 Thessalonians	
3:6-9	72
3:10	72,75
3:11-12	72
1 Timothy	
5:8	172,211
6:4-5	58
6:6	53
6:7-10	53
6:9	58,221
6:10	57,214,222
6:17	66
6:17-19	63
6:18-19	66
2 Timothy	
2:16,18	59
Hebrews	
13:5	12
13:8	150

Scripture References (cont'd)

verse	page #
James	
1:12-15	15
1 Peter	
1:15-16	263
4:10	46
1 John	
1:7	215
1:7-9	216
2:15-16	15
3:17	153, 172, 182
3:16-17	66
Revelation	
2:7	254
22:1-2	254
22:2,14	254

BOOKS by B. Lee McDowell
Dowadad Press, Publisher
A division of Lee McDowell Christian Ministries, Inc.
www.blmcm.net
www.amazon.com/-/e/B083LQXJZ4

Books in Print

Seagulls Don't Lie!
The Truth will MAKE you free!

God's Words Bring *Life*
Christ's Life becoming your Life

all i want is Jesus!
His Love, His Grace, His Sound Mind, His Shepherding

The Images of God & Man
17 diagrams explaining "spirit, soul, & body"

Study Guide – The Images of God & Man
Questions & discussions for The Images of God & Man

Putting the Handcuffs on God
False beliefs & actions stifle God's Power

The Math of Life
Experiencing the Life of Christ in your personal finances

Books to Come

The Parable of the Two Souls
Examining the two spiritual souls of Saints

The Pane of Christianity
Two sides to one Truth

Christ's Life as My Life
A Daily Devotional giving Truth about Christ's Supernatural Spiritual Life Lived through me

The Overlooked Fundamentals of Christianity
  Growing in God's Grace – MUCH more than "unmerited favor"
  Definitions, Diagrams, and Foundational Truths

all i want is Jesus! – Vol. 2
  His Presence, His Acceptance, His Faith, His Peace, His Joy, His Hope, His Mercy

Putting the Handcuffs on God – Vol. 2
  More false beliefs and actions stifling God's Power

Made in the USA
Middletown, DE
14 April 2024